MANAGING STRATEGIC AIRLINE ALLIANCES

Managing Strategic Airline Alliances

BIRGIT KLEYMANN
HANNU SERISTÖ

ASHGATE

Published by
Ashgate Publishing Limited
Gower House
Croft Road
Aldershot
Hampshire GU11 3HR
England

Ashgate Publishing Company
Suite 420
101 Cherry Street
Burlington, VT 05401-4405
USA

Ashgate website: http://www.ashgate.com

British Library Cataloguing in Publication Data
Kleymann, Birgit
 Managing strategic airline alliances. - (Ashgate studies in
 aviation economics and management)
 1.Airlines - Management 2.Strategic alliances (Business)
 3.Business networks
 I.Title II. Seristö, Hannu
 387.7'068

Library of Congress Cataloging-in-Publication Data
Kleymann, Birgit.
 Managing strategic airline alliances / by Birgit Kleymann and Hannu Seristö
      p. cm. -- (Ashgate studies in aviation economics and management)
 Includes index.
 ISBN 0-7546-1327-5
 1. Airlines--Management. 2. Strategic alliances (Business) I. Seristö, Hannu. II.
Title. III. Series

 HE9780.K645 2004
 387.7'068--dc22

                                            2004014739

ISBN 0 7546 1327 5

Printed in Great Britain by TJ International Ltd, Padstow, Cornwall

Contents

The Authors

Birgit Kleymann, PhD
Dr. Kleymann is Senior Assistant Professor of Strategy and Organisation Theory at IÉSEG School of Management, Catholic University of Lille, in France. Her main research interest is the application of Organisation Theory to the development of multilateral alliances. In addition to assignments with international airlines in Europe and South America, she has worked in internal consulting for a multinational company and as a sales executive for a manufacturer of transport aircraft. She holds a PPL and is a certified Aircraft Dispatcher.

Hannu Seristö (D.Sc. in Economics)
Dr. Seristö is Professor of International Business at the Helsinki School of Economics in Finland. Prior to his academic career he has worked for Finnair and McKinsey & Co.

Aviation has been both a hobby and of professional interest to him since having pilot's basic training in the Finnish Air Force in the early 1980s.

Authorship of individual chapters

Chapter 1 by Birgit Kleymann
Chapter 2 by Hannu Seristö and Birgit Kleymann
Chapters 3 and 4 by Birgit Kleymann
Chapters 5, 6, 7, 8 by Hannu Seristö
Chapter 9 by Birgit Kleymann
Chapter 10 by Hannu Seristö
Chapter 11 by Birgit Kleymann and Hannu Seristö

Preface

When discussing airline strategy in the 21st century, the first thing that comes to mind is probably the issue of alliance membership. Indeed, intensive, multilateral cooperation between airlines is a relatively new phenomenon that arose out of significant changes in the carriers' operating environment. Since the liberalisation of air transport, airlines have lost the protection of their markets, which increased competition between carriers; many a former state-owned carrier has been privatised, and to a large number of flag carriers there is the new obligation to operate under a real profit motive. In this situation, airlines find themselves facing two challenges simultaneously. They have to compete in terms of service levels, but also face pressure to lower the fares and consequently have to strive to reduce costs. The reaction of the participants in the newly liberalised markets was to consolidate on some fronts to avoid the potentially detrimental effects of over-competition. Broadly speaking, an airline needs to find a way to increase its scope without having to incur the costs of serving all desirable markets by itself. At the same time, it must strive to avoid excessive vulnerability from the uncertainties of loose, shorter-term cooperative agreements with other carriers. This leads to a setting where the airline has to manage a 'trade-off between autonomy and survival'.[1]

Even though the absolute number of agreements to cooperate is impressive, many of these agreements have turned out to be rather short lived or suboptimal for one or more of the partners involved.

As has been the case within other industries, airlines need to give very careful consideration to their alliance strategies as tools for growth or at least for survival. In addition, airlines differ so much from each other – for example in terms of size, mission, infrastructure, objective, company culture – that contributions to, and expectations from, an alliance are very diverse. Therefore, the question is not so much whether or not to enter into an alliance, but rather with whom, in what market, and to what extent.

Also, because airline alliance groups are a quite novel form of inter-firm cooperation, there is no existing blueprint for them, and no suitable models exist that can be 'borrowed' from other industries.

In management research, quite a bit is known about alliance forms such as bi- or trilateral consortia, R&D cooperation, or joint ventures. Typically, these alliance forms involve (a) a very limited number of partners, and (b) often have a definite boundary, be it in temporal or operational terms. Where research has investigated multipartner arrangements, this has almost exclusively concentrated on looser ties, temporary contracts, or social networks.

The alliance groups that airlines have been building among themselves, however, are a different form of cooperation: they involve many partners, they concern the whole firm, and they are mostly of indeterminate duration. Especially because of the increasing complexity linked to a relatively large number of partners, there is a limit to what knowledge of 'classical' alliances can teach the airline manager whose company has joined an alliance group.

To the airline manager, alliance group membership is an issue that requires careful steering. Challenges to managers include finding their way in an organisational form that is only loosely coupled, consists of very heterogeneous members, still displays considerable flux in terms of membership base and types of links between members, and that has to accommodate both an overarching rationale for the well-being of the alliance group itself, and the 'local' rationales of individual member airlines. Power imbalances have to be mitigated, interdependencies need to be managed, and – beyond the rationales of any one particular member airline – consensus must be established to allow the alliance group to evolve as an organisation in its own right.

It is our aim to shed some light on these issues; we therefore will look at micro and macro levels of alliancing; from the individual manager's sensemaking processes up to issues of alliance group governance. The main issues dealt with in this book are, first, why airlines cooperate, and to what extent, and, second, what happens inside this cooperation, and along which lines does this cooperation evolve. As the book is about the very managing of alliances, the broader economic issues concerning airline alliances is beyond the boundaries of our discussion; for instance, we do not deal with the impact that alliances have on the industry structure per se or on the welfare in an economy. Moreover, while we fully acknowledge the increasing significance of cargo for airlines, our discussion focuses on the passenger side of the industry.

This book has been written on the basis of our joint and individual studies of the airline industry over the past ten years. Most chapters are derived from articles and papers that were written for an academic audience, but we consider ourselves to pursue *applied* research, and we do believe that concepts and models used in management science can indeed help practitioners to understand some of the dynamics of a complex phenomenon such as multilateral alliances. This book is therefore written for both an audience of practitioners, who want to gain some theoretical insights into the dynamics of their industry, and also for the growing number of academics who are interested in approaching multilateral alliances from the many perspectives organisation theory has to offer.

We wish to thank all the airline practitioners that gave us valuable insights into their business and took the time to discuss alliancing with us. We also thank our employers for giving us the time and resources to finish this project, and our families for their patience and understanding. A special thank you goes to Mrs. Ann-Mari Wright-Hyttinen for her competent and invaluable help with putting the book into its final form.

Note
[1]   Pfeffer, J. and Salancik, G. (1978), The External Control of Organizations. New York: Harper and Tow.

Foreword

Fariba Alamdari
Head, Air Transport Department
Cranfield University

Alliances are generally a strategy that companies use when acquiring another company or when internal development as a means of growing is not an option. Although there have been cross-border mergers in most other industries, the restriction in foreign ownership in aviation is still maintained, which has led to a rapid move towards the formation of alliances in the industry. The restrictions on who may own and control a national airline, and the right of a country to refuse or accept the designation of an airline under a bilateral air services agreement if that airline is not majority owned and controlled by citizens of the country of designation, have hindered airline cross-border mergers or takeovers. Of course these rules have been relaxed in the EU, and it is intended to gradually remove nationality clauses from bilateral air agreements following the decision of the European Court of Justice to that effect. However, many major markets are still subject to these rules. Therefore, until such time that air transport is completely free of ownership and control restrictions, airlines will carry on forming partnerships in order to grow and expand their networks.

The alliances, however, by their nature are open-ended and ever changing. The industry has witnessed the exit of members from global alliances due to clashing cultures, business conflicts and competition. This raises the question of what forces shape the organisation of airline alliances and how airline alliances should be managed to ensure an effective cooperation amongst members. The problem arises from the nature of the loose partnership between airlines. In effect, each partner is an independent organisation with a separate management board and financial accounting. Ultimately, each airline is concerned with its own results, and wishes to ensure a positive balance sheet for its own shareholders. However, the partnership often requires compromises that could be in conflict with individual member's motives and objectives.

Birgit Kleymann and Hannu Seristö, in their book *Managing Strategic Airline Alliances*, address the issues related to the organisational structure of airline alliances and the challenges facing airline executives in creating a healthy balance between managing their independency on the one hand, and the interdependency with their partners on the other. The authors provide an insight into the difficulties that executives face in managing alliances in an unstable environment within which they operate.

For a successful partnership, alliances need to have a clear governance policy which does not undermine individual partners. *Managing Strategic Airline Alliances* clearly highlights the difficulties in managing multilateral partnerships and suggests an organisational structure which could reduce the potential conflicts between partners.

The book does not provide a complete answer to the dilemma of independency and interdependency within airline alliances, but certainly identifies the problems and suggests possible solutions as a way forward. The ultimate solution is, clearly, in freeing up the airline industry, like many other industries, from ownership and nationality rules which currently hinder industry development in accordance with the market forces. *Managing Strategic Airline Alliances* is certainly a useful source of information for readers interested in both the governance of airline alliances and organisational theory.

Chapter 1

Characteristics of the Airline Industry and Alliances

The regulatory framework of air transport

The airline industry has traditionally been characterised by a high degree of regulation, not only on the technical, but also on the economic side. On international routes, airlines mostly operated within a very rigid framework set by air services agreements (in short ASAs), which are intergovernmental agreements concerning traffic rights between two countries. The regulation of air traffic stems from the Paris Convention of 1919, where it was recognised that each state is sovereign over the airspace above its territory and thus responsible for defining the nature and extent of air traffic serving it. In addition to heavy domestic regulation of air traffic in most countries, ASAs between nations regulated the international market in terms of fares to be charged, frequencies to be flown, and capacities to be offered. In practice, two countries that decided to set up air services between each other were to designate a specific airline (the so-called 'flag carrier') each to serve that particular market from their side. Except for the case of the United States of America, most flag carriers were government-owned. An airline enjoying flag carrier status was provided with route rights by its government, and did not face any competition except from the designated flag carrier of the country at the other end of the route. Even that competition was usually quite limited, since capacities and fares (and at times even the standard of in-flight services offered to passengers) were defined in the ASA. At the same time, flag carriers were not free to enter or exit routes on economic or operational grounds, because their status often dictated operations to serve public convenience and political considerations. Similar regulations governed the domestic services operated by airlines. This system did not encourage airlines to operate efficiently, but it assured a fairly stable and predictable operating environment.

The Oil Crisis of the 1970s triggered a call for more efficiency and an increased profit motive within airline operations. In the United States, a debate arose concerning the merits of the regulatory system. The main point of criticism was the obsolescence of rules, which were initially intended to protect an infant industry in the 1930s. Now it was argued that the airline industry had matured enough that it could operate in a competitive environment. The main new ideas were that air fare levels should indeed be decided in the marketplace, that there should be freedom for airlines to enter and exit a given market (a route or set of routes), and that competition should stimulate the drive for more efficiency in airline operations.

In 1978, the Carter Administration introduced the so-called 'deregulation package' concerning its domestic market. In 1992, deregulation was for the first time established at international level by a step-wise process that was initiated within the European Union, and which eventually moved towards full liberalisation of intra-EU air traffic. Eventually, air traffic within the EU would be considered domestic traffic, subject to very few restrictions. The key issues of this EU liberalisation package include the following:

- EU airlines will be free to operate from any airport within the EU (subject to infrastructure restrictions such as slot availability, noise regulations etc).
- A route can be operated by several carriers (the reciprocal two-carrier rule is thus eliminated).
- Cabotage[1] rights will be granted. That way, several national airlines lost their domestic monopoly.
- Increased freedom to set fares on economic grounds.
- Negotiation of traffic rights with non-EU countries will be undertaken by an EU-authority, rather than by the authorities of a specific county.
- Decrease and eventual termination of government subsidies to airlines.

Outside the (so far) unique EU scene, air transport between countries is sometimes governed by a specific type of air services trading arrangement, namely the so-called 'Open Skies' regime. The name is slightly misleading, since such an agreement does not provide for 'free flight' between two signatory states – genuine open skies only exist in Europe.[2] In reality, they are a significantly relaxed form of regulation. For example, an Open Skies agreement that a country might sign with the United States currently involves the following main points and limitations (which apply to both airlines from the signing nation and to US airlines):

- Full 5th freedom rights (for a description of the freedoms of the air, see endnote[3]).
- No restrictions on capacity, fares or routings.
- Access to all points in each country.
- Unrestricted designation (i.e., no flag carrier status for any airline).

On the 'negative' side of points still impeding truly free flight, this agreement lays down

- No provision for the possibility of exercising 7th or 8th freedom.
- Strict national ownership and effective control restrictions.[4]

Typically, ASAs are of a bilateral nature, i.e., between two countries. There are currently thousands of bilateral air services agreements in place between some 180 nations. The extent of airline activities between these countries depends very much on the outcome of those negotiations. In a further step to simplify the negotiation processes, some countries agree on a *multilateral* Open Skies regime. In November 2000, one of the first such agreements on a significant scale was signed by the United States, Brunei, Chile, New Zealand and Singapore.

This increasingly liberalised, albeit not completely deregulated, regime of global air transport means that former flag carriers would lose their hitherto well-protected position. Being a national airline no longer suffices as a reason to be present in certain markets. The airlines' reactions to liberalisation and deregulation have, to some extent, been different on the two sides of the Atlantic. In the United States, where deregulation was introduced in a single step in 1978, there ensued fierce competition between the established carriers as well as against many a start-up airline. This has left the market now, more than twenty years later, with a smaller number of contenders than were present in the initial phase, when the prospect of free market entry attracted (and created) many competitors. The airlines that still exist today owe their survival mainly either to their size and the resulting benefits of scope, density and market dominance or to their specialist position as feeders and niche carriers. In some cases, and where allowed by competition authorities, larger incumbents also purchased majority stakes in potential competitors and merged them fully into their own operations. As became evident in the cases of American Airlines purchasing TWA, and United Airlines investing in US Air, this process of consolidation did not always prove beneficial to the investing airline.

The reaction on the European scene has been different in that most airlines there aimed, at least from the outset of liberalisation, more at consolidation in the marketplace, rather than at direct confrontation with competitors. The main competitive advantage held by European airlines prior to deregulation, namely the dominance of their respective national home markets, is still held in many cases. This is partially due to the relatively slow, step-wise establishment of a deregulated regime in Europe. Start-up airlines have been gradually challenging some of these positions, mostly in low-cost niches. A few airlines have established operations outside their home country, but, so far, relatively few EU airlines make full use of their rights to fly cabotage outside their home country, or to serve routes between two countries other than their own. However, the scene is changing with increasing speed, and the question for an individual airline is now to re-define its role and to find a strategy that takes into account its specific resource endowment. It will be the exploitation and expansion of these resources, rather than pure government endorsement, which will become an airline's 'raison d'être'.

As to the possibility of consolidation through mergers and acquisition, this was and is still limited in the airline industry. It is mainly impeded by three factors: the first being the high cost associated with such a step, the second one being clauses that still require most airlines' shares to be held by a majority of nationals of their country of registration (this is true even within Europe), and the third being antitrust concerns. Antitrust issues even prevent or limit non-equity seeking cooperation between airlines. In some cases, the US authorities have granted *antitrust immunity*[5] to alliances between a US airline and a foreign carrier, provided that the partner carriers' home government had signed an Open Skies agreement with the US. In Europe, authorities are unlikely to approve cooperation between two carriers in a market unless there are clear possibilities for competitors to establish themselves as well in that market.[6] Indeed, airlines are nowadays operating in a competitive environment where regulation in some markets prevents full competition on one hand and full freedom of reaction to competitive pressures on the other. The regulatory situation is, however, in constant flux, with a clear tendency towards liberalisation. Full global liberalisation can however be considered to be a highly unlikely scenario,[7] at least in the medium term, and it appears unlikely that even a – hypothetical – fully and globally liberalised air transport market would completely eliminate the need for alliancing.[8]

It will not be discussed here whether a (hypothetical) fully liberalised air transport market would lead to more efficiency or to lower cost for the consumer. There is a possibility that a fully deregulated air transport industry would move towards a small-numbers oligopoly (i.e., a few mega-carriers), with duopolies and monopolies in regional markets. If this is assumed, the current stand by antitrust authorities, which limits the possibilities for mergers or tight cooperation between airlines, could indeed be seen as a way to preclude some of these oligopolies and ensure some competition between firms.

Economic characteristics of the airline industry

> Three passengers less per flight, costs increasing by two per cent, and ten DM [approx. €5] less yield per ticket sold are all it takes to put us down to a zero in results.
> (Senior Manager, Lufthansa)

The deregulation of the airline industry was an attempt to drive the industry towards the perceived ideal of perfect competition with its supposed benefits of pricing related to costs, optimal output and the disappearance of inefficient producers.[9] However, even after the deregulation of air transport in the US, the European Union, and other parts of the world, markets are far from contestable.[10] In most of the world's markets, one can observe a regional segmentation into geographically different market zones which are characterised by strong oligopolies where a set of weaker competitors have almost no significant individual market leverage. The reasons for the existence of these oligopolies might lie in the size and scope effects discussed further below, and in two salient characteristics of the airline industry.

First, studies on the cost structure of airlines[11] have shown that this industry is highly sensitive to variations in external factors such as fuel prices, wage levels, and demand. This sensitivity has increased in recent years as the average yield per RPK (Revenue Passenger Kilometre) has been dropping continuously [12] In other words, profit margins are small and competing in the airline industry is costly and risky. There have been, especially in the first years of deregulation in the US, small start-up airlines, which tried to attack the established larger carriers head-on by offering significantly lower fares on certain routes. Frequently, this move triggered a price war between the two competitors. For some time, consumers could benefit from airlines undercutting each other on a route or set of routes. However, it was normally the larger incumbent airline which eventually won the war: they could sustain extremely low (and if need be even unprofitable) fare levels on a route for the time it took to drive the competitor out of that market by cross-subsidising that market with funds from other, more profitable routes. After the beaten competitor withdrew, fares went up to previous levels.

Second, entry barriers to most markets are still considerable, be it due to airline-specific reasons such as market power (e.g. hub dominance, CRS ownership) or external factors such as infrastructure availability (e.g. airport slots) or remaining regulation in certain international markets (bilateral agreements limiting the number of airlines that can serve a route between two countries).

The airline industry can therefore be characterised as very sensitive to outside factors, highly cyclical, and featuring significant barriers to open competition. In addition, the fact that most air transport markets are oligopolistic in character contributes to the industry's inherent instability: since in oligopolies the actions of one competitor have significant influence on the other(s), there is a continuous process of re-adaptation and re-positioning of firms.[13] Equilibrium is difficult to obtain, or maintain, and the airline industry can be considered to be in a state of constant flux.

Benefits of scale, scope, and density in air transport[14]

Economies of scale

Since the early 1990s, the airline industry has followed a general tendency towards establishing alliances, which could at that time also be observed as a trend in other industries, both in the manufacturing and the service sectors. One of the classic reasons for firm growth – whether organically or through mergers – has been the reaping of economies of scale. Scale economies occur when unit costs go down as total production is increased. They evolve mostly from the spreading of fixed costs over an increasing volume of output. In the air transport industry, however, there appears to be a limit to economies of scale that an airline can derive purely from being large in size. True scale effects have only been observed among growing smaller airlines: increasing an airline's size from, say, two aircraft to twenty does carry scale benefits. However, beyond this relatively low threshold, no significant long-run scale economies have been found;[15] in other words, there appear to be no differences in unit costs between carriers of different size as long as factors such as the average stage length, traffic density and input prices remain the same.[16] This is partially due to the fact that the airline product (a seat travelling from A to B) is a *service*, whose production is labour intensive and cannot be performed at a single location, or in bulk in advance and then stored. Most importantly, the airline industry is characterised by a relatively high proportion of Direct Operating Costs. An airline's variable, or direct operating costs typically range between 30 and 50 per cent of total costs.[17] The way these numbers are calculated and what costs are considered to be variable depend on the timeframe considered, or on the 'escapability' of the costs: immediately escapable costs are those which are not incurred if a single flight does not operate. This includes fuel, landing and navigation charges, direct engineering costs (related to flight cycles or hours operated), passenger service costs (e.g. meals), and aircrew subsistence costs (hotels etc). Immediately escapable costs are also called Direct Operating Costs. If the time horizon is extended to the medium term (one schedule period or a year), the proportion of escapable costs increases, as aircraft that do not fly can be sold (thereby reducing fixed insurance costs, maintenance overheads etc), sales offices can be closed, etc. With more than 50 per cent of total costs being variable (or directly related to production at least over the medium term[18]) it is possible to say that the possibilities for reaping savings from spreading the fixed costs over a greater production output are limited, especially since the increase in output is linked to relatively high direct costs.

Economies of scale (or of 'size') have been divided[19] into 'technological economies' (based on large scale production and large plants), 'managerial economies' (improved division of labour) and 'financial economies' (reductions in unit costs when purchases, sales and financial transactions are made on a large scale). Applied to the case of airline alliances, one can say that technological economies are achieved to a very limited extent, except at 'plant level',[20] i.e., in relation to aircraft size.[21] The extent to which managerial and financial economies can be reaped from alliancing is still limited, due to the relatively low level of integration between partner airlines. In the airline case, there are still limited possibilities for reaping scale economies from alliancing: some of the fixed costs (especially aircraft and personnel related) are still very airline specific and many cannot be fully spread over alliance partners due to the regulatory environment in which an airline operates, which in many cases includes very tight and restrictive labour contracts. There is, however, some potential for cost economies to be reaped from alliancing in terms of *synergies*; for example, through joint procurement (such as fuel in case of the Star alliance), facility sharing, etc. Here, it is important to note that in horizontal cooperation, the strength of synergetic effects between partners decreases considerably if markets are isolated.[22] In airline terms, this means that synergies from joint facility operations can mainly be reaped at points of linkage between two partners' route systems. This is most likely to refer to each partners' main hub airport. Route system-related features and hub location are therefore attributes of considerable importance to an airline's positioning in, and benefiting from, cooperation agreements with other carriers (see section on economies of scope, below).

Further potential for reaping size-related economies from alliancing lies in joint procurement of technical material (aircraft and aircraft spares). This, however, requires a significant homogeneity in the carriers' operational profile (in terms of fleet structure and operating procedures). Harmonising the technical side is in itself a costly process. In addition, the existing synergies must be offset against the fact that operating in a tighter multilateral alliance group implies increased overhead costs, the payment of membership or entrance dues, and some inefficiencies due to coordinating efforts.

Economies of density

A further type of economies are the scale-derived economies of density (related to Penros's (1956) managerial economies), which occur when unit costs go down as the volume provided increases at a fixed network size. Two kinds of economies of density have been proposed in the air transport context,[23] namely *Link Density*, which is related to the load factors on a flight or city pair, and *Network Density*, which measures the efficiency of fleet utilisation over the entire network or a set of routes. Link densities occur because of the indivisibility of the airline product: an aircraft flying from A to B 'produces' a fixed number of seats per flight on this stage. Network densities can be reaped through increased efficiency, e.g. through optimising partner feed (hubbing, harmonisation of schedules), or through higher frequencies (in the case of longhaul routes, this reduces costs related to overly long crew layovers at remote outstations and, more frequently, it improves aircraft utilisation). In an alliance, this type of economies can only be realised if the coordination and feed between partners is optimised or if one airline gives up the route and leaves its operation to its partner. This type of cooperation therefore requires high degrees of partner integration, which in turn are costly to establish and maintain. In some cases they might also jeopardise an airline's standalone capability (see Chapter 3). It is important to keep in mind that in the alliancing context, benefits of scale and scope are sought through cooperation of two or several separate organisational entities, and not through the growth and expansion of one single entity. Limits to such cooperation are frequently set in regulatory constraints (such as air services agreements between two countries laying down the flags of registration of aircraft providing the service) or related to labour agreements (pilot unions' demands can effectively veto cross-crew utilisation, as can national licensing requirements for aircrew; scope clauses prescribing size of aircraft operated).

Economies of scope

A highly significant type of economies to be reaped in this type of horizontal alliances are scope economies. These are related to one of the key objectives of alliancing, namely route system enlargement. In general terms, economies of scope occur when unit costs go down as the *variety* of products produced increases. Economies of scope occur generally when products are distinct, but related. In the airline case, this would refer to the number of markets, or city pairs, served – in other words, to the extent of the joint route system. In airline terminology, they can also be called 'economies of network size'.[24] Alliances offer an airline the opportunity to reap economies of network size without having to physically expand the number of points they serve themselves. Possible sources of these economies are codeshares, a broadening of the marketing presence through joint branding, and access to well-distributed Frequent Flyer Programmes. A related concept is that of 'benefits of scope'. The most visible scope benefit is value enhancement, i.e., the airline's customer gets seamless access to a large number of points across the world. In addition, there is the so-called 'reputation effect'[25] which relates to the fact that, frequently, an alliance membership is seen as a sign of approval, or a seal of quality.

In practical terms, growth in scope through alliancing might bring more immediate passenger benefits than pure growth in scale: for example, there are disadvantages related to operating a route system around one single hub.

> Inconvenient transfers and lengthy routes are the disadvantage of such [centralised] networks. The savings in operating costs may eventually be outweighed by the loss of customers searching for more convenient service. In order to remain competitive, major carriers tend to upgrade hub-and-spoke networks with multiple hub facilities.
> (Chou, 1990)

Thus, instead of increasing the scale at one hub beyond the realistic capacity of that hub, airlines might fare better to increase their scope first, by distributing traffic across several hubs. Using alliance partners' route systems and hubs is one quick and relatively inexpensive way to achieve this.

Three basic types of airlines

There have been numerous suggestions on how airlines can be classified.[26] It is proposed here to categorize airlines according to a feature which is highly relevant to their membership in a strategic alliance, namely the *nature* and *scope* of services provided; in other words, the characteristics of their route system. The focus is not on competition on certain routes, but rather on the firm's positioning in relation to other firms – competitors, alliance partners, and competing alliance partners. In the following classification, airlines are grouped according to the relative importance they put on serving their home markets versus intercontinental flights to feed that home market, or transcontinental flights that do not concern the home market at all. The notion of 'home market' is feasible because all of the current actors in the alliance game are airlines which have traditionally served a medium- to short-haul market around their hub(s), an area where they enjoy a strong market presence and possibly even dominance. An airline's home market is thus the set of routes on which it has the highest operating density. To mention two examples, Finnair's home market is within North-Eastern Europe, and connecting this region through its hub in Helsinki to European capitals; Lufthansa's home market is Central Europe.

We can distinguish three types of internationally operating airlines, namely the Local Champion, the Long-haul Operator, and the Global Connector. The Local Champions are typically short- to medium-haul airlines. They operate limited long-haul services, and some of these intercontinental operations – for example, Finnair's routes to Asia – are high-yield and generate significant revenue, but these often constitute a relatively small part of overall operations. Often (but not always), Local Champions are true niche carriers in that they serve markets where they enjoy a strong presence and relatively little competition. Some of these markets can be quite attractive due to their wealth (for example, Northern Europe). Examples of Local Champions include Austrian Airlines, Finnair, SAS Scandinavian Airlines, and TAP Air Portugal.

The Long-haul Operators are very similar to Local Champions in that they concentrate on feeding a home market, but intercontinental flights constitute a somewhat higher proportion of their total flight operations and revenues. Most of these airlines are in this category due to the geopolitically 'remote' location of their home, such as Australia/New Zealand or South America. As flag carriers, their mission was, or is, to link their country to the 'Rest of the World'. They typically connect their home market, where they enjoy a dominant or close to dominant position, with the respective important business centres on other continents. Examples of this type are Air New Zealand, LAN Chile, or South African Airways.

Lastly, there are the Global Connectors. These airlines truly aim to serve the whole world; they operate to several continents and have extensive capability to link two continents through their home hub on a third. They often also operate dense local networks, but these do not necessarily constitute their primary 'raison d'être'. The role of Global Connector requires a centrally located home base, such as in Europe, North America or a central location in Asia. Examples for airlines that operate transcontinentally are Lufthansa (linking North America to Africa or the Middle East via their Frankfurt Hub), American Airlines (linking Europe to South America via Miami or Dallas), or Singapore Airlines (linking Europe to Australasia).

The requirements and some examples for each type of airline in this broad classification are summed up below:

- 'Local Champion': Low relation of intercontinental destinations to domestic / regional destinations. Low absolute number of intercontinental destinations. Examples: bmi British Midland Int'l; Olympic Airways; CSA Czech Airways; Finnair; Aer Lingus; SAS; Austrian Airlines; TAP Air Portugal.
- 'Longhaul Operator': Slightly higher absolute number of intercontinental destinations. Remote geographic location of hub (i.e. here, 'remote' for connecting two continents through hub on third). Examples: Aerolíneas Argentinas; LAN Chile; Varig; Japan Air Lines; Air New Zealand; South African Airways.
- 'Global Connector': High absolute number of intercontinental destinations, covering all or almost all continents. Connecting two continents via a hub in a third. Centrally located hub(s). Examples: Air France; British Airways; KLM; Lufthansa; Singapore Airlines.

In sum, the Local Champions are oriented towards a specific market level, the Global Connectors operate on a global level (linking markets), with the Long-haul Operators constituting a special case of Local Champion. There can be, and in fact are, some cases of overlap of roles where a Global Connector also has a Local Champion function (such as Air France). However, and as will be discussed in Chapter 3, there appears to be a tendency among airlines to specialise in one role; Global Connectors are increasingly letting smaller operators feed them on what was formerly their local route system. The classification is thus still useful in the sense that these airlines' primary strategic interest in alliancing is driven by their ambitions as Global Connectors.

Three generic airline strategies

The three generic airline strategies are Growth, Focus, and Lowest-cost strategy (Seristö 1999; see also Chapter 5). Each of these has certain limitations, which push airlines towards establishing some alliance links.

Growth

The first option is organic growth of an airline. This refers to growth without mergers or acquisitions. The viability of this option is, however, severely limited, due to the following main restrictions to organic growth of an airline:

- Regulatory: in a number of markets, access is still governed by bilateral agreements where only designated carriers can serve a route. This means that an airline is not always free to decide on which markets to expand.
- Infrastructure: even in a deregulated market, a newcomer might face significant slot restrictions at airports.

- Market capacity: a market only supports a certain capacity. Doganis (1991; 2001) has shown that new entrants to a market are often tempted to induce a fare war which cannot be sustained in the long run and which is likely to end with the exit of the challenger.
- Economical: there is a limit to the degree of internalisation possible. One reason is that beyond a certain size, a firm may become inefficient. Another reason is that the (hypothetical) cost of organic growth is significantly higher than the cost of teaming up with a partner.
- Competition dampening: by alliancing with an airline, this carrier becomes a partner. In the case of organic growth into that carrier's market, it would have been a competitor.

Another growth option would that be of mergers, or the acquisition of a controlling stake in another carrier. The merger issue will be discussed in more detail at the end of this chapter. The main obstacle to this kind of growth is financial. Because demand for air travel is derived demand, the airline industry is highly cyclical and significantly impacted by outside events. At the same time, the provision of air travel is cost intensive with a fairly high amount of fixed costs and low margins. Deregulation has aggravated this. The difficulties airlines have with fleet planning (i.e., the in-time procurement of adequate machinery to produce their service) and the increased practice of aircraft leasing instead of purchasing reflect the fact that planning on long time horizons is difficult, and airlines are reluctant to make significant investments into other carriers and face the integration costs.[27] Nevertheless, there has been evidence of some airlines seeking equity stakes especially in smaller partners, and then not merging them into their own operations, but merely exercising control over these partners' operations. Examples include Lufthansa's investment in the German regional airline Eurowings, which influenced Eurowings' operational profile in terms of fleet planning, route network, and sales. Another example is the investment SAS made in Spanair in late 2001. Spanair has now been operationally re-oriented to stop serving its route to Washington DC (cooperating with Star partner United on North Atlantic routes instead), and concentrate instead on expanding in the Spanish/Western Mediterranean market plus a very small set of long-thin routes out of Spain where SAS (and/or the Star alliance) have a certain strategic interest in presence. SAS has also invested in Star partner bmi British Midland (as has Lufthansa), and Singapore Airlines in Star partner Air New Zealand. The clear tendency in equity investments seems to be that if these investments are taken, they must be large enough to allow the investing airline to exercise leverage over the partner's operations. Small minority investments, which could be observed in the past (ANA having held a small stake of Austrian Airlines, British Airways holding ten per cent of Iberia) have not be observed recently.

The growth option also includes the possibility for alliances and will be discussed later.

Focus

Focus is the pursuit of a niche strategy. The airline can focus either on a certain geographic market or on a customer base. In the case of focusing on a geographic niche, an alliance with other carriers is a feasible option in that it provides the niche carrier with feed for its market, by having the partner airlines connect the specialist to the world. The other niche strategy, one which appears to be impervious at least to the current alliance movement, is that of *functional* differentiation, for example, that of low-fare, no frills services, and we currently see no low-fare carrier participating in the big alliance game. One straightforward reason for this is the need for a more or less homogeneous fare structure as well as an at least theoretical requirement for similar service levels across alliance partners. There appears to be what we can call a 'minimum required structural compatibility level' for an alliance to take place, and sharp differences in service concepts or fares seem to be factors which move the strategic group of low-fare/ no-frills carriers below this minimum threshold level. There could be, however, some scope for cooperation with other airlines in the field of joint resource utilisation.

Lowest-cost strategy

Lastly, there is the lowest-cost choice, which means a concentration on high load factors, minimum operating and overhead costs, and a standardised fleet. This in practice refers to scheduled low-fare carriers as described above, and also to non-scheduled carriers serving tourist destinations under contract for tour operators. These airlines do not carry connecting traffic, which implies that allying with other airlines will carry very limited benefits. Some benefits might, however, arise in the field of cost reduction, and we can currently observe a tentative alliance formation between several European charter carriers. It seems that, currently, a true lowest-cost strategy is difficult to pursue if the airline wants to uphold features that would make it structurally compatible with current alliances, as these features refer to sales infrastructure and passenger amenities.

Types of alliances between airlines

In the broadest sense, alliances as they occur in the airline industry can be understood this way: '… an alliance involves collaboration between two or more firms that retain their autonomy during the course of their relationship.'[28] Important to the understanding of alliancing specifically in the airline industry, is (a) the possibility for more than two firms entering an alliance, and (b) the fact that in tightly integrated alliance groups, the retention of an individual airline's autonomy is difficult. The extent to which airline managers try to retain their firm's autonomy within the alliance group will be discussed in Chapters 3 and 4.

What is commonly termed 'airline alliance' consists in fact of several different types of cooperative links. The following list briefly describes the most common forms of cooperation between airlines:

1. *Cost sharing ventures.* This involves two or more airlines jointly purchasing equipment, thereby benefiting from bulk discounts. An example from the late 1990s is the joint purchasing of a fleet of around 100 Airbus A 318/319 aircraft by three – otherwise not cooperating – Latin American airlines (Grupo TACA, TAM, and LAN Chile).
2. *Asset pools.* These occur often in the area of maintenance, where airlines might pool the spare parts (in some cases even engines) they store at outstations or joint warehouses.
3. *Pro-rate agreements.* An agreement on the revenue which airline A pays airline B if B carries A's passengers on a route operated by B. This is the simplest form of commercial agreement.
4. *Codesharing* (on single routes or across larger parts of the respective networks. Airline A sells a flight under its own airline designator code, even though that flight is operated by another airline, B (i.e., A and B 'share' a designator code). The advantage for A lies in its access to markets without having to physically operate its own aircraft there; for B the advantage lies in being able to better fill the aircraft it operates on that route, namely with its own *and* A's passengers, and to be eventually able to move to operating a larger aircraft type sooner on that route, thereby benefiting from the typically lower seat-mile costs a larger aircraft has. In codesharing, revenues are split between A and B according to an agreed formula. There is commonly a distinction between strategic, regional, and point-to-point codesharing: the first type covering a large part of the partner's route system, the second type focussing on cooperation within a specific geographic area, and the third type being of a merely 'tactical' nature on single routes. Codeshares can be fairly short-term (1-2 schedule periods) and just concern one route, or they can in fact constitute the very backbone of an alliance, being multilateral (where two or more airlines place their codes on flights of a third), long-term and involving significant changes in operational arrangements in order to harmonise schedules. This can be called an 'equal partner network',[29] even if one codeshare partner is of overall smaller size, there is often *relative equality* in that particular market.
5. *Feeder.* This is a special form of codesharing between a larger and a smaller partner. This cooperation tends to be hierarchical. A smaller, typically regional, airline flying under its own brand operates a codeshare to a larger airline's hub. A typical example was Eurowings prior to Lufthansa's investment in that airline: Eurowings used to be a fully independent regional airline, feeding KLM's Amsterdam hub from several cities in Germany, cooperating with Air France on routes to Paris, and also operating some routes solely on their own code (see also 'integrated feeders', point 8).

6. *Marketing alliances.* This includes joint advertising (sometimes under an alliance brand name), joint sales, and joint frequent flyer programmes; these typically go together with strategic and sometimes regional codeshares. Marketing alliances are frequently multilateral, and require extensive coordination between partners. A typical marketing alliance is oneworld.

7. *Joint Ventures.* A JV is, in a way, a 'complete' marketing alliance, in that the JV partners apply joint pricing and revenue sharing on a route or set of code shared routes. A Joint Venture requires the partners to seek antitrust immunity. Typically, the authorities grant antitrust immunity for a number of years, after which partners have to apply again. One of the Senior Executives interviewed called Joint Ventures 'Route Mergers' and mentioned that one of the advantages of JVs is that airline management can achieve a merger-like situation on certain markets, deepen cooperation and bypass ownership issues without having to ask for shareholder endorsement for this. Joint Ventures occur between partners either on markets where there would be a Route Set overlap (Example: JV between Lufthansa and SAS on Germany-Northern Europe market, Joint Venture between Lufthansa and United on North Atlantic routes), or on jointly exploiting a new third market. These are truly strategic alliances in the sense that they involve the merging of a part of the activities, but not all. A route or market Joint Venture might imply that one airline gives up its presence in a certain market.

8. *Integrated Feeder.* Possibly the most hierarchical form of cooperation, typically between a larger carrier and a regional airline where the smaller airline operates fully and exclusively under franchise to feed its partner. The large airline thus establishes a 'clan', or 'dominated network', around it. This practice exists frequently in the USA, where almost all major carriers have their integrated feeders. In Europe, a dominated network is maintained by Lufthansa with regional airline Lufthansa Cityline and those carriers under its 'Team Lufthansa' sub-brand (Augsburg Airways, Cimber Air, Cirrus Airlines, Contact Air, Rheintalflug), and also by British Airways (British Regional Airlines, SUN-Air of Scandinavia, Comair, Loganair).

9. *Equity stakes.* Often, these involve only minority stakes (due to home country legislation which in many cases limit foreign ownership of airlines). Equity stakes are sometimes a way to pre-empt competitors from teaming up with a third airline. In other cases, they are sought because they are assumed to 'cement' an alliance, providing the investor with better control over its partner. An airline which, up to 2001, pursued a policy of buying equity in its alliance partners was Swissair. Other equity links include SAS/Lufthansa in Spanair, SAS in bmi British Midland International, the former stake British Airways had in Deutsche BA, the stakes held by Singapore Airlines in Virgin Atlantic and Air New Zealand. The operational influence of investors in their partner varies.

An alliance group is thus in many cases more than a simple arrangement of codeshare agreements between partners. As cooperation between partners exceeds simple exchange agreements, the need for tighter coordination – and therefore, integration of efforts – increases. In a fully multilateral alliance network (i.e. where each member cooperates with every other member), a single member's decisions will affect the network. These alliances are based on integration,[30] and they feature increased interdependence between members. The degree of integration between members will also define organisational boundaries.[31] At high levels of member integration, airlines will move towards constituting organisational units of an alliance, which can then be considered a supra-organisation. The increased mutual interdependence will imply a need for stability of the supra-organisation (or task environment). These requirements will be further discussed in Chapters 3 and 9.

Formality and scope of airline alliances

In general terms, a tie between two firms can be described according to (a) its nature, as defined by the degree of formal resource commitment, and (b) by its extent, or scope. The degree of formal resource commitment can be said to measure the 'qualitative side' of a relationship. It depicts whether it has been 'sealed' by a contractual agreement and of the type of contract involved. One can broadly distinguish between formal agreements where parties pledge a certain type of cooperation or coordination without specifying too many details, and such agreements where the nature of that cooperation (the 'how') is laid down and prescribed in more detail. As stated, airline alliances can be seen to reside at the upper end of the formality continuum.

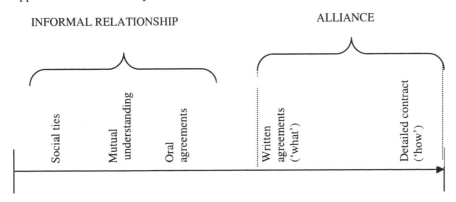

Figure 1.1   The continuum of alliance formality

In addition, one can use a second concept, that of relative scope,[32] in order to be able to describe an alliance. This concept illustrates the 'quantitative' nature of the interaction. It can be defined as 'the extent of activities in markets unrelated to the alliance as a proportion of all activities conducted by the firms'.[33] This is highly relevant for the analysis of alliancing dynamics, since 'the opportunity set of each firm outside the particular alliance crucially impacts its behaviour within the alliance'.[34]

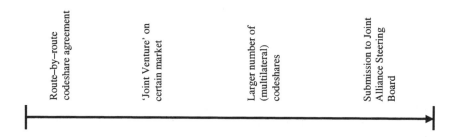

Figure 1.2   The continuum of relative alliance scope

In the airline case, low relative scope of an alliance means that an airline cooperates on certain routes with a partner, typically through a codeshare, or a block-space agreement. This cooperation constitutes but a relatively small part of overall operations. At a higher level of relative scope, a certain set of routes, typically comprising a geographical market, could be covered by a Joint Venture with a partner or several partners. A yet higher level of relative scope would be membership in a multilateral alliance, where a large part of an airline's operations is within the context of cooperation with one or more partners from an alliance group. The highest alliancing level in terms of scope would be the submission to a joint alliance steering board, where the airline moves towards constituting a sub-unit of the supra-organisation of the alliance group.

It must be noted that the two continua are interlinked; the above continuum of relative scope starts on the formality continuum at a relatively high level, i.e., at least that of a written agreement. Less formal relations with limited scope do exist; they can apply to management contacts between airlines whose route sets do not overlap, or to relations between functional areas of two airlines. A fairly common example is the contact and cooperation between airline personnel at outstations: station managers of different airlines – competing or not – sometimes join forces in negotiating with the local airport authority as their landlord. Similarly, in several countries there are 'Boards of Airline Representatives', comprising managers from foreign airlines operating into that country. They typically have a lobbying function. At a higher level of relative scope, informal relations are frequently a stage which precedes formal cooperation. Informal relations with a higher degree of scope are the area of, for example, tacit collusion, or the stage of preliminary talks in preparation for alliance group membership or a merger. Apart from seeing informal relations as a step towards formalisation, they also merit attention *within* formalised relationships. Within an airline alliance group, the decision making is frequently carried out by 'task groups' or 'working committees' on specific topics, such as for example IT-integration or harmonisation of Frequent Flyer Programmes. Tacit understanding and goodwill may be of some importance within these task groups, but it is proposed here that in the formation and partner choice phase of airlines, informal links are of relatively less importance than market and resource characteristics of a specific potential partner (partially due to the fact that each airline has a clear 'speciality resource', or core market, which it contributes to an alliance).

An interesting and important feature of cooperative agreements between airlines is that it is frequently the extensive and strategically important marketing agreements or alliance group membership agreements that specify the nature and extent of a cooperation in much less detail than, say, a pro-rate agreement, which would typically be highly formal, but of limited scope and of a purely tactical nature. Less detailed agreements thus frequently embrace a much larger scope, and require a higher amount of non-structured, ad-hoc coordination and continued negotiation. This implies a higher need for consensus between partners, or a need for a hierarchical alliance structure. This will be discussed in more detail in Chapter 9.

The degree of alliance integration

As we have seen, membership in an alliance group offers the airline an opportunity to reap benefits of cooperation without the need for physical growth while evading most of the regulatory impediments to mergers. It is therefore assumed that, due to the global nature of air travel, no airline (with the exception of some functionally highly differentiated ones) can operate in a vacuum; even a purely domestically operating carrier needs some link with an international airline to obtain feed. A characterising feature of an alliance is the degree of interconnectedness, or tightness of coupling, between partners. There are four prominent factors which influence the differences in tightness of coupling, namely regulation, passenger expectations, the uncertain competitive environment, and internal (managerial) resistance.

A very strong factor that provides for a 'domino effect' in the tendency towards the formation of marketing alliances between airlines is customer expectations. The requirements of the travelling public tend to go towards 'seamless' travel to a maximum number of points across the globe, and this goes beyond what a single airline could provide. As some airlines start to cooperate and provide a global route system, other airlines are 'forced' to follow suit: a significant characteristic of the product has changed, and producers must adapt to be able to provide it.

Two factors positively influence the tightness of cooperation between alliance members. First, and as discussed above, passengers have come to demand a type of service that is impossible for a single airline to provide. The need to fulfil these enhanced expectations induces tighter cooperation between carriers. Second, the increased level of possible competition between airlines and the continuing deregulation of markets has led to greater uncertainty in the airlines' operating environment. They are turning to cooperation in an attempt to control this uncertainty.[35]

The next two factors work *against* tight cooperation between partner carriers. Within airline management, there is still a considerable reluctance to give up independence and to relegate decision making to some external entity (see Chapter 4). There is also the hurdle of cultural friction: as firms cooperate, distinct company cultures – and, in the case of airlines, invariably nationalities – meet; and even though procedures at the 'production-level' of airlines (i.e. maintaining and flying the aircraft, dispatching the passengers) are highly standardised world-wide, culture is still likely to have an important influence on how and why things are decided. Even though they might consciously favour alliance membership, managers are likely to put their own airline's interests above those of the alliance, thereby working against integration.

Lastly, it is interesting to note the impact of the regulatory environment. On one hand, there is strong resistance against approving alliances that would dominate a certain market or a certain hub airport. This has a negative effect on the tightness of member coupling, as it can prevent codeshares and joint ventures. But regulation also has its impact on customer expectations as well as on the airlines' requirements for environmental control. As discussed, the opening of markets has changed what customers expect from air travel. Moreover, the mere fact that strong regulatory forces govern air transport is inducing airlines to cooperate with each other in order to maximise their influence on regulators. A further factor increasing the need for environmental control is that uncertainty levels and competitive pressure on airlines increase due to the gradual reduction of traffic regulation; as 5th, 6th and 7th freedom rights become more common, competitors are freer in their actions – such as fare and frequency setting – in many markets.

Three tiers of alliance membership

Examining airline alliances from the perspective of tightness of integration, one can conceptualise an airline alliance group as a three-tier structure with a dense 'core', where members are tightly linked to each other, a sphere of 'second tiers', which are typically linked to one of the core actors, but less tightly among each other, and a surrounding halo of 'contributors', who cooperate on a route-by-route basis, but are not true members of the alliance network.

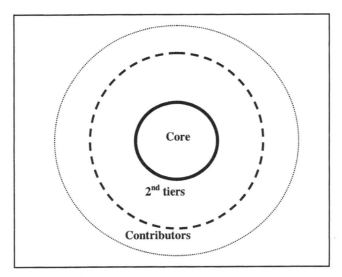

Figure 1.3   Levels of alliance integration

The *core* is ideally a true multilateral alliance, operating to some extent under an alliance brand name, and governed or at least coordinated by a joint alliance steering board. The relationship between core members is almost non-hierarchical, or at least is intended to be so. In some cases, core members serve determined markets as Joint Ventures (such as Lufthansa with SAS in the Germany - Northern Europe market).

Second tiers are airlines that typically have close links with one or two core members. They often provide coverage of geographical regions that are of strategic importance to the alliance, but not sufficiently covered by any core member. Regional feeders are also typical second tiers. There are typically few links between second tiers themselves, but one can observe a form of clan[36] building, or clustering, where each core member has a set of close links to second tiers; these affiliates constitute a 'clan' within the alliance.[37] Examples for clans are the 'Team Lufthansa' airlines (regionals which operate as feeders under LH-code), or the TWA network feeding American Airlines in the domestic US market.

The *contributors* are airlines outside the alliance; they can cooperate with carriers from different alliances in a 'portfolio of bilaterals' (see below).

If the list of alliance objectives, or benefits, is examined as to which objectives are met at what level of integration, one obtains the following pattern:

Managing Strategic Airline Alliances

	Competitor taming	Strengthening of position on home market	Value enhancement	Efficiency gains through joint resource utilisation	Economies of Density	Learning	Hub	Network enlargement	Environmental control
Core Member	yes	yes	yes	yes	yes	yes	yes	yes	yes
Second Tier	yes	yes	yes	some	some	some	no	some	few
Contributor	some	no	yes	no	yes	no	no	no	no

Figure 1.4   Benefits gained from alliancing
Source: Kleymann and Seristö, 1999.

This pattern shows that there are benefits to be gained from alliance for any type of airline, and at any level of integration, with loosely-tied contributors reaping at least the benefits of value enhancement (that is, their passengers have a greater choice of convenient onwards flights at connecting hubs), and economies of density (where partners channel passengers onto the contributor's flights).

However, weighing the benefits of alliancing against the need for managerial discretion – still of importance as long as a firm's managers are responsible to those who hold stakes in their firm, not in the alliance – one can also use a framework proposed by Doganis (1991), which states that an airline's profitability depends on management's ability to manipulate and match three key profitability variables, namely (a) Unit Costs, (b) Yields, and (c) Loadfactors, as well as manage five key product factors, which are (1) Fares and Conditions, (2) Schedules, (3) Comfort, (4) Access, and (5) Image. Of these factors, those which are likely to be affected to the largest extent by alliance membership are loadfactors (through hubbing/achievement of economies of density), schedules, access, and image. There might be, for some airlines, a gain in 'comfort' factors. But it must be noted that Doganis explicitly states that the airline must be able to 'manage' and 'manipulate' these factors. Membership in an alliance is likely to curtail some of an airline's freedom of strategy-devising, and recipes devised at alliance level and imposed on members might not be optimal for an individual carrier. There is, therefore, a clear trade-off between membership benefits and benefits of (and indeed the need for) individual strategy making. As to actual integration levels, currently most airlines position themselves as either core members or as contributors. However, evidence from interviews (see Chapter 4) suggests that beyond a certain size, alliance cores become unwieldy and difficult to manage. By observing the currently existing airline alliance groups and their attempts to establish a joint governance mode, one can note the following two tendencies in alliance group organisation. The first is a tendency to maintain a moderately sized, but tightly integrated and truly multilateral alliance core while allowing a slow expansion of a second tier sphere, the members of which will be tightly bound to one core airline. A relatively small core size implies less complex core management, but it possibly encourages 'empire building' by core members and requires the submission to a strong, unilateral hierarchy for the second tiers.

The second tendency in alliance group organisation seems to be efforts to create an additional hierarchical level in the form of a superstructure (an alliance governing body), which exercises authority over all members (see Chapter 9). This alliance governing body would require that group members bestow it with a certain authority over their own policymaking; it therefore requires member airlines to give up a certain degree of governance autonomy *ex ante*. Both tendencies clearly aim at complexity reduction: it appears that a federation of multiple, autonomous but interdependent firms which differ from each other in terms of resource endowments and policy goals cannot be efficiently governed on a 'democratic' basis. The development of airline alliances in the past years has indeed included the search for some alliance group governance mode.

Portfolio of bilaterals versus multilateral alliances

Even though the present discussion focuses on multilateral alliances, it is useful to keep in mind that there are two principal kinds of alliance arrangements that can be distinguished in the airline industry, namely portfolios of bilaterals, and multilateral alliances. In a 'portfolio of bilaterals' type of alliance, a focal airline remains a 'contributor' to any airline alliance group in that it maintains a set of bilateral agreements with partners who do not necessarily need to be related to each other.

In a multilateral alliance, each partner has a bilateral agreement with every other one, or at least with the supra-organisation.

A portfolio of bilaterals would need to be examined from the perspective of the single airline, which maintains a set of links with other airlines. It is thus not a true 'network' in the strict sense of the word. The currently largest carrier pursuing a portfolio strategy is Japan Air Lines: JAL is not a member in any alliance group; they operate a portfolio of bilaterals instead. In mid-2001, they had bilateral agreements with a total of 19 airlines. These airlines together provided for 26 per cent of world traffic.[38]

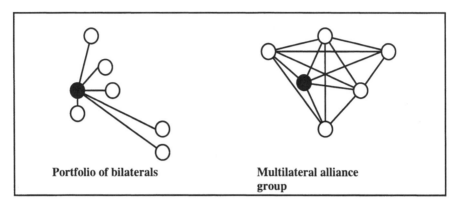

Figure 1.5   **Two basic types of alliances**

A multilateral network, on the other hand, can be examined both from the perspective of a single actor, and of the network itself. A true multilateral alliance can imply exclusivity, i.e., no right for members to forge agreements outside the alliance network (for example, cases of exclusivity apply in the Star-alliance). This is an interesting aspect for consideration upon joining an alliance, since a portfolio of bilaterals has the advantage of less complicated dissolution, whereas in a multilateral net, a member is considerably more tied up. But on taking a portfolio approach, a carrier is unlikely to reap significant gains in marketing scope.

The following table lists the main strategic differences for an airline between maintaining a portfolio of bilaterals versus joining a multilateral alliance.

Table 1.1 Multilateral alliances versus portfolio of bilaterals

	Multilateral alliance	**Portfolio of bilaterals**
Gains in market scope	very high	moderate to high
Provision of "shelter"	high	none to low
Sunk costs	high	low
Complexity of dissolution	high	low
Operating autonomy	low to medium	high

It appears that the option of a portfolio-of-bilaterals approach as opposed to membership in an alliance group is particularly feasible for airlines that do not strongly require the integration benefit of sheltering from competition. In practice, this would apply to airlines with a home market that features high entry barriers for geographical and/or political/regulatory reasons, and it is indeed this type of airline that tends to opt for a portfolio approach, staying outside any alliance group.

Current airline alliance groups

Alliances have two purposes: Stop competing with each other, and jointly beat upon the other guy. All the rest is fluff.
(Senior Manager of US Air in a TV interview)

At present, the existing four airline alliance groups account for more than half of globally produced RPK. This section gives a broad overview over the existing alliance groups. The current alliance groups can be described as follows:

Star alliance. This currently largest airline alliance group was founded in 1997. It is a multilateral network of currently 15 core airlines, most of which have agreements with all other members of the alliance and a fairly large number of regional feeders. Star is marketed as a brand in its own right. Star members are frequently bound by exclusivity agreements, which limit the extent to which they are allowed to seek cooperation with airlines that are not members of that alliance group. The alliance is governed by consensus achieved by members during meetings that occur on a fixed rota at several managerial levels. There are also airlines that assume a leadership role in a certain region: the most prominent is Lufthansa in Europe. Star can be considered the most truly multilateral alliance group so far, where each member collaborates (albeit to a varying extent) with every other member.

However, the formal governance of the alliance group is still based on bilateral agreements between individual carriers. In a step to achieve multilateral governance, a Star management board called AMT (Alliance Management Team) has been set up with around 80 full-time employees, staffed partially by member airlines' managers and partially by outsiders.

In 2002, the Star alliance was registered as a limited liability company under German law.

Within Star, some members are even linked tighter than by mere codeshares. There are Joint Venture type agreements in place which involve joint fare setting, schedule coordination and a sharing of costs and revenues on certain routes or markets. Importantly, Lufthansa and United Airlines enjoy antitrust immunity on North Atlantic routes. In addition, Lufthansa has set up Joint Ventures in the markets between Germany and Scandinavia, Austria and Thailand with its partners SAS, AUA and Thai Airways respectively.

Recently, Star has negotiated joint IT infrastructure solutions for its members with a large IT systems firm; they also have established the 'Star Alliance FuelCo', a joint company that purchases aircraft fuel for members at a number of airports around the world.

To accommodate for the fact that growth in membership would require the alliance group to take a different structure from the present one in order to remain functional, Star has acknowledged that they are planning to move to adopting an official tier-structure while extending their membership base:

> [Star spokesman] Klick said the board expects at its [May 2002] Shanghai meeting to approve a major recasting of its evolving growth strategy to recognize the varying sizes and regional presence/interests of potential new members by 'packaging' and defining for the first time the requirements for various levels of membership participation.
> (ATW online, 26 February 2002)

For the time being, however, Star clings to its principle of 'one member, one vote', implying that in alliance voting, each airline has the same say, regardless of size.

oneworld   oneworld can best be described as two clusters of airlines, one evolving around American Airlines and the other evolving around British Airways. Initially, a very close Joint Venture type cooperation on North Atlantic routes between the two carriers was planned. Opposition from the regulatory authorities, who feared that a monopolistic situation on the large UK-US market could ensue, places severe limitations on the degree to which the two carriers can cooperate. There were repeated attempts to achieve antitrust immunity for British Airways and American Airlines on the North Atlantic market, which failed mainly due to the US authorities' condition that they would have to give up a fairly large number of slots at London Heathrow airport to open that hub to more competition. Both BA and AA considered this too high a price to pay. As a result, oneworld is the only alliance group where the lead carriers do not enjoy antitrust immunity on the important Europe–US market. While British Airways and American Airlines are barred from cooperating too closely, recent moves within the alliance have shown a strengthening of other ties. For example, in February 2002, American Airlines increased its codeshares with Iberia and Qantas and struck a ten-year agreement concerning joint aircraft procurement and sharing facilities at airports with the latter airline. British Airways extended its codeshares with Asian partner Cathay Pacific.

oneworld members are not as strictly bound by exclusivity stipulations as Star members. The governance of oneworld has been described by various interview partners as very democratic and consensus-seeking. In 2000, a oneworld management company was set up in Vancouver, Canada. The role of that company is that of a forum for communication and of a coordinator for cross-airline working groups. The oneworld management company is planned to be given greater authority over alliance governance in the medium term.

SkyTeam This latest alliance group was formed in 1999 between Air France and Delta Air Lines. It currently comprises six carriers. The declared aim of this alliance is to stay small and concentrate on high-quality services. One significant infrastructure-related advantage of this group is its dominant position at Charles de Gaulle airport in Paris, which is the last large hub in Europe that does not suffer from severe congestion problems and which has possibilities for further enlargement. The most tightly-linked unit within SkyTeam is a US Cargo Sales Joint Venture between Air France, Delta and Korean Air, headquartered in Atlanta.

SkyTeam was granted antitrust immunity by the US Department of Transportation in January 2002. The aim was to give passengers access to all destinations beyond the four carriers' hub airports, a vital condition for being able to reap full scope benefits, especially for this rather small group. SkyTeam has a dedicated governing board which consists of senior executives from member airlines who meet twice a year to 'provide senior approval to alliancing initiatives, and outline goals and strategies to enhance the alliance's strength' (Alitalia Press Release, Nov 15, 2001). This sort of 'governance structure' is considerably less formal than those of Star and oneworld, both of which have dedicated 'management companies' which also include staff at middle levels.

'Wings' In 1992, Dutch KLM and Northwest Airlines established a cooperation and integration agreement covering codeshares and joint marketing and involving all of the respective partners' operations. A global Joint Venture agreement over a period of at least 13 years was established in 1996. By 1998, both airlines had integrated their sales organisations. In 1999/2000, KLM prepared to merge with Alitalia, a deal that was unsuccessful (see below). Both KLM and Northwest have separate sets of partners with whom they codeshare and to which some features of the 'Wings' alliance (such as Frequent Flyer Points, and codeshares) are extended. In 2001, Continental Airlines, which had hitherto cooperated with Northwest only, established an extensive codeshare partnership with KLM. (Note that 'Wings' is still an unofficial name for this alliance, which is still officially referred to as the 'KLM-Northwest alliance'). After KLM was integrated with Air France in a joint holding company in 2002, industry observers expect the 'Wings' alliance to dissolve, with the cluster around KLM joining Skyteam.

Cases of failed airline alliances

The past two decades have also seen a number of major alliance failures. One interviewed senior manager listed what he saw as the three main failure factors for airline alliances:

- Overextension of financial resources (e.g. Swissair - Qualiflyer).
- Political reasons and unwillingness to cooperate (e.g. KLM/Alitalia; KLM/British Airways).
- Strategic overlap (e.g. Finnair/SAS during EQA). Strategic overlap is a significant problem if both partners consider themselves 'equals', and no one thus agrees to take a 'feeder' role. Currently, strategic overlap is overshadowing the relationship between Lufthansa and SAS within Star.

Interestingly, the early (and now defunct) alliances were, with the exception of *Alcazar*, all initiatives by one single airline to establish a partnership network (Iberia, Swissair), or a portfolio of bilaterals (SAS), based on equity investment in those partners. The following is a short description of some major alliance failures.

SAS-group In the late 1980s, SAS bought stakes in a number of airlines, including Danair of the UK, LAN Chile, Continental Airlines, and the (then) charter carrier Spanair. Cross-shareholdings were planned (but never materialised) with Swissair and Finnair. This strategy has subsequently been criticised[39] for being too expensive and involving links with carriers that would not bring real scope benefits to SAS. In addition, even though SAS held equity stakes in its partners, it failed to secure sufficient management influence over them.

EQA/Alcazar In the early 1990s, SAS, Swissair and Austrian Airlines established the 'European Quality Alliance' (EQA), which was centred on technical cooperation and the marketing of EQA as a 'seal of quality'. In 1993, the group expanded into codesharing, and KLM was to join what by then had become known under the new alliance name 'Alcazar'. The establishment of Alcazar stalled during the second half of 1993, primarily due to disagreements on who the US partner to this airline group ought to be; KLM was adamant about maintaining its strong ties to Northwest, even though that airline was at the time in financial difficulties and its North American network was not large compared with its US competitors. Swissair insisted on its partner Delta Air Lines and strongly objected a partnership with Northwest, because this would have jeopardised the triangular cooperation Swissair/Delta/Singapore Airlines which had been in place prior to EQA/Alcazar and was highly valued by Swissair management. SAS in turn cooperated with Continental Airlines and feared that the integration of another very strong transatlantic partner would force them to cut back on their (already limited) transatlantic services. A further problem was that one of Alcazar's main aims was to achieve cost reduction through consolidation. There were significant variations especially in labour costs, between the member airlines, with Swissair's salary and benefit costs per employee being 70 per cent higher than those of KLM.[40] Achieving cost reductions would have implied a significant shift of functions (and jobs) from Zürich to Amsterdam; this met resistance at union and even government level and was unacceptable to Swissair. In short, pre-existing alliances and agreements between airlines, differences in cost structures, and unwillingness to give up sovereignty hindered the development of a common agenda for a new, larger alliance group.

Grupo Iberia The Spanish airline Iberia announced in 1990 its strategy to establish itself as the leading European carrier on routes to South America. Iberia sought to take advantage of the ongoing privatisation of several South American airlines at that time by investing in Aerolíneas Argentinas, VIASA of Venezuela, and LADECO of Chile, taking management control of the first two. Iberia also established three regional hubs in Miami, Santo Domingo and Buenos Aires, which were fed by intercontinental flights from Madrid and then provided onward connections within the subcontinent by a fleet of Iberia DC9s in fairly luxurious cabin configurations, which were permanently based at these hubs. For a variety of reasons, most of which were related to costs, extreme management problems in cooperating with their South American partners, the lack of operational viability of the Santo Domingo and Miami hubs, as well as the general economic situation in that part of the world, Iberia gradually withdrew from its engagement in Latin America. VIASA has since disappeared; LADECO is now merged with former competitor LAN Chile, and Aerolíneas Argentinas, in which Iberia held a stake until 2001, is now controlled by another Spanish consortium with no links to Iberia.

KLM/Alitalia Merger In 1998, Dutch KLM and Alitalia announced a full merger of their activities. This merger was approved by the EU competition authorities on the grounds that it involved little overlap between partners. Apart from having to give up a relatively small number of slots in Amsterdam to open competition on routes between the Netherlands and Italy, the partners were very free to create a merged airline. KLM provided financial assistance to Alitalia, mainly to help that airline setting up operations at its newly opened – and at the time poorly performing – hub at Milan-Malpensa airport. The Malpensa hub was seen to be one of Alitalia's main strategic assets. After several months of preparing the deal, however, KLM announced that they would cancel the proposed merger. Officially, this was on the grounds that Alitalia had failed to restructure its internal organisation, and that, more importantly, the Italian carrier had not achieved an acceptable level of operational reliability at Malpensa airport. Unofficially, the de-merger is also believed to be grounded in a certain incompatibility of company and national cultures.

Qualiflyer was to date the only airline alliance group that involved one lead airline holding equity stakes in its partners. In an effort to gain independence from cooperation with other, large carriers, Swissair sought to establish a small, but tightly integrated airline alliance group in Europe. They invested in the Belgian national carrier Sabena (thereby gaining a hub within the European Community), in the French airlines Air Outre Mer, Air Littoral, and Air Liberté, in the Polish national carrier LOT as well as in the German charter carrier LTU. Swissair also sought equity stakes in its Qualiflyer partners TAP Air Portugal, Portugália, and THY Turkish Airways. However, Swissair's strategy failed to bear fruit. All partners in which they had equity stakes and frequently significant operational influence started to have severe financial problems toward the end of the 1990s. Three main points of criticism were that Swissair's partners were rather small, not optimally organised, and rather weakly performing airlines, and that Swissair had failed to extend its alliance group to a global level, concentrating on covering Europe instead. Also, the policy of seeking equity stakes in each partner was considered by most analysts to be too costly. At the end of 2000 and the beginning of 2001, Swissair's parent company SAir expressed unwillingness to support further the present alliancing strategy. In an attempt to cut costs, Swissair sold a part of its stake in LTU, divested its French portfolio, and entered renegotiations about the future of the Sabena stake. In September/October 2001, however, Swissair operations were grounded due to the airline's incapability to meet even current operating expenses (e.g. fuel, catering, ramp services). At the beginning of 2002, some of Swissair's operations were integrated with those of the (more successful) Swiss regional airline Crossair to create a new airline called 'Swiss'. The end of the Qualiflyer alliance was formally announced in February 2002. Swiss and American Airlines are currently in negotiations to gain antitrust immunity. Swiss will join the oneworld alliance in 2004.

Mergers and acquisitions – an alternative to alliances?

As discussed above, the possibilities for merging airlines are still limited, mostly for financial and regulatory reasons, and also due to antitrust concerns. However, it is very likely that in the future some mergers will take place. There are, in theory, three hierarchical possibilities of one airline investing in another: (a) an acquisition, where Airline X buys (and more or less integrates) an (often smaller) Airline Y; (b) a hierarchy *beyond* the original organisation boundaries, where airline Z emerges out of a full merging of airlines X and Y; and a third merger option (c), which is the route taken by Air France and KLM: a holding company is formed as a superstructure to both airlines, which then might be able to continue operating as separate brands for some time, while still reaping some (but by no means all!) of the benefits of integration. In the current airline industry environment, it seems that option (a) – the acquisition – is taken up primarily in cases where a larger airline buys a majority stake – or control – in a much smaller carrier. Full integration is not the goal here, as the larger carrier has every reason to run its acquired target as a separate firm – mostly for labour cost reasons. The strategy of Lufthansa acquiring controlling stakes in German and Central European regional airlines bears testimony to this. Option (b) – the creation of a new entity out of two merged ones – would require a major re-structuring within both partners to make them compatible, and it would be extremely hard to disband, because the original organisational boundaries of airlines X and Y would have been dissolved.

The rationale for this type of true merger seems to be mainly scope related, or aiming at cancelling out competition, as scale economies derived from growing in size appear to be limited in the airline industry (see above).

Up to this date, acquisitions do happen between partners of very different sizes and operational profiles, while true mergers are likely to remain very rare, and can be expected to start along the lines of the Air France–KLM structure. This latter venture still bears many of the characteristics of an alliance: there are still separate identities and organisational boundaries for both carriers, and decision-making will remain up to certain levels with the individual carrier; structures need to be aligned (instead of merged), and there are different stakeholders for each unit. The advantage of such a set-up is – apart from it being politically more palatable to the smaller partners' share- and stakeholders – that both airlines can continue to operate as designated flag carriers under existing Air Services Agreements. Had option (b) been chosen for KLM-Air France, the newly created entity would have lost some of the traffic rights held by the original companies. A further advantage of this setup is that while the full cost of integration is not undergone – or can be spread over a larger time – there is the immediate advantage of a pre-emptive move. In colloquial terms, Air France could 'snap up' KLM, and secure it, before KLM and its very attractive hub at Schiphol could become interesting partners (or targets) to one of Air France's competitors.

Thus, even if the number and extent of equity ties between airlines can be expected to increase in the future, many of these links – especially if they are between partners of roughly equal size and market importance – are still likely to retain the characteristics of an alliance, and due to the continuing regulatory and financial constraints to full mergers and acquisitions, the total need for collaboration between airlines is expected to far exceed the possibilities for acquisitions. In fact, the Star alliance has passed a statute whereby no member can hold more than five per cent equity in another member. It is therefore very likely that even in an increasingly deregulated and liberalised operating environment for airlines, alliances – in whatever form they can take – are going to be the primary mode of linkage between carriers.

Notes

[1] Cabotage rights mean that an airline from country A has the right to pick up and transport passengers between two points in country B, thus operating a domestic service in B (see endnote 3).

[2] Williams, 2000.

[3] *The "freedoms of the air"*
First Freedom: The right for an airline from country A to overfly another country B's airspace without landing.
Second Freedom: The right for an airline from country A to make a landing in another country (B) for technical reasons (e.g. refuelling).

Third Freedom: The right to carry revenue traffic (i.e. fare paying passengers) from own country (A) to country B.

Fourth Freedom: The right to carry revenue traffic from country B back to home country A.

Fifth Freedom: The right for an airline from country A to carry revenue traffic between countries B and C or D on flights starting or ending in home country A.

Sixth Freedom: The right for an airline from country A to carry revenue traffic between countries B and C via its base in home country A as a transit point (de facto a combination of 3rd and 4th freedom rights).

Seventh Freedom: The right for an airline from country A to carry passengers between countries B and C directly, without the need for that service routed via, or originating in, home country A.

Eighth Freedom: The right for an airline from country A to operate domestic services in country B ("cabotage rights").

The 1st to 5th freedom rights are typically negotiated in bilateral air services agreements. The 6th to 8th freedoms are called "supplementary rights", with the latter two being granted very rarely. Open skies in Europe means that EU airlines enjoy all eight freedoms within the EU; to give a somewhat far-fetched example, Lufthansa could theoretically establish a hub in Paris and serve the markets between France and Italy from there, or Air France could establish a hub in Berlin serving German domestic destinations. So far, few European airlines have made full use of the eight freedoms. The reasons for this are mostly operational, such as the difficulty of establishing remote hubs, penetrating already saturated markets, or airport constraints.

[4] For example, the minimum 'domestic' ownership share is 75% in the US and Canada, 72.6% in Singapore, 66.6% in Japan, 65% in China, and 50.1% in the EU.

[5] Antitrust immunity, as bestowed by the US Department of Transportation to a group of airlines, allows them to discuss and coordinate routes, schedules, marketing (including Frequent Flyer) and sales programmes, pricing and, possibly most importantly, pricing and yield management issues.

[6] In reality, however, a large number of routes is in fact still dominated or monopolistically operated by one carrier or alliance group. The possibility for challenging this dominance is in many cases merely theoretical. Entry barriers are very high (for example, to be able to set up attractive frequencies at attractive times).

[7] Oum, Park and Zhang, 2000.

[8] Pels, 2001.

[9] Alamdari, 1989.

[10] Nyathi, 1996.

[11] e.g. Seristö, 1995.

[12] Doganis, 1991; 2001.

[13] Nyathi, 1996.

[14] For an in-depth discussion of these economies in air transport, see Holloway, 1997.

[15] Caves et al., 1984; Holloway, 1997; Doganis, 2001.

[16] Doganis, 1991; Bissessur, 1996.

[17] Doganis, 1991:123ff.

[18] In the very long run, all costs can be considered to be ultimately escapable, but when considering the airline industry, a schedule period – or six months – can be taken as a good time horizon for applying changes such as starting or ceasing to serve routes, increasing or decreasing frequencies etc.

[19] This discussion is partially based on Penrose's, 1959, very detailed treatment of economies of size.

[20] ibid.

[21] In general, larger aircraft have lower seatmile costs over a given stage length than smaller aircraft (cf. Doganis, 1991; Seristö, 1995).

[22] Paprottka, 1996.

[23] Youssef, 1992.

[24] Bissessur, 1996.

[25] Besanko et al., 1996.

[26] See, for example, Gialloreto, 1986); Kling and Smith, 1995; Ter Kuile, 1997; Staniland, 1997; and Berardino and Frankel, 1998. Smith et al., 1997 have classified airlines in the US into strategic groups according to cost position, marketing expenditures, management characteristics, and the scope of operation. They found three clusters, which they called "Niche Seeker", "High-End Flyer", and "Entrenched- Dominant". They found no evidence of competitive behaviour being predictable on the grounds of cluster membership ("*in terms of actions and reactions, rivalry cannot be predicted by strategic group membership*"). This might be due to the fact that in air transport, rivalry depends on a route. In other words, airlines from two different clusters frequently compete on one route or set of routes.

[27] An example for an airline suffering from having invested into another carrier just prior to a major downturn is that of American Airlines, whose results were severely impaired by a combination of the general industry downturn after the terrorist attacks of September 11, 2001, and the cost of purchasing and integrating TWA.

[28] Ring, 2000.

[29] Child and Faulkner, 1998.

[30] Brewer and Hooper, 1998.

[31] For a discussion of boundaries in hybrid organisations, see Borys and Jemison, 1989.

[32] This notion has been introduced by Khanna et al., 1998.

[33] ibid.

[34] ibid.

[35] However, Chapters 3 will discuss how cooperation can also create new uncertainties through specific dependencies.

[36] Note that in this context, 'clans' are rather hierarchical; this is in contrast to the terminology used by Jarillo, 1988, who uses the term 'Clan' to describe groups that are less hierarchical than 'strategic networks'.

[37] A similar differentiation between partner levels has been put forward in KLM's 1997 annual report, where the airline divides the carriers with which it cooperates into "Global partners", "Network Partners", "Route Partners", "Leisure Flight Partners" and "Cargo Partners".

[38] *Air Transport World*, June 2001.

[39] See e.g. Doganis, 1991.

[40] *Avmark Aviation Economist*, November 1993.

References

Alamdari, F. (1989), Airline deregulation: an analysis under different regulatory and operating environments. Cranfield Institute of Technology, Bedford, UK.

Berardino, F. and Frankel, C. (1998), Keeping Score. *Airline Business*, September 1998.

Besanko, D., Dranove, D. and Shanley, M. (1996), Economics of Strategy. New York: Wiley.

Bissessur, A. (1996), The identification and analysis of the Critical Success Factors of strategic airline alliances. Unpublished PhD-dissertation, Cranfield University, Bedford, UK.

Borys, B. and Jemison, D. (1989), Hybrid Arrangements as Strategic Alliances: Theoretical Issues in Organizational Combinations. *Academy of Management Review*, Vol. 14, No. 2, pp. 234-249.

Brewer, A. and Hooper, P. (1998), Strategic Alliances Among International Airlines and their Implications for Organizational Change. Working Paper ITS-WP-98-10, Institute of Transport Studies, Graduate School of Business, The University of Sydney.

Caves, D., Christensen, L. and Tretheway, M. (1984), Economies of Density versus Economies of Scale: Why trunk and local services differ. *Rand Journal of Economics*, Vol 15 No 4.

Child, J. and Faulkner, D. (1998), Strategies of Cooperation. Managing Alliances, Networks, and Joint Ventures. Oxford: Oxford University Press.

Doganis, R. (1991), Flying Off Course - The Economics of International Airlines. London: HarperCollins.

Doganis, R. (2001), The airline business in the 21st century. London: Routledge.

Gialloreto, L. (1986), The Multi – Mega: A trend of the 1990's? *The Avmark Aviation Economist*, October 1986.

Holloway, S. (1997), Straight and level: Practical Airline Economics. Aldershot, Hants.: Ashgate.

Jarillo, J.C. (1988), On Strategic Networks. *Strategic Management Journal*, Vol. 9, pp. 31-41.

Khanna, T., Gulati, R. and Nohria, N. (1998), The dynamics of Learning Alliances: Competition, Co-operation, and Relative Scope. *Strategic Management Journal*, Vol. 19, pp. 193-210.

Kling, J. and Smith, K. (1995), Identifying Strategic Groups in the U.S. airline industry: An application of the Porter Model. *Transportation Journal*, Winter 1995.

Nyathi, M. (1996), Strategic Alliance Partner Choice in International Aviation. PhD Dissertation, Institute of Transport Studies, Graduate School of Business, The University of Sydney.

Oum, T., Park, J. and Zhang, A. (1996), The Effects of Airline Codesharing Agreements on Firm Conduct and International Air Fares. *Journal of Transport Economics and Policy*, May 1996.

Paprottka, S. (1996), Unternehmenszusammenschlüsse: Synergiepotentiale und ihre Umsetzungsmöglichkeiten durch Integration. Wiesbaden, Germany: Gabler.

Pels, E. (2001), A note on airline alliances. *Journal of Air Transport Management*, Vol. 7, pp. 3-7.

Penrose, E. (1959), The Theory of the Growth of the Firm. Oxford University Press.

Ring, P. (2000), The Three T's of Alliance Creation: Task, Team and Time. *European Management Journal*, Vol. 18 No. 2 , pp. 152-163.

Seristö, H. (1995), Airline Performance and Costs. An Analysis of Performance Measurement and Cost Reduction in Major Airlines. PhD Dissertation, Helsinki School of Economics and Business Administration, Finland.

Smith, K., Grimm, C., Wally, S. and Young, G. (1997), Strategic Groups and Rivalrous Firm Behaviour: Towards a Reconciliation. *Strategic Management Journal*, Vol 18 No 2, pp. 149-157.

Staniland, M. (1997), Surviving the Single Market: Corporate Dilemmas and Strategies of European Airlines. Conference Proceedings of the 1997 Air Transport Research Group of the WCTR Society, vol. 1 No. 3, University of Nebraska at Omaha.

Ter Kuile, A. (1997), Hub Fever. *Airline Business*, December 1997.

Williams, G. (2000), Achieving Open Skies. Lecture Notes, Cranfield University, Bedford, UK.

Youssef, W. (1992), Causes and effects of international airline equity alliances. PhD dissertation, series UCB-ITS-DS-92-1, Institute of Transportation Studies, University of California, Berkeley.

Chapter 2

Alliancing Objectives

Beyond the primary argument that airlines seek alliances in order to improve their international competitiveness, the precise objectives that airlines seek to attain by joining an alliance group are not always that clear. Moreover, they differ considerably according to the type of airline concerned. This chapter examines alliancing objectives in more detail and as a function of airline type, first briefly from a history point of view, and then distinguishing different types of objectives against the background of industry dynamics.

A historical glimpse at alliancing objectives

The airline industry has evolved quite recently into one of real global competition. European carriers have led the way in developing international alliance strategies. Although first alliance agreements were made some seventy years ago, the first major airline actively to seek and develop modern alliances was the Scandinavian Airlines System (SAS), which deserves a brief presentation as an example of the expressed objectives of airlines.

SAS's CEO Jan Carlzon wrote the following in 1987:

> We base our efforts on two main strategies: broadening our passenger base through co-operation in Europe, and establishing new gateways on other continents. By establishing alliances with local airlines in these foreign locations, we can extend our fully integrated system to our passengers in their continued travel.

In the 1992 annual report Carlzon continued:

> SAS's goal in its search for partners has been to join a constellation which can operate a profitable global traffic system with strong hubs in Europe and which meets our basic task of developing services to, from, via and within Scandinavia. The best alternative is an extensive strategic co-operation with at least two of the medium-sized companies or one of the giants. In our opinion it is more advantageous for our shareholders and our home market for SAS to be an equal partner in a 'fourth force' in Europe rather than a small part of one of the three major carriers.

By 1985, Carlzon had already predicted that there would be only five major airlines in Europe by 1995 and declared that SAS wanted to be 'One of Five in 1995'. During the latter part of the 1980s, SAS tried to build alliances of various types but was unable to raise sufficient interest. In SAS's words the 'long-term visions were shadowed by thriving economies'. The recession of the early 1990s forced SAS to reconsider its strategies and, in 1995, the new CEO Stenberg wrote:

> Scandinavia has been given greater prominence in SAS' strategy. It is the task of SAS as an independent company to serve the home market with an effective and in every way attractive air transport product. Reliable co-operation partners, with good traffic systems which complement SAS, will be an important part of what we have to offer. But we no longer regard the partners issue as a matter of survival.

SAS started with a strategy of building alliances with airlines that were either smaller or of the same size as SAS itself. In the 1990s the alliance strategy was refocused on partnering with large airlines. Also, experience had taught that equity-based arrangements are very difficult to manage, and therefore further alliances would be pursued without ownership. Moreover, the emphasis in its own operations was shifted from global reach to being a dominant player in the markets of the home region. In any case, the objective in the early alliances was almost solely to enhance market presence and thus revenues. It appears that the present home of SAS, the Star Alliance, is also expected to produce significant benefits in the short and medium-term in the area of marketing. However, in the longer term, additional benefits are expected from operational cost savings in maintenance, sourcing and handling.

Reasons for airlines building alliances

Past research has categorised a number of reasons for alliances, including risk sharing, scale economies, access to markets or technology, learning, or attacking a competitor. As to airline alliances, it has been suggested[1] that there are two main drivers: first, the search for more market power and second, the search for lower operating costs.

We can find drivers of different level and different type, and they could be put into three categories:

- deregulation of the industry,
- changes in customer preferences,
- changes in technology and infrastructure.

Deregulation has opened up markets, and led to intensifying competition and consequently also to a battle to secure market presence and cut costs. The history of airline industry alliances suggests that the role of authority control is an area which in itself deserves to be brought up as a reason for alliances. The following factors can be seen as regulation-related drivers of alliances in the airline industry:

- generally tight control over mergers and acquisitions in the industry,

- restrictions by governments on foreign ownership in airlines,
- protection of markets with bilateral agreements.

Changes in customer preferences comprise such factors as overall globalisation of business (services follow clients; people need to travel more), the diminishing role of airline nationality in customer choices, and the preference by customers for high flight frequencies and seamless connections to about any point of the globe. Technological and infrastructural changes include on the aviation infrastructure side the introduction of medium-sized long-range aircraft, the development of sales and distribution technology – including the Internet, and the congestion of airspace and airports in many areas.

Objectives of alliances

Research on strategic alliances – typically concerning manufacturing industries – has pointed to two primary categories of objectives in alliance arrangements: product objectives and knowledge objectives. As to product objectives, there have been two primary goals: either the enhancement of product offering or the reduction of production costs. As to knowledge objectives, the goal has typically been to learn a new technology or process from a partner; the goals of knowledge transfer have often been rather specified and particular. Research on airline alliances has listed several objectives for the co-operative arrangements. These objectives could be tactical or strategic in nature and are mostly product objectives, comprising, for example, access to a larger route network, higher load factors, larger market share, joint fare setting and sales efforts, shared loyalty programmes, and pooling of labour and other resources.

Rhoades & Lush (1997) have suggested two dimensions on which airline alliance arrangements differ, namely commitment of resources and complexity of arrangement. Partly following that division, marketing-related alliance arrangements can be split into three types: 1. code-sharing and schedule coordination, 2. joint frequent-flyer programmes and facility-sharing (e.g. airport lounges), 3. broad marketing co-operation. The fourth type is technical co-operation, mainly in maintenance and handling. Obviously the airlines' objectives for alliance arrangements are reflected in the types of alliance that they have arranged. The four types of alliance arrangement of six major airlines – two from each of the three major regions of North America, Europe and Asia – are presented in Figure 2.1, which also shows how arrangements evolved from 1990 to 1999, the decade when the alliancing got started in large scale.

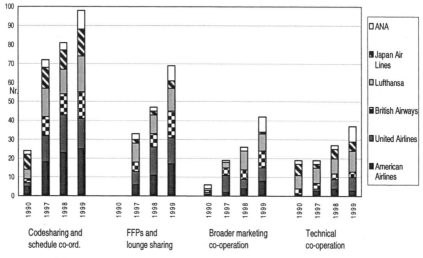

Figure 2.1   Alliance arrangements by six leading airlines 1990-1999
Source: Compiled by author from statistics by Airline Business.

Most of the arrangements involved code-sharing and schedule co-ordination. Overall, the marketing-related arrangements clearly outweighed technical co-operation, which is more concerned with cost reduction.

The major objectives for airlines in alliance arrangements can be divided into three categories: market-defensive, market-offensive and efficiency-seeking objectives. This division corresponds partly to the findings of Lorange and Roos (1993), and Murray and Mahon (1993), and can be used when placing alliances into a strategy framework for airlines.

Defensive objectives aim at reducing the level of environmental uncertainty for the airline. The pursuit of defence from these uncertainties can include 'entrenchment', where an airline seeks integration into an alliance group that will provide a more stable immediate operating environment. It can also mean the consolidation of one's position through traffic feed from an allied partner. An example for this is Lufthansa's shareholding in German regional carrier Eurowings. The link with the regional carrier stopped Eurowings from cooperating with Lufthansa's rival KLM (Eurowings channelled a substantial amount of traffic from Northern Germany on to KLM medium and longhaul flights via Amsterdam), and allowed Eurowings to feed Lufthansa hubs in Frankfurt and Munich instead. Thus, Lufthansa reduced the level of competition (and therefore uncertainty) in a specific market.

Passive market defence aims at sheltering from competition. In a 'shelter', the airline can temporarily reduce capacity in order to restructure or undergo cost-cutting measures without fully losing its presence in certain markets. A recent example of this is All Nippon Airways, which, in an effort to cut costs, will increase its codesharing with its partners Lufthansa and United Airlines, while reducing its own international operations for a certain period.

Furthermore, entering an alliance dampens or completely eliminates competition with partner airlines and strengthens the carrier's position against outside competitors ('Competitor taming'). The deregulated environment and the fact that competitors might have joined an alliance put a carrier in a potentially weak position. Joining an alliance provides access to resources to strengthen that position.[2]

Past research on alliances in general has suggested that making friends out of foes would be a motivation for many alliances. Making strong competitor airlines partners rather than rivals would appear to be a very valid objective in today's airline business, too. What is called competitor taming here is very close to what Doz and Hamel (1998) have termed 'co-option'. It is typically, however, not very openly expressed in airline industry talk; perhaps the airlines' rush for market presence and for resource utilisation overshadows competitor taming as a motivator for alliances, but it would nevertheless appear to be a background factor in some alliances.

Market-offensive objectives include value enhancement through offering better connections and, in some cases, being linked to a 'prestigious' brand (either that of a partner, or that of the alliance itself, which becomes a 'seal of quality'). Another factor is the learning of new skills, especially in the fields of yield management or exploiting new sales channels (such as through the internet). Furthermore, there is the objective of hub dominance. This refers to those airlines which have a base at an important hub airport, and which seek to hold a maximum number of slots, favourable gate and facility locations, and the possibility to accommodate partners' flights, in order to offer optimally coordinated and smooth connections.

Efficiency-seeking objectives include efficiency gains through joint resource utilisation, for example, sharing airport facilities (both airside and landside), or establishing maintenance joint ventures and spare pools. Furthermore, there are economies of density (for example, increased load factors) to be reaped from schedule harmonisation.

Lastly, there is the objective of *environmental control*. This could be linked to the defence motive in the described sense of 'competition dampening'. On a more active account, a single airline has, to some extent, influence over its *immediate* environment, but relatively less leverage over the larger general environment. The alliance, if acting as a representative of its members, is likely to have more negotiating clout vis-à-vis external suppliers or (possibly in the future) regulators.

In addition, there are capability objectives, in other words objectives related to learning. Environment control has mostly concerned the ability of airlines to cope with the various forms of regulation in the industry. A framework of dynamics in international alliances, linking drivers in the airline business and the objectives of alliances is suggested in Figure 2.2. Let us briefly run through the suggested logic.

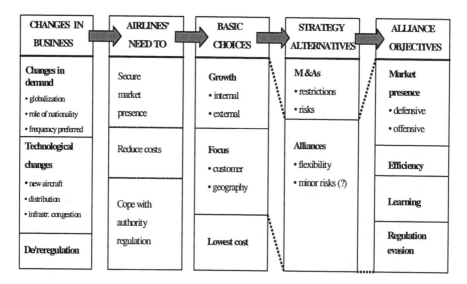

Figure 2.2   Framework of international airline alliances dynamics

The basic strategic choices of airlines are limited to three: growth strategy, focus strategy and lowest cost strategy. Growth can be sought either internally (organic growth) or externally. As internal growth is often slow, it is attractive for many airlines to seek growth externally; then the further options are mergers, acquisitions or alliances. As there are many regulatory limitations on airline mergers and acquisitions, alliances often provide a less complicated route for growth. Alliances provide more flexibility than mergers and acquisition, require less capital, and may carry fewer risks than M&As.

If an airline chooses focus as its basic strategy, there are still pressures in the competitive environment that support the use of alliances. Whether the airline bases its strategy on different customer groups (e.g. business travellers) or on a certain geographic area (e.g. traffic between Europe and Africa), it is nevertheless likely to benefit from some sort of partnership with suitable airlines. No matter what the niche or specific geographic market is, an airline is likely to benefit from a larger catchment area and better connections.

As to the final objectives, first, the changes in the industry have made it essential for most carriers to seek growth and to secure presence in a larger market. Second, there is a pressure to use resources better, i.e. to reduce high operating costs. Securing market presence can be seen either as an offensive objective of alliances, typical for large airlines, or a defensive objective, typical for medium-sized and small airlines. Larger airlines seek market power and consequent enhanced value for customers by pursuing larger network coverage, higher frequencies, more extensive loyalty programs and dominance of 'hub' airports through alliance arrangements. Medium-sized and small carriers appear to be more interested in market coverage rather than outright market power in responding to the challenge of expanding larger airlines; smaller carriers seem to consider participation in alliances essential in trying to avoid shrinking into mere regional operators. For the market presence objective it is necessary to distinguish between global level and specific market level sub-objectives, which may require arrangements of conflicting interests.

The second major objective, efficiency or better use of resources, can be pursued either through higher productivity or simply lower costs of inputs. Higher productivity is sought, for instance, through sharing aircraft and air crew capacity, using the partner's ground handling and airport passenger services at foreign stations instead of the airline providing them by itself, and making better use of possible excess aircraft maintenance capacity by servicing partner airlines' aircraft. As to direct cost savings, joint sourcing of fuel, catering, aircraft, spare parts, or information and marketing services may, for example, produce significantly lower costs than sourcing by each partner alone.

As to the relative role of the two major objectives, it is the pursuit of stronger market presence that has so far been clearly more apparent and dominant, the need for better resource utilisation being clearly secondary and also a longer-term objective in nature. It appears that resource utilisation is a factor increasingly acknowledged but pursued rather slowly. One explanation for this slow action is, of course, the rigidity that airline management face due to both very strong labour unions and regulation by authorities. In a typical multi-partner alliance, the alliance-driven improvement in member airline profits comes during the first few years mostly from revenue enhancement, but in later years increasingly from cost reduction. The third objective, learning, is discussed in more detail below. The fourth objective, coping with regulation can be seen as an intermediate objective for alliances. As governments are still significant owners in many internationally operating airlines and often place specific limitations on the share of foreign ownership in the airlines of their nationality, antitrust legislation and the fact that bilateral agreements between countries still form much of the basis for international air transportation drive airlines towards alliances instead of mergers or acquisitions.

The objectives for alliancing can be assessed through categorising the different kind of airlines. Chapter 1 introduced the distinction between three different types of internationally operating airlines: Local Champion, Long-haul Operator, and Global Connector. Local champions operate typically short- and medium-haul routes, and include carriers such as Austrian Airlines and Finnair. Long-haul

Operators are in many ways like local champions, but a large share of their operations are on intercontinental routes. These carriers include Air New Zealand and South African Airways. Global Connectors aim to serve the whole world market, and comprise such large carriers as American Airlines and Lufthansa. Figure 2.3 presents the different components of market-defensive, market-offensive and efficiency-seeking objectives and also suggests what the key objectives for different types of airlines could, or perhaps should, be.

The role of learning

It appears that the role of learning from partners in airline alliances has so far been very limited. In contrast to many manufacturing industries, where the ability to learn from a more experienced or otherwise 'better' partner is often given as a reason for building alliances, in airline alliances it rarely emerges as a reason. Perhaps the history of airlines as national icons, at least in Europe, has created corporate cultures that are not the best environments for absorbing new practices. Or, as the airline industry is in such turmoil, airlines are overly concerned about the threat of losing their proprietary assets and capabilities to partner airlines. Past research has suggested that firms are able to learn from alliance partners more easily when the level of transparency or openness between them is high[3] and that mutual trust between partners reduces the fear of opportunistic behaviour, i.e. 'stealing' other partners' proprietary know-how and capabilities.[4] Finding a balance between opening up for more learning opportunities and being concerned about partners copying too much of their core capabilities would appear to be a challenge for many airlines. It appears that in today's situation many airlines would benefit from greater 'relational capital', which refers to mutual trust, respect and friendship that reside at the individual level between alliance partners, as suggested by Kale et al. (2000, 221; see also Chapter 3).

It seems that airlines would need to emphasise building more informal coordination and control mechanisms to enhance learning; the control and coordination aspect has been brought up in many earlier studies concerning mainly manufacturing industries, for instance by Calori et al. (1994) in the cross-border acquisitions context. Learning, coordination and control in turn are linked to HRM development. Lei and Slocum (1991) charted the four key elements of alliances and alliance research: 1. rationale, 2. benefits and costs, 3. success factors, 4. and human resources management. Past research has emphasised the role of HRM when firms are aiming at enhanced organisational learning in a setting where corporate and national cultures may differ markedly.

	LOCAL CHAMPION	LONGHAUL OPERATOR	GLOBAL CONNECTOR
Market-defensive			
• Home market position improvement	■		
• Competitor training	■	■	
Market-offensive			
• Value enhancement	■	■	■
• Network enlargement			■
• Hub dominance			■
Efficiency seeking			
• Shared resource utilisation			■
• Economies of scale & density			■
• Learning	■	■	

Figure 2.3   Key objectives of alliances for different types of airlines

As most of the airline alliances have primarily marketing-related objectives in the first phase and resource-utilisation objectives only in later phases of the alliance, there is a reason to expect that learning will become a more explicit objective as the 'relative share' of resource utilisation or cost reduction objectives increase in airline alliances.

Concluding remarks

Changes in the industry have made it essential for most airlines to seek growth and to secure presence in a larger market. There is pressure to reduce operational costs in airlines through better utilisation of resources. The many types of regulation in the industry make alliances the only feasible way to grow and seek presence in a larger market. Airlines appear somewhat frustrated by the fact that a natural evolution into being trans-national companies is in fact blocked by authorities.

Market presence and global reach appear to play an essential role in airlines' strategic planning for survival and prosperity. Therefore, the primary motivation for international alliances so far has been the need to secure an extensive catchment area or a large onward connection network. It seems that resource utilisation is often acknowledged in international airline alliance arrangements. However, airlines have in fact been rather slow in pursuing higher productivity or lower costs through concerted efforts with partners; there seems to be rigidity in airlines in operationalising the changes.

As to managerial challenges, it seems that the area where there appears to be much potential for improvement is that of learning. Earlier research[5] has emphasised the role of trust between the partners as a contributor to successful learning. It is the very notion of trust that makes airline alliances different from those in other industries; so far alliances in the airline industry have been either very short-lived or limited in scope, or both, and therefore trust has not been developed between the partners. It seems that the learning aspect of alliance management should be given much more emphasis, which would in practice require, first, strong and specific initiative from the highest management, and second, allocation of sufficient capacity and perhaps the best talent to the management of key alliances.

Notes

[1] See Alamdari and Morrell, 1997.
[2] Pfeffer and Salancik, 1978.
[3] Doz and Hamel, 1998.
[4] Gulati, 1995.
[5] See e.g. Inkpen, 1998.

References

Calori, R., Lubatkin, M. & Very, P. (1994). Control mechanisms in cross-border acquisitions: an international comparison. *Organization Studies*, 15(3), 361-379.

Doz, Y. & Hamel, G. (1998). Alliance Advantage: the Art of Creating Value through Partnering. Harvard Business School Press, Boston.

Gulati, R. (1995). Does familiarity breed trust? The implications of repeated ties for contractual choice in alliances. *Academy of Management Journal*, 38, 85-112.

Inkpen, A. (1998). Learning, knowledge acquisition, and strategic alliances. *European Management Journal*, 16(2), April 1998, 223-229.

Kale, P., Singh, H. & Perlmutter, H. (2000). Learning and protection of proprietary assets in strategic alliances: building relational capital. *Strategic Management Journal*, 21(3), 217-237.

Lei, D. & Slocum, J. (1991). Global strategic alliances: payoffs and pitfalls. *Organization Dynamics*, 19(3), 44-63.

Lorange, P., Roos, J. & Simcic Bronn, P. (1992). Building successful strategic alliances. *Long Range Planning*, 25(6), 10-17.

Murray, E. & Mahon, J. (1993). Strategic alliances: gateway to the new Europe? *Long Range Planning*, 26(4), 102-111.

Pfeffer, J. and Salancik, G. (1978), The External Control of Organizations. New York: Harper & Row.

Rhoades, D. & Lush, H. (1997). A typology of strategic alliances in the airline industry: propositions for stability and duration. Conference Proceedings of the 1997 Air Transport Research Group of the WCTR Society, vol. 1, no. 1. University of Nebraska at Omaha.

Chapter 3

The Dynamics of Interdependence

Generalists vs. specialists in an increasingly unstable environment: Lessons from organisational ecology

A very interesting description of firms building federations has been put forward by a relatively small but influential group of academic researchers known as Organisation Ecologists. Applying concepts used in ecology to understanding firm behaviour, they examine the adaptation of populations of firms to changing environmental conditions. They describe the relative fitness of specialist versus generalist organisations in settings of various degrees of environmental stability. One of their findings is that in a stable operating environment, firms will be more able to afford specialisation. This is because specialisation is generally the preferred (because more efficient) operating mode, but a specialised firm is only fit over a relatively small range of environmental conditions, whereas a generalist firm might be overall less efficient (because less streamlined), but can ride out the tides of economic shifts much easier, since at least one part of it will always be capable of dealing with whatever state the environment happens to be in. Hence, if the environment is perceived as very unstable by a firm, it is likely to operate more as a generalist, in order to be fit across a greater range of environmental contingencies. Organisation ecologists also argue that the only way a firm can remain a specialist under unstable conditions is through federating with others: the federation of specialists is a generalist in the aggregate, and by being tightly bound to each other, the vulnerable specialists create a somewhat more stable immediate operating environment.

These principles also hold for the airline industry, even though it behaved differently from the organisation ecologists' descriptions in the beginning of its history. Up into the 1980s, most internationally operating airlines strove for a generalist role, even though their operating environment was comparably stable. In airline terms, a generalist is a carrier that operates a mixed fleet over a variety of routes, for example, regional commuter and short-haul as well as intercontinental routes. These routes require different aircraft types (because of range and capacity considerations), all of which require specific maintenance and operations procedures, spare parts etc. Thus, the production of Passenger Seat Miles is spread not only over a greater *number* of plants (i.e., aircraft), but also over a greater *variety* of plants. This is problematic in that, for any airline, operating a mixed fleet over a variety of routes is considerably more costly than operating a homogeneous fleet.[1]

The reason for airlines having been generalists in a stable (pre-deregulation) environment is that, in contrast to the manufacturing firms examined by the organisational ecologists, there was seldom an urgent profit motive for airlines, and they did not need to be fit across a range of environmental contingencies: they were mostly government owned, and the nature of their operational profile (i.e. airports served, aircraft operated, frequencies, fares etc) was largely determined by government policy. Consequently, there was little competition between airlines: each international route was usually served by the respective designated flag carrier of the countries concerned, with very tight specifications on price, quantity and type of services offered. In this protected environment, airlines developed into generalists, that is, they simultaneously operated domestic services, regional services, and long-haul flights to connect their country to the rest of the world (in some cases even purely for prestige or political reasons). With the onset of the deregulation of air transport, an increasingly unstable environment was thus looming for a highly capital-intensive industry, with many an airline finding that operating a generalist profile was becoming unaffordable and unjustifiable. At the same time, deregulation increased customer expectations; airline passengers now demanded seamless service between almost any two points on the globe, at competitive fares. The airlines thus faced pressure to save costs, while at the same time they had to increase the scope of their services. Increasing scope through internal growth or mergers is costly, complicated, and in many cases not even possible due to regulatory constraints and would, in any case, never reach the global scope required by customers. Hence, a natural option for airlines at this stage was to link up among each other in order to provide a truly globe-spanning route system. The airline industry moved from an environment where stability was provided by the virtual absence of competition and steady funding from government sources to an unstable, deregulated and highly competitive one, where the high capital costs involved in airline operations aggravated the fact that 'Generalism is costly', and where specialisation becomes increasingly attractive in that it entails a lower requirement for excess capacity (ibid.[2]). And this is the situation where organisational ecologists predict that firms will move towards alliancing. Using the distinctions proposed by Hannan and Freeman (1977), the new environment encountered by airlines can be considered 'coarse grained' and 'unstable', and the predicted reaction of organisations to such an environment is that '[o]rganizations may federate in such a way that supra-organizations consisting of heterogeneous collections of specialist organizations pool resources' (ibid.). The relationship would thus be one where due to the increased uncertainty of the wider environment (brought about by deregulation and in a large number of cases the privatisation of former flag carriers), airlines have reacted in a way to ensure collective survival,[3] in other words, they sought to (re)gain control over their environment by establishing federations.[4] At this point, it is very important to keep in mind that in the case of the airline industry, clear limits exist regarding the possible extent of federation. Mergers and even extensive Joint Ventures between airlines are often restricted by the regulatory authorities, and where they are allowed, they carry a high price tag (often in terms of having to give up slots at key hubs to competitors). Also, alliance groups themselves are not yet very tightly integrated. So far, there has been very little cross-subsidising between airlines, which are still separate organisational entities. Even within equity alliances, each carrier typically continues to operate as a separate unit responsible for its own profit and losses. Thus, even though an airline alliance group can indeed be visualised as a kind of supra-organisation in its own right, the defensive advantages the alliance group can draw from such polymorphism are still limited. There are, however, already significant benefits from alliance group formation that can be reaped on the market-offensive side: specialists link their resources (i.e., route systems) to be able to satisfy a type of demand (seamless, global travel) that no single partner could have satisfied on its own. This is a form of growth where the firm itself grows in scope (i.e., the route system offered to customers), but not in scale. In other words, the airline alliance group can be seen as a federation of specialists where airlines ideally complement each other within an alliance, each adopting a certain role. It appears that the reaping of advantages of federation on the offensive side (such as benefits of scope) does not require as tight integration as would the reaping of advantages on the defensive side (such as sheltering from competition). When observing future developments in multilateral alliances, this is indeed an important point: the offensive advantages of greater market access are reaped already at relatively low levels of integration. Firms which are thus integrated into a multilateral alliance have access to these advantages while still needing to protect themselves from environmental uncertainties; the alliance group cannot yet fully do this for them. It is only in a second, tighter stage of alliance integration that partners can create a true supra-organisation which can then represent a stable task environment for the individual airline, and permit it to specialise. Again, specialisation is only likely to come about in a firm that feels safe in a stable, predictable environment. For an airline joining an alliance, this means that their structural adaptation to alliance membership ought to take into account these two stages: it seems that only at a high level of stability and predictability of the airline's task environment (i.e., the alliance group) can the firm afford what can be called carefree specialisation. The necessarily fairly tight federation, however, increases the interdependence between the federated firms. To understand these interdependencies between airlines in alliance groups, the Resource Dependence Perspective (RDP) has been a much-used tool for organisation theorists to understand alliancing.

A resource dependence perspective on airline alliances

The resource dependence perspective (RDP) can be seen as a development of the broader resource-based view,[5] which focuses on conceptualising the firm as the holder of a set of resources.[6] It assumes that firms face environmental uncertainty and scarcity of resources, and supposes that managerial action is primarily directed at protecting organisations from dependencies that come about from the external environment. In a famous phrase which characterises the thrust of RDP very well, Pfeffer and Salancik (1978) state that management is continuously engaged in 'negotiating a tradeoff between autonomy and survival'. One of the strengths of the resource dependence perspective is that it can explain uncertainty *management* (rather than simply uncertainty *avoidance*), in organisational behaviour. The environmental uncertainty is in fact held to be so important a factor that firms are understood to base any long-term strategy *primarily* on their resources and capabilities, instead of on customer's wishes or needs. Resources and capabilities thus constitute an important determinant of direction and possibilities for the firm.[7] In the resource dependence view, firms seek to (a) reduce uncertainty within their operating environment and, related to this; (b) minimise their dependence on other firms, mainly because such a dependence on a specific partner firm would give that firm power over the focal actor;[8] or at least (c) modify their resource dependencies on other firms.[9] It is especially the modification of dependencies that is of interest in this chapter.

The resource dependence view is related to the previously introduced perspective of organisation ecology in that both approaches emphasise the impact of the environment on the organisation, and thus acknowledge a *limited extent of autonomy for the firm*. In addition, both views see the firm's resource configuration as an important origin of structural inertia, which limits and influences the firm's adaptation to its environment. Both views also share a certain interest in firm interdependencies and industrial niches. But where organisation ecology often takes a population logic, the resource dependence perspective focuses on the single firm,[10] and it also accords the firm relatively more autonomy over the *deployment* of its resources. This, in turn, requires the firm to make efforts to *protect* its resources, and to retain authority over them. It must be underlined at this point that any attempt to understand inter-firm coordination from a resource dependence perspective must take into account the peculiarities of the industry or type of firm under examination; for example, Buvik and Grønhaug (2000) highlight the crucial role of the degree of asset specificity in the industry or organisational field under scrutiny when determining the impact of environmental uncertainty on inter-firm coordination. In other words, RDP can be used as a tool to understand concrete industry contexts, but might be less powerful in explaining megatrends. For the present purpose of understanding airline alliance groups and what goes on within them, RDP and the concepts it yields can indeed explain a considerable extent of airline behaviour, such as specialisation, and positioning within alliance groups. It appears that, especially within multilateral alliances, autonomy and dependence are not mutually exclusive; one frequently encounters a situation where firms are simultaneously highly autonomous, and highly dependent on their partners,[11] or in fact on the alliance itself.

The following discussion concentrates on the relation of individual airlines to their partners and, in the aggregate, to their alliance group. It can be argued that the airline alliance group constitutes an environment in its own right, an immediate environment, or task environment. This task environment buffers the individual airline from the outside environment (and from head-on competition with other airlines or federations), but it also requires the airline to negotiate its role, position, and power *within* it. A task environment that consists of airlines which are formally tied to each other displays a certain degree of stability, or at least predictability, to the members of that federation. But because this federation is a structured form, and because it involves symbiotic interdependence, it also displays hierarchical elements. Thus, issues of domination and power asymmetries as well as tensions between individual and collective advantages[12] are present and must be negotiated. In other words, alliance membership might provide a somewhat more stable and predictable operating environment and it might also buffer an airline from having to compete on its own, but in their current form, alliance groups are still environments where firms compete with each other, or at least strive to exercise power over each other. It is suggested here that the resource dependence approach offers concepts that are useful for understanding the mechanisms of inter-firm coordination within multilateral alliance groups, and that it can also help explain the stability – or lack of stability – of such groups.

The alliancing aptitude

Managing its dependencies and interdependencies with other alliance partners can thus be seen a crucial skill for any airline in an alliance environment. If one assumes that managerial efforts are indeed directed to a significant extent at ensuring a firm's autonomy (see also Chapter 4) but recognises that some dependencies have to be entered into in order to ensure survival in a hostile and unstable environment, it is possible to say that a firm seeks to avoid or at least manage dependencies through what can be called an *alliancing aptitude*. The alliancing aptitude of an airline comprises features which

- give it negotiating clout within the alliance group (once joined) to cancel out or at least reduce asymmetries: 'The power of the participant [in a coalition] is a function of the dependence of others in the organisation on his contributions, activities, capabilities';[13]
- allow the airline to enter dependencies which are largely unspecific, and avoid specific dependencies on other airlines;
- and thus allow it to retain a certain Standalone Capability in case the alliance fails, loosens or changes shape.[14]

The following sections will discuss each of these points in turn, in the specific context of airline alliances. The term 'environment' will refer here primarily to the airline alliance group itself (i.e., what will be termed 'network' or 'federated environment'). This appears justified in that the primary environment for an allied airline is indeed the alliance group, and resource configuration issues are relevant in relation to other network members, both at the formation and the implementation/management stages of the alliance. The resources of an airline can be classified into route-system related, technical, and nontangibles. Route-system related resources are traffic rights, slots at airports, and hub location and characteristics.[15] Technical resources refer to the airline's operating infrastructure and include its fleet, IT systems and know-how, and installations at hubs and outstations. Nontangible resources refer to the customer basis,[16] the airline's overall reputation, and its brand.

Living with power imbalances in multilateral airline alliances

A point that significantly shapes the alliancing behaviour of firms is the issue of power imbalances between partners.[17] Asymmetries are indeed a fact of life in a partnership, and arising asymmetries are not necessarily a sign of failure. In an open-ended relationship, asymmetries and possible instabilities must be anticipated and accommodated.[18] The expression 'power imbalance' carries a fairly negative connotation which it should not, if one considers that *any* hierarchical arrangement implies, and is based on, power imbalances, and that hierarchical arrangements are in fact necessary for the coordination of organisational efforts of any kind. On the one hand, the relation in a multilateral airline alliance group is very much one of symbiosis between partners that have different needs, and contributions: Local Champions offer their expertise on a determined market, and seek access to large hubs in order to improve their marketing scope. Global Connectors, in turn, seek to access markets where it would be too costly for them to be present by themselves, and provide a link of these markets to their hubs, and between each other. Ideally, the alliance turns into a win-win situation for any kind of partner, provided – and this is an important point – that there are few issues of contention, such as route system overlaps, or hubs that are located too close to each other. By choosing a strategic position that fits the resources at their disposal, and avoiding overlaps, even a relatively small airline can dampen the effects of asymmetries by creating *reciprocity in asymmetry*,[19] where A depends on B for resource x, and B on A for resource y. Obviously, the relative value of resources x and y also plays a role, but the issue under discussion here is the management (and not the complete elimination) of asymmetries. Especially from the viewpoint of a small to medium sized airline, then, the issue should not be to seek to eliminate inequalities in a multilateral federation – a quest best described as utopian – but to seek to handle them in such a way that they do not threaten that airline's self-determination, and its option to leave the federation.

Another factor somewhat limiting the impact of power imbalances in a multilateral alliance group is their *dynamic* component, i.e., the development of an alliance over time: when there is mutual dependence – indeed, multilateral *inter*dependence – into the foreseeable future, game-theory-like scenarios are less likely to occur.[20] To use a concept described by Sheppard and Tuchinsky (1996), with increasing interdependence and a future ahead, *distributive* bargains (involving a single, critical dimension, and opposing positions) turn into *integrative* bargains, where each partner attempts to get his fair share, but wishes are in most cases not fully confrontational. That this is indeed the case in the airline industry has been shown by Shibata (2001) who describes how alliances between US and European airlines allow each partner to reap individual benefits from cooperation on North Atlantic routes. Shibata's results contribute to the hypothesis that integrative bargains are more likely to be achieved between specialists, that is, between partners that occupy distinct, i.e. non-overlapping, niches. Cooperation on a set of routes can, however, also be a scene for power play between partners. If two partners decide to operate and codeshare jointly in a market between their countries, they might (provided they are cleared to do so by the competition authorities) eventually come to an agreement regarding the *market share* allotted to each partner. A much more important question, however, would be that of *yield share*. This is a salient issue especially on European short-haul routes. If two airlines coordinate their services on a route, the carrier which operates the early morning or late evening flights is more likely to reap high yields (because of a higher percentage of full-fare paying business passengers on those flights) than the airline that operates the flights during the middle of the day. Hence, even though the capacity (in terms of e.g. available seat kilometres) might be evenly distributed between two cooperating carriers, the yield distribution may not be. Similar issues arise where one partner merely feeds another partner's hub, from where passengers are then carried on that second partner's mid- or long-haul flights.

It is suggested here that in fact yield share ought to be used as a much more accurate proxy for market power of an airline on a given route. It is likely that a significant part of internal wrestling between alliance partners will in fact occur over the allocation of yield share on jointly operated routes. This problem is especially acute in case of codeshare agreements where each partner remains responsible for his own operations, cost and revenue. If he loses out in the yield-share allocation, he is at risk of being barred from operating more profitable routes for the sake of his partner. If the alliance agreement consists mainly of codeshares on single routes, one partner might easily get into a disadvantaged position when operating a multiple-codeshare relationship, whereas partner asymmetries would be mitigated in a Joint Venture situation where partners share expenses and revenues on a route or set of routes. It is in this sense that smaller partners can benefit from the very tight integration of a Joint Venture with a larger airline.

Specific and unspecific dependence

The alliancing aptitude can then be seen as the firm's capability to manage its dependencies within an alliance. In this context, it is useful to distinguish between two different types of dependence, namely *specific*, and *unspecific* dependence.[21] Dependence can be said to be *specific* if it refers to a firm's dependence on one particular resource (and on the partner who controls that resource). That resource can then be said to be imperfectly substitutable[22] in the sense that a firm needs access to that resource, and to no other, to perform a certain vital function. There are two main problems related to entering specific dependencies. The first is that holding, or controlling access to, resources implies power. The power difference between two firms where one is specifically dependent on the other can possibly lead to an unstable situation in the case of a lack of goal consensus between partners.[23] A second problem related to specific dependencies is that the structural changes a firm makes to accommodate cooperation with a partner on which it is specifically dependent represent sunk costs. Once these costs are incurred, the firm will seek to amortise this investment, and is in a way held hostage to the cooperation.

A different situation occurs if the dependence is *unspecific*. In the case of unspecific dependence, a firm might still depend on partners for resources, or sheltering, in the sense that it cannot survive on its own. But it is of less importance with which partner(s) the firm enters cooperation. In other words, the focal firm does not depend on any one particular partner; thus, partners (and the resources they control) are substitutable. The problems associated with a lack of goal consensus between partners still apply once cooperation is entered; but in the case of unspecific resource dependence, a firm always retains the option to choose among, and if necessary switch between, partners. The firm which is unspecifically dependent on cooperation with other firms is 'able to procure valuable resources from another party without losing control of one's own resources'.[24]

Specific dependence on an alliance: trust and sunk costs

It is important at this point to consider that a firm can in fact be specifically dependent not only on a partner but also on an alliance group. If one sees the alliance network as the firm's immediate task environment, it is this environment that needs to be stable and non-turbulent in order for a firm to reap the important membership benefit of a chance for what could be called carefree specialisation. Carefree specialisation refers to a firm's ability to be able to specialise (i.e., concentrate on the provision and exploitation of core resources) while affording to curtail non-core ones, the maintenance of which had been hitherto needed in order to provide for the mastering of environmental uncertainties. Specialisation involves considerable risk and requires tight integration within the protective alliance environment. There is, however, another type of risk inherent in tight integration into an alliance, namely *relational risk*[25] or opportunistic behaviour by partners. There are, in addition to contractual stipulations which aim at limiting opportunistic behaviour by a partner, two interrelated mechanisms in place which can to some extent mitigate the risk involved at high levels of integration, namely *trust* and *alliance-specific investments*.[26] Tight linkages imply gains in terms of efficient coordination, but also significant compromises in the form of sunk costs or alliance-specific investments. These sunk costs can occur either in terms of concrete expenses (for example, in the airline case, marketing a joint brand, moving airport facilities or jointly building a dedicated alliance concourse at an airport, switching to alliance-compatible IT systems, or payment of an up-front fee for joining an airline alliance group), or in terms of opportunities given up (for example, ceding operations on certain routes to one of the partners or submitting to exclusivity stipulations). The tighter the cooperative integration between partners becomes, the higher the risk level related to alliance-specific investments, and the need for trust between partners. Figure 3.1 illustrates the role of sunk costs and alliance-specific investments.

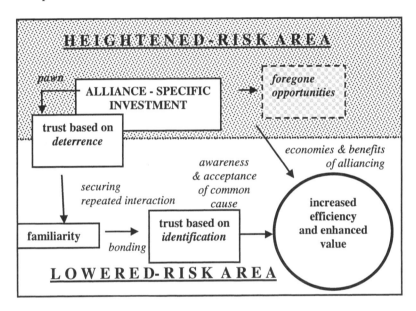

Figure 3.1   Risk and alliance-specific investment
Source: Kleymann and Seristö, 2001.

Alliance-specific investments provide stability in that they somewhat deter partners from opportunistic behaviour or defection. For example, in manufacturing industries, equity Joint Ventures (involving sunk cost) are frequently preferred to contracts for governing a relationship when a partner's component or input is specific to the purchaser (in other words, if the purchaser is specifically dependent on that resource) as a means to prevent the holder of that resource from behaving opportunistically.[27] Generally speaking, in a relationship which involves specific dependencies and sunk costs, there is greater incentive to cooperate (or dissuasion to shirk) and thus a greater inherent stability in the federation. This can be illustrated by the following quote:

We have now nine companies in Star and they have ten different reservation systems. Building one joint system is expensive and takes time. It could also make it impossible for an airline to leave an alliance.[28]

Sunk costs thus have a double efficiency-creating function; one direct, and the other derived: alliance-specific investments are the basis which guarantees efficient and effective alliance operations. At the same time, they provide derived benefits, as they serve as a form of pawn, or pledge: investment in a relationship deters a partner from opportunistic behaviour; trust is based on deterrence.[29] At this level of trust, the sunk cost incurred can be considered a *safeguard of goodwill*.[30] With partners discouraged from behaving opportunistically, closer interaction is facilitated and secured. Having thus cooperated over a period of time allows the build-up of knowledge about partners' behaviour and priorities. For example, in an interesting link between game theory and the institutionalist perspective, Das and Teng (2000b) see an alliance as an infinitely repeated game, with firms seeking to gain legitimacy through a reputation for being cooperative or showing goodwill. Hence, there is a certain motivation for unilateral commitment of one partner as a signal of goodwill. At this stage, another form of trust within the firm has emerged. This form is not based purely on deterrence and on the motivation of 'getting one's money worth', but rather on familiarity,[31] awareness of a common cause and, ultimately, identification with the alliance itself. This *trust-based identification* with the alliance will, eventually, be a catalyst of efficient behaviour in itself, on both front-line as well as managerial levels.[32] An example is the (somewhat) risky subordination of an airline's brand to the alliance's own brand in a specific market; this subordination to an umbrella brand might indeed create managerial identification, if not familiarity, with the alliance. It should be noted that this process takes time. Meyerson et al. (1996) examined temporary groups, which displayed behaviour that assumes the existence of trust, although there was no time or occasion for any trust-building activity to take place. Instead, the kind of trust developed was of a more generic nature, what they term 'swift trust', based on the prerequisite that all group members agree to trust one focal actor (the 'contractor') and his decisions. Trust was thus deflected to the contractor. The problem here is of course that the contractor is given authority; therefore the contractor's position is hierarchically superior to those of other partners. The process of choosing a contractor was assumed to have taken place prior to the formation of the ad-hoc group, and from each side independently. In fact, a hierarchically superior contractor appears to be useful even in coalitions that are of longer-term nature, when that coalition faces non-routine decisions that might potentially put a strain on the coalition itself. In the airline context, an alliance steering group could well assume the role of such a contractor. This, in turn, requires at least bilateral trust between the firm and the contractor. Tyler and Degoey (1996) describe the 'identity-based model' of trust, which describes how actors develop trust in a hierarchically superior authority when they identify with that authority. At that point, then, there is a zone of indifference where actors accept a decision made by the authority without consciously questioning it. This zone of indifference is in fact the leeway for action which the authority is given and within which it does not have to justify itself.[33]

Lastly, trust greatly influences the degree and kind of learning taking place between partners. In the context of airline alliances, it might be useful to distinguish between two kinds of learning, namely the learning of (technical or operational) skills on one hand, and the learning of how to manage the alliance, i.e., the build-up of an alliance capability, on the other.[34] Related to the former type of learning, past research has suggested that firms are able to learn from alliance partners more easily when the level of transparency or openness between them is high[35] and that mutual trust between partners reduces the fear of opportunistic behaviour, i.e., stealing other partners' proprietary know-how and capabilities.[36] In the airline industry, which is much less dependent on R&D than other industries, technical learning concerns mostly a relatively small set of sensitive issues such as Yield Management Systems and marketing-related IT infrastructure such as Frequent Flyer Programme-related capabilities. The production of the service itself (i.e., flying aircraft from A to B and selling capacity on them) is a highly standardised procedure and, in contrast to many manufacturing industries, there is no sensitive production knowledge or proprietary technology related to producing air transport services. Concerning the latter type of learning, i.e., that of *how* to cooperate, it seems that in today's situation many airlines would benefit from greater relational capital, which refers to the mutual trust, respect and friendship that reside at the individual level between alliance partners.[37] A closer relationship can enhance the potential to create value, which in turn would support the argument for higher relational capital. The experience of having built up relational capital is a type of knowledge that can be used in other, future relationships, and is an important ingredient of alliancing capability.

Managing dependencies: the concept of standalone capability

Members of an airline alliance group are required to relinquish some amount of authority to a joint governing entity, and they frequently carve up markets between themselves. This implies that an airline might have to cease being directly present in one market for the sake of a partner. If the alliance dissolves, the airlines will be weakened at those points where they were formerly linked to partners. In an extreme case, the alliance members might operate to a large extent under a joint brand name, thereby sacrificing their own brand presence in some markets; in case of alliance dissolution, they will find themselves crippled, with the need to rebuild brands. If, say, a European airline that operates transcontinentally cedes a set of its routes to Asia to one of its Asian alliance partners and the alliance dissolves, that airline would need to incur the costs and efforts to re-establish itself on that market. This is one aspect of the opportunity cost related to tight integration into an alliance. A further example of opportunity cost related to alliancing is members being bound by exclusivity agreements: in tightly integrated airline alliance groups such as Star, members are not very free to design their private alliancing strategy beyond the airline alliance group itself, or to enter cooperative agreements with airlines outside the alliance group even though such a cooperation might make sense for that particular member airline. Instead, alliance partners are bound to cooperate exclusively with partners from within their airline alliance group, with very strict limits set on the nature and extent of cooperation with outside airlines. This, in turn, has a set of effects on the individual airline's overall internal structure: in the event that the alliance fails, or if the airline leaves the airline alliance group, it may find it has developed structurally too much as an alliance member, and may have lost a certain standalone capability. The concept of standalone capacity is in fact very important as one of the pillars of airline success in a federated universe. It is based on the assumption that the firm is compelled to undergo some changes upon federating with others, but that the internal restructuration of resource configurations to match the needs of the alliance or a partner is costly to a firm and detrimental to its overall flexibility; in the words of Pfeffer and Salancik (1978):

> The price for inclusion in any collective structure is the loss of discretion and control over one's activities [...] Organizations seek to avoid dependencies and external control, and, at the same time, to shape their own contexts and retain their autonomy for independent action.

In an operating environment where federation among organisations is a necessity, the concept of standalone capability does not imply a firm's ability to remain outside *any* federation; instead, it refers to the firm's continued capability to be a free, autonomous agent *within* its environment. In a network environment, this means *an agent capable of managing its interdependencies*. Standalone capability, thus, refers to the capability of a firm

- to survive for a certain (albeit limited) amount of time by itself in order to allow for the possibility of severing ties with existing partners,
- to have guarded enough key (or core) resources and capabilities under its own jurisdiction to make it an attractive partner sought for association with others, and
- to maintain sufficient operational flexibility and linkage resources to adjust parts of its structure to membership in a new alliance group.

Core resources

Standalone capability guarantees that an airline maintains a role – and some power – within an alliance group by guarding its contribution to it, and that it is strong enough to be able to afford looser coupling – or decoupling – from an existing partnership in order to seek a more optimal arrangement. Conserving standalone capability helps to de-specify the dependence of the airline on its partner(s) or the alliance group, in that it ensures the airline's ability to switch partners and buffers its core from shifts and changes within the alliance group. It is one of the features that an airline which aspires to maintain itself as a separate entity must most jealously seek to guard. Standalone capability rests on the protection of a firm's core resources and that firm's capability to interface these core resources with partners, without harming the core. In the airline case, core resources are likely to be route system related. Examples include the dominance of a hub airport and a large share, if not dominance, of a certain market. Core resources are thus those resources that provide the unique contribution of that firm to the alliance; they are the resources that partners seek to obtain from that firm. The value of a core resource is a function of (a) internally to the firm: how many resources that resource can create (i.e., its value as a 'resource-creating resource'[38]), and (b) externally: of how many firms are (specifically) dependent on it. These core resources will provide a basis for existence to an airline if and when a transition phase between two alliances occurs, and they also help ensure that this transition phase is reasonably short. On linking to a new airline alliance group or integrating tighter into an existing group, airline management needs to be aware of this core, which should not be bent too much to the particular requirements of any one alliance group.

Linkage resources

Airline management also need to be aware of those non-core resources that serve as interfaces, or linkage points, to potential partners. Many linkage resources are sales-related. A typical linkage resource is a Frequent Flyer Programme (which is then joined with those of partners) or participation in a specific Computer Reservations System (CRS). Additionally, some routes can be considered a linkage resource if they connect the airline's core market to a major hub airport. Linkage resources need to be managed under the aspect of flexibility; they need to be able to provide an interface with different, and potentially changing, partners. Because linkage resources can be likened to a bridge in that they provide access to the firm's core, it is important that the firm maintains as much control as possible over the deployment of these resources. The challenge lies in allowing for flexibility requirements and compromises with partners at the other end of the link, while maintaining some control over the development and deployment of these linkage resources. An example of this is a mediumsized airline of the Local Champion type which dominates a certain regional market (core resources) and which operates a limited set of intercontinental routes. Upon joining an airline alliance group, this airline would seek to adjust its linkage services to inter- and transcontinental hubs of partner carriers in a manner to accommodate, and integrate with, its alliance partners. This is likely to require the shifting of services, refraining from serving some destinations but stepping up services to others, etc. It will also imply that this airline adapts its Frequent Flyer Programme to those of its partners. Further link resource adaptations will concern sales offices abroad, marketing campaigns etc. At the same time, however, the core of that airline's operation, i.e., what it really contributes to the airline alliance group (the market where it is the Local Champion), must be relatively protected from these movements. One reason for this is the high costs related to restructuring any part of a firm, and especially the densest; the second reason is that the airline seeks to retain maximum control over what constitutes its unique contribution to that, or any further, alliance.

Evidence from recent strategic moves

> Inevitably we're [as a medium-sized airline] always dealing with big brother, but I think we've been reasonably successful in the position we're in, so that we bring in these things to the party, and [alliance group X] wanted us in as much as we wanted to get in. And that's in effect a background to the relationship, but we never allow ourselves to be dominated by that asymmetry, but you're right that the asymmetry is there, and I've always used the analogy of marriage in this context, of course, the courtship was particularly interesting and positive and the honeymoon was fine, but once you start living together permanently it starts to get real, and managing a relationship that's both asymmetric and multilateral is particularly difficult.
> (Senior Manager in an interview)

This section will apply the previous discussion to the actual situation in the airline industry, based on events in the industry that were recent at the time of writing. It considers an airline alliance group as a network of interdependencies where airlines contribute a resource or set of resources. Since one primary aim of airline alliances is to seek geographical scope, the core resources consist of what can be called the airline's home market. This refers to the route-system related, technical and nontangible resources in the set of markets where that particular airline has its highest operating density. Exploiting these resources can be seen as the airline's 'raison d'être'. The home market resource base is an aggregate of the two separate criteria used by Weber and Dinwoodie (2000), namely 'Business Strength' and 'Market Attractiveness' and can be classified according to the following criteria:

1. the *attractiveness* of that resource (e.g. in the airline case, access to a wealthy, high yield market and/or a central, uncongested hub)
2. the *uniqueness* of the resource (e.g. the degree of market dominance in the home market; *substitutability*)
3. the *remoteness* of the resource (e.g. the difficulty of market entry from the outside. In the airline case, this refers to cultural remoteness, geographical remoteness, regulatory barriers and other factors which would render a potential competitor's establishment in those markets slow and costly; *imitability*).

The concept of resource attractiveness is akin to what Pfeffer and Salancik (1978) call 'Resource Importance', and the uniqueness of a resource is closely related to their notion of 'Concentration of Resource Control'. Resource uniqueness refers to the asset specificity of that resource or how easily that resource can be obtained from another provider.[39] Resource remoteness indicates the contestability of the market, e.g. how difficult or costly it is for an outsider to start operations in that market if there are 'resource position barriers'.[40] In the airline case, a carrier ideally obtains a powerful position in the network of airlines if it is *dominating* an *attractive* (i.e., wealthy, high yield) market which is *difficult to enter from the outside* (even in case of a completely deregulated environment, some locations are just geographically too remote to be economically exploited by newcomers, or there are cultural barriers).

The possible combinations of the three resource characteristics in the airline industry are described in table 3.1.

This table highlights the problems of not having a core resource whose contribution is attractive to potential partners and of operating in an easily contestable market. Easily contestable markets are likely to be in a geographically central location and/or within a fully deregulated environment where there are no infrastructure barriers (such as airport slot restrictions) to setting up airline operations.

Table 3.1 Resource Characteristics

Situation	Possible strength of position in alliance	Airline examples
One of several players in a less attractive, remote market	Weak position for alliancing	The casualties of the recent Privatisation/Deregulation wave in South America: LAB, LAP, Pluna
Dominance of a less attractive, remote market	Weak position for alliancing	Air Madagascar, Air Seychelles, Airlines in South Pacific region
One of several players in a less attractive, easily contestable market	Very hard to grow out of	Second-level US domestic carriers
Dominance in a less attractive, easily contestable market	Weak position	Essential Air Services providers in the US
One of several players in an attractive, remote market	'Beauty Contest'. Moderate to good position for alliancing	ANA, JAL
Dominance of an attractive, remote market	'Coveted Beauty'. Very good position for alliancing.	Finnair, LAN Chile, VARIG, Air China, South African Airways
One of several players in an attractive, easily contestable market	'Sandwiched in'. Strong need for differentiation and/or alliancing for sheltering. Weak negotiating position within alliance.	US domestic carriers, SABENA, Thai Airways, MAS
Dominance of an attractive but easily contestable market	'Stressed out'. Have to seek scope and entrench simultaneously. Can move towards being Global Connectors.	Lufthansa, Air France, KLM, British Airways

A further important issue is that of market dominance. Even if the contributed market is attractive, the airline that does not clearly dominate this market finds itself in competition with other players for a potential partner's attention. In real life, this problem is somewhat mitigated by the fact that there are several airline alliance groups, so there is a possibility for each airline to find a home. A larger problem in this context however is the negotiating stand that a non-dominant player has once the alliance is joined; he could theoretically be replaced or overridden. This is in fact close to what contributed to the problems which Thai Airways faced in the Star alliance: its market resources are not unique enough to give it a firm stand in that alliance; with the inclusion of Singapore Airlines (with which Thai has significant route overlap) as a Star member, the relative position of Thai – the uniqueness of its contribution – was weakened. On the other hand, domination of an attractive market that is not easily contestable might also allow an airline to stay out of any alliance group at all, and opt for a portfolio-of-bilaterals approach instead. When discussing the portfolio of bilaterals strategy during an interview, one senior manager mentioned the example of Japan Airlines, which successfully operates a portfolio of bilaterals: 'Everybody wants JAL [as an alliance partner], they have a huge domestic market, they can afford it [to stay outside an alliance group]'.

It is interesting to note that remaining outside an alliance group was pictured as an attractive option that was not open to any airline. Indeed, the management of Japan Airlines themselves openly stated that to them, joining an alliance group was not necessary as long as they could operate a useful portfolio of bilaterals. Interestingly, in November 2001 and after having repeatedly hinted at their commitment to the portfolio-approach, Japan Airlines stepped up its position in the Japanese domestic market by merging with domestic airline Japan Air Services (JAS). Japan Airlines can only afford its portfolio strategy if it has a strong hold on a coveted resource, in this case the Japanese domestic and regional market.

Putting the market characterisation in the alliance context further strengthens the hypothesis that alliancing increases specialisation amongst airlines. While changing an airline's route structure (and, consequently, a considerable part of its physical infrastructure such as fleet composition) is a process which takes time, one can already observe some of this development in practice: recent examples of specialisation due to alliance membership include a move by ANA of Japan; their value to the Star alliance resides in the contribution of the (highly attractive, remote) Japanese market. The airline recently announced that they would reduce their own intercontinental flights, increase codeshares with their partners Lufthansa and United (thereby assuring continuity of good overseas links for ANA's passengers) while concentrating more on serving domestic and East Asian routes. In a similar vein, MAS of Malaysia announced that they would concentrate on serving their region and let their partner KLM (a Global Connector) operate their routes to Australia. Most recently, Alitalia announced that upon joining the SkyTeam alliance, they intend to cut some long- and medium-haul routes and concentrate on the Italian and western Mediterranean markets. None of these moves are radical, but they certainly depict a tendency. As to large firms operating as Global Connectors, they could theoretically remain generalists and perform the double-act of being a Local Champion around their home hub themselves, at the expense of becoming a very complex airline. However, the evidence from Global

Connectors like Lufthansa, Air France or British Airways suggests a tendency for this type of airline to employ smaller regional carriers as feeders, under tight operational integration and often under the likes of an 'Express' or 'Team'-sub-brand to perform the role of local champion in markets around their main hub(s). The regional feeders typically have lower operating costs. They are frequently paid for their services on a so-called fee-for-departure basis, which means that they receive a flat fee for every departure under their partner's code, irrespective of seats filled. This guarantees the regional a relatively stable income, and additional cost savings because they do not have to incur marketing and sales costs themselves. For example, Lufthansa relied heavily on the route system of its (lower cost, regional) CityLine subsidiary while it cut down heavily on its mainline route system and frequencies after the industry crisis induced by the terrorist attacks of 11 September 2001. In the words of one Lufthansa executive;

> So far we have not yet touched our regional capacity at CityLine. It is possible that CityLine business will increase in the current environment and that our regional jets might replace Lufthansa Classic planes on certain routes and destinations in the future. So the future of our CityLine operations given its lower cost base, different wage structure and smaller planes, looks quite promising to us.[41]

An examination of changes in route systems with airlines since 1995 yielded a number of tendencies that could be well matched with the resource-configuration types described above:

Table 3.2 Recent moves by different airline types

Situation	Typical recent moves
One of several players in a less attractive, remote market	Disappear upon withdrawal of government financing (e.g. LAB, LAP, Pluna).
Dominance of a less attractive, remote market	Increasingly seek foreign carriers to operate their routes (e.g. Air Seychelles).
One of several players in a less attractive, easily contestable market	Seek to operate as feeders to larger carriers (e.g. second-level US domestic carriers).
Dominance in a less attractive, easily contestable market	Stay in niche, eventually codeshare with larger airline serving local area (e.g. Essential Air Services providers in North America).
One of several players in an attractive, remote market	*Either* operate a portfolio of bilaterals (e.g. JAL) *or* integrate into alliance and assume a specialist role (withdrawing from some longhaul routes, stepping up regional services) (e.g. ANA).
Dominance of an attractive, remote market	If home market is small, seek alliance integration; defend niche / 'specialist' position (e.g. Finnair, LAN Chile). If home market is large, alternative possibility for portfolio-of-bilaterals approach exists. (VARIG did not opt for this, South African did, Air China might.)
One of several players in an attractive, easily contestable market	Insecure future as government funding is withdrawn. Seek feeder role to larger carriers.
Dominance of an attractive but easily contestable market	Extend role as Global Connectors. Hub control becomes vital. Increasingly pulling out of local/regional routes, letting those be operated by tightly controlled feeders or franchisees under their own brand.

The majority of airlines moved visibly towards a more specialist position between 1995 and 2002. Interestingly, in the two recent cases of airline failures (Swissair and Sabena) it was the smaller, integrated, specialised regional carriers (Crossair and DAT, respectively), that survived their generalist parent.

One must also mention some examples of interesting apparent exceptions to this general tendency, where allied airlines somewhat moved towards a more generalist profile: one example is that of bmi British Midland International, an airline which fits into the 'one of several players in an attractive, easily contestable market' category: a medium-sized airline based in England, which has traditionally operated domestic and European routes in competition with British Airways and a number of smaller carriers in a home market (the UK) which is, by European standards, quite liberal and displays relatively low barriers to entry. British Midland joined the Star alliance in July 2000; its traditional role within Star would have been that of a Local Champion, contributing the UK market to the alliance. However, and in addition to this, British Midland significantly expanded its service portfolio (i.e., it generalised) in 2001 by starting to serve transatlantic destinations (currently Chicago and Washington DC out of Manchester, and several Canadian destinations out of London Heathrow).

A second example is Finnair, another typical Local Champion who dominates an attractive and remote, albeit relatively small, market. Finnair has always operated a limited set of long-haul routes to North America and the Far East. In 2001, Finnair (by then a member of the oneworld alliance group, but which also codeshared with non-oneworld carrier Swissair on several long-haul routes out of Zürich), actually increased its frequencies from its base in Helsinki to the Far East. Finnair depicted its aim to maintain a certain standalone capability this way:

> Finnair does not have a dominant role in the restructuring of the industry. Our position as a Northern European airline networking with strong partners allows us to steer our own future. We can only retain this ability if we can produce a healthy profit, keep our production costs competitive with those of our main rivals and if we have top notch, highly skilled and motivated staff.[42]

These two airlines appear to be going against the assumed tendency towards specialisation, by expanding their services to intercontinental flights and operating, in addition to their short-to-medium-haul fleet (which both airlines have been homogenising during recent years), a fairly small fleet of long-haul aircraft. This move can be seen as a sign that alliances are not yet considered to be a sufficiently stable operating environment which allows full carefree specialisation. In other words, the assumption, or strengthening, of selected long-haul routes can be seen as a contribution to conserving that airline's standalone capability, a necessary move in a perceived unstable environment. It remains to be seen whether British Midland will, in the long run, be allowed to compete on the North Atlantic with its alliance partner United. One sign of British Midland already turning away from its strategy of offering high-quality service in direct competition with alliance partners was its sudden announcement on 12 November 2001 to somewhat alter its operational profile and turn into a low-cost carrier. Similarly, Finnair's expansion on certain Far East routes still clearly avoids head-on competition with any of its partners by concentrating on the relatively small (but high-yield) market of Scandinavia-Far East routes and catering to a mainly Finnish business clientele. Even though the connection to Far Eastern destinations from central Europe via Helsinki is actively marketed by Finnair (benefiting from Helsinki's location under the great circle route from central Europe to China and Japan), Finnair clearly stays within, and consolidates, its niche; in other words, it is actively protecting its standalone capability.

These examples seem to suggest that it is, in fact, at only very high levels of integration, and alliance stability, that airlines can feel safe enough to truly specialise. A Local Champion's move to maintain some longhaul routes – which implies having to operate a dedicated fleet at significant cost – can be interpreted as a sign that a firm's aim to maintain standalone capability is countervailing to the tendency towards specialisation.

Thus, only if it is embedded in a very stable federated environment does a firm not need to undergo the full costs of generalism, while still being buffered from environmental uncertainties. It then needs to cover relatively less of the spectrum of overall needed resources itself. But through its specialisation, it can concentrate on dominating access to, or control, one or a set of resources. Provided that these resources are attractive to other actors in the field, a firm that controls an attractive resource can be best off if it specialises in the provision of these core resources. A generalist firm, however, which seeks to cover a large spectrum of functions, is likely to enter into direct competition with specialists in any one functional field or to enter into a set of multiple specific dependencies on several specialists. Nevertheless, and especially in the case of an industry or organisational field where scope issues are relevant (such as the airline industry), the generalist does have a vital role in the function of linking specialists to each other. This does create a certain dependence of the specialist (who also has to seek scope) on the generalist, but this dependence is likely to be unspecific because a specialist is likely still to have an option as to which generalist it uses as a scope provider. One senior manager of a smaller airline underlined the importance of not sacrificing too much independence and described very well the principle behind unspecific dependencies: 'You only lose part of your independence, on certain issues, which are strategically very important for the alliance, but not for you'.

It is in this sense that specialists, even if possibly of overall small size, are not necessarily disadvantaged in a networking environment. The ultimate aim of an alliancing strategy, especially for a smaller partner would, thus be (a) to deploy and protect resources in order either to achieve reciprocal asymmetries, or, possibly, to get on the 'good' side of an asymmetry by having partners specifically dependent on one's core resource(s) and (b) to conserve its standalone capability.

Chapter conclusions

It has been proposed in this chapter that an airline's behaviour in a federated environment (which represents that carrier's immediate task environment) is determined to a significant extent by the stability of that firm's task environment. This stability in turn is a function of the reciprocal interdependencies that exist between partners, and of the degree and grounding of trust and goodwill. The airline's position in its task environment depends on the deployment and protection of a set of core resources. In addition to this core, the airline needs to operate a set of ancillary or peripheral link resources, which serve the protection of the core and/or the linking of that core to other airlines' route systems. The alliancing competence of an airline can thus be described as

1. the ability to maximally exploit core resources, and to successfully and flexibly build ties with other firms through linkage resources without harming, or endangering, the core,
2. the ability to make partners specifically dependent on its own core resources, while striving to enter only unspecific dependencies by itself,
3. the ability to balance benefits from lean, specialist operations on one hand and the need for retention of standalone capability on the other.

It was also suggested that while entering specific dependencies with one particular partner may be dangerous to an airline (unless it acquires equity and/or establishes a joint venture with that partner), the entering of specific dependencies with a federation, or alliance group, while still representing a risk, carries certain advantages in terms of provision of a stable operating environment without the need to seek equity investment in each or every partner. One crucial requirement for the minimisation of risk related to investing in specific dependence on an alliance is, however, that *all* partners involved in that federation must have entered similar specific dependencies: the federation can only provide stability (which is what is bought with alliance-specific investments) if all partners are tied to it and are equally deterred from instability-causing behaviour.

In an alliancing environment, firms which have access to an attractive, imperfectly substitutable resource can afford to specialise to a greater degree because they have other partners specifically dependent on them for the provision of a coveted resource or resource bundle (in the airline case, this is most frequently domination of an attractive market). On the other hand, airlines which do not control such an exclusive resource, but which are based at a central location and which operate more generalist services (for example, most large Western European carriers such as British Airways, Lufthansa, KLM or Air France) tend to position themselves as link providers, connecting the specialists' markets between each others' and to their own route systems. An airline alliance group needs both types of airlines in order to offer adequate scope benefits to its customers.

In the larger context of corporate governance, the discussion of interdependencies and standalone capability can be a basis for understanding managerial action, since the ability of decision makers to make a choice depends frequently on how far they could preserve autonomy in the environment.[43] A good complement to this structural view is thus research on the managerial side, to investigate whether there exists some countervailing power to alliance integration in the managerial quest for independence[44] and to depict the features of an alliance mindset[45] of key actors as a function of the balancing of standalone requirements with dependence on an alliance. This issue will be addressed in the following chapter.

Notes

[1] see e.g. Seristö, 1995.

[2] Hannan and Freeman, 1977.

[3] Astley and Van de Ven, 1983.

[4] Provan, 1983.

[5] A large part of alliance literature does in fact assume a resource based perspective, but often with a focus on vertical alliances and dyadic relationships. Eisenhardt and Schoonhoven (1996) offer a resource-based view on the *formation* of alliances; they argue that the motivation for alliance formation comes about at the two extremes of the resource spectrum: while vulnerable firms need resources, strong firms seek to capitalise on their assets. Similarly, Koza and Lewin (1998) argue that it is important to understand alliancing behaviour in function of a firm's strategic choice portfolio and prior history. In the context of airline alliances, however, the distinction between 'strong' and 'vulnerable' firms might be less applicable, since both 'vulnerable' and less 'vulnerable' firms are scope-seeking, and thus highly dependent on obtaining resources, or access to resources, from partners. Alliancing will influence the market power, as well as dependencies, of both types. Taking network *dynamics* into account, Håkansson and Snehota (1995) examine both structural and process characteristics of business networks. They posit that stability and change are interdependent: 'Much of the change in business networks aims at achieving a certain degree of stability'. They also provide an interesting twist to classical resource dependence views by saying that 'Companies not only economize on use of resources. They use resources, their own and others', in order to provide resources for others. Thus they create and develop resources and it may well be that creating and developing resources rather than economizing on resources is their primary purpose.'

[6] see e.g. Penrose, 1959; Wernerfelt, 1984; Conner, 1991; Grant, 1991; Mahoney and Pandian, 1992; Monteverde, 1997; and especially the recent discussion by Barney, 2001 and Priem and Butler, 2001 a-b.

[7] Wernerfelt, 1984; Grant, 1991; Ahuja, 2000.

[8] Spekman and Sawhney, 1992.

[9] Provan, 1982.

[10] Pfeffer, 1987.

[11] Dant and Gundlach, 1998.

[12] Jones et al, 1998.

[13] Pfeffer and Salancik, 1978.

[14] It is important to make this distinction: Most literature paints things in black and white, i.e., alliance failure or not. In reality, there are many 'shades of grey', each of which demand response capability.

[15] For example, Air France benefits from dominance of Charles de Gaulle airport, one of Europe's few uncongested hub airports.

[16] With the increased proliferation of frequent flyer programmes and corporate accounts, customers are increasingly bound to a specific airline or alliance group.

[17] For example, Bucklin and Sengupta (1993) link alliance success to the partner's ability to dampen power imbalances between them. Khanna et al. (1998) state that because of asymmetric incentives, no two partners in an alliance operate within the same context. Doz and Hamel (1998) describe how, in an alliance based on co-specialisation, partners' bargaining power depends on asymmetries in the uniqueness of their contribution. One can expect this to be further aggravated in the case of a multilateral alliance.

18 Koza and Lewin, 2000.
19 Pfeffer and Salancik, 1978.
20 Jarillo, 1988; Gulati et al, 1994.
21 Kleymann, 2002.
22 Morgan and Hunt, 1999.
23 Borys and Jemison, 1989.
24 Das and Teng, 2000a, b.
25 Das and Teng, 1999; 2001.
26 Kleymann and Seristö, 2001.
27 Hennart, 1988.
28 Executive responsible for Management Information Systems, Lufthansa. Source: *Kauppalehti,* 6 July 1999.
29 Sheppard and Tuchinsky, 1996; Gulati, Nohria and Zaheer, 2000.
30 Child and Faulkner, 1998.
31 Gulati, 1995.
32 Creed and Miles, 1996.
33 For a related discussion on the process and challenges of institutionalising 'alliancing', see Kleymann, 2002.
34 Kale et al., 2000.
35 Doz and Hamel, 1998.
36 Gulati, 1995.
37 Kale et al., 2000.
38 Håkansson and Snehota, 1995.
39 Auster, 1994.
40 Wernerfelt, 1984.
41 Karl-Ludwig Kley, CFO Lufthansa, at UBS Warburg Transport Conference, London 1 Oct 2001.
42 Finnair C.E.O. Keijo Suila, Finnair Annual Report 1999/2000.
43 Child, 1997.
44 Galbraith, 1967; Dant and Gundlach, 1998.
45 Spekman et al., 1998.

References

Ahuja, G. (2000), The Duality of Collaboration: Inducements and Opportunities in the Formation of Interfirm Linkages. *Strategic Management Journal*, Vol. 21, No 3, pp. 317-344.
Astley, W. and Fombrun, C. (1983), Collective Strategy: Social Ecology of Organizational Environments. *Academy of Management Review*, Vol. 8, No. 4, pp. 576-687.
Auster, E. (1994), Macro and Strategic Perspectives on Interorganizational Linkages. In: Shrivastava, P., Huff, A. and Dutton, J. (eds), Advances in Strategic Management, Vol 10B, JAI Press, pp. 3-40.
Barney, J. (2001), Is the Resource-Based "View" a Useful Perspective for Strategic Management Research? Yes. *Academy of Management Review*, Vol. 26, No. 1, pp. 41-56.

Borys, B. and Jemison, D. (1989), Hybrid Arrangements as Strategic Alliances: Theoretical Issues in Organizational Combinations. *Academy of Management Review*, Vol. 14, No. 2, pp. 234-249.

Bucklin, L. and Sengupta, S. (1992), Balancing Co-Marketing Alliancing for Effectiveness. *Working Paper, Report No. 92-120*, Marketing Science Institute, Cambridge, Ma.

Bucklin, L. and Sengupta, S. (1993), Organizing Successful Co-Marketing Alliances. *Journal of Marketing*, Vol. 57 (April), pp. 32-46.

Buvik, A. and Grønhaug, K. (2000), Inter-firm dependence, environmental uncertainty and vertical co-ordination in industrial buyer - seller - relationships. *Omega*, Vol. 28, pp. 445-454.

Child, J. (1997), Strategic Choice in the Analysis of Action, Structure, Organizations and Environment: Retrospect and Prospect. *Organization Studies*, Vol. 18, No. 1, pp. 43-76.

Child, J. and Faulkner, D. (1998), Strategies of Cooperation. Managing Alliances, Networks, and Joint Ventures. Oxford: Oxford University Press.

Conner, K. (1991), A Historical Comparison of Resource-Based Theory and Five Schools of Thought Within Industrial Organization Economics: Do We Have a New Theory of the Firm? *Journal of Management*, Vol. 17, No. 1, pp. 121-154.

Creed, W. and Miles, R. (1996), Trust in Organizations: A Conceptual Framework Linking Organizational Forms, Managerial Philosophies, and the Opportunity Cost of Controls. In: Kramer, R. and Tyler, T. (eds): Trust in Organizations. Thousand Oaks: Sage.

Dant, R., and Gundlach, G. (1998), The Challenge of Autonomy and Dependence in Franchised Channels of Distribution. *Journal of Business Venturing*, Vol. 14, pp. 35-67.

Das, T. (1983), Qualitative Research in Organizational Behaviour. *Journal of Management Studies*, Vol. 20, No. 3, pp. 301-314.

Das, T. and Teng, B. (1999), Managing risk in strategic alliances. *The Academy of Management Executive*, Vol 13 No. 4, pp. 50-62.

Das, T. and Teng, B. (2000a), A Resource-Based Theory of Strategic Alliances. *Journal of Management*, Vol. 26, No. 1, pp. 31-61.

Das, T. and Teng, B. (2000b), Instabilities of Strategic Alliances: An Internal Tensions Perspective. *Organization Science*, Vol. 11, No. 1, pp. 77-101.

Das, T. and Teng, B. (2001), A risk perception model of alliance structuring. *Journal of International Management*, Vol. 7, pp. 1–29.

Das, T. and Teng, B. (2001), Trust, Control, and Risk in Strategic Alliances: An Integrated Framework. *Organization Studies*, Vol. 22, No 2, pp. 251-283.

Doz, Y. and Hamel, G. (1998), Alliance Advantage. Boston, Mass.: HBS press.

Eisenhardt, K. and Schoonhoven, C. (1996), Resource-based View of Strategic Alliance Formation: Strategic and Social Effects in Entrepreneurial Firms. *Organization Science*, Vol. 7, No. 2, pp. 136-150.

Galbraith, J.K. (1967), The Concept of Countervailing Power. In: Mallen, B. (ed.), Marketing Channel: A Conceptual Viewpoint. New York: Wiley.

Grant, R. (1991), The resources-based theory of competitive advantage: Implications for strategy formulation. *California Management Review*, 33 (3), pp. 114-135.

Gulati, R. (1995), Does Familiarity Breed Trust? The Implications of Repeated Ties for Contractual Choice in Alliances. *Academy of Management Journal*, Vol. 38, No. 1, pp. 85-112.

Gulati, R., Khanna, T. and Nohria, N. (1994), Unilateral Commitments and the Importance of Process in Alliances. *Sloan Management Review*, Spring 1994, pp. 61-69.

Gulati, R., Nohria, N. and Zaheer, A. (2000), Strategic Networks. *Strategic Management Journal*, Vol 21, No 3, pp. 203-216.

Håkansson, H. and Snehota, I. (1995), *Developing Relationships in Business Networks*. London: Routledge.

Hannan, M. and Freeman, J. (1977), The Population Ecology of Organisations. *American Journal of Sociology*, Vol. 82, No. 5, pp. 929-964.

Hannan, M. and Freeman, J. (1984), Structural Inertia and Organisational Change. *American Sociological Review*, Vol. 49, pp. 149-164.

Hennart, J.-F. (1988), A Transaction Costs Theory of Equity Joint Ventures. *Strategic Management Journal*, Vol. 9, No. 4, pp. 361-374.

Jarillo, J.C. (1988), On Strategic Networks. *Strategic Management Journal*, Vol. 9, pp. 31-41.

Jones, C., Hesterly, W.S., Fladmoe-Lindquist, K. and Borgatti, S.P. (1998), Professional Service Constellations: How Strategies and Capabilities Influence Collaborative Stability and Change. *Organization Science*, Vol. 9, No. 3, pp. 396-410.

Kale, P., Singh, H. and Perlmutter, H. (2000), Learning and Protection of Proprietary Assets in Strategic Alliances: Building Relational Capital. *Strategic Management Journal*, Vol 21, No 3, pp. 217-238.

Khanna, T., Gulati, R. and Nohria, N. (1998), The dynamics of Learning Alliances: Competition, Co-operation, and Relative Scope. *Strategic Management Journal*, Vol. 19, pp. 193-210.

Kleymann, B. (2002), The Development of Multilateral Alliances- the Case of the Airline Industry. PhD Dissertation, Helsinki School of Economics. Helsinki, Finland.

Kleymann, B. and Seristö, H. (2001), Levels of Airline Alliance Membership: Balancing Risks and Benefits. *Journal of Air Transport Management*, Vol. 7, No. 5, pp. 303-310.

Koza, M. and Lewin, A. (1998), The Co-evolution of Strategic Alliances. *Organization Science*, Vol. 9, No. 3, pp. 255-264.

Koza, M. and Lewin, A. (2000), Managing Partnerships and Strategic Alliances: Raising the Odds of Success. *European Management Journal*, Vol. 18, No. 2, pp. 146-151.

Mahoney, J. and Pandian, J.R. (1992), The Resource-Based View Within the Conversation of Strategic Management. *Strategic Management Journal*, Vol. 13, pp. 363-380.

Meyerson, D., Weick, K. , and Kramer, R. (1996), Swift Trust and Temporary Groups. In: Kramer, R. and Tyler, T. (eds.): Trust in Organizations. Thousand Oaks: Sage

Monteverde, K. (1997), Mapping the Competence Boundaries of the Firm: Applying Resource- Based Strategic Analysis. In: Thomas, H., O'Neal, D., and Ghertman, M. (eds.), Strategy, Structure and Style. New York: Wiley.

Morgan, R. and Hunt, S. (1999), Relationship-Based Competitive Advantage: The Role of Relationship Marketing in Marketing Strategy. *Journal of Business Research*, Vol. 46, pp. 281-290.

Penrose, E. (1959), The Theory of the Growth of the Firm. Oxford University Press.

Pfeffer, J. (1982), Organizations and Organization Theory. London: Pitman.

Pfeffer, J. (1987), New Directions for Organization Theory. Oxford: Oxford University Press.

Pfeffer, J. and Salancik, G. (1978), The External Control of Organizations. New York: Harper & Row.

Priem, R. and Butler, J. (2001a), Is the Resource-Based "View" a Useful Perspective for Strategic Management Research? *Academy of Management Review*, Vol. 26, No. 1, pp. 22–40.

Priem, R. and Butler, J. (2001b), Tautology in the Resource-Based View and The Implications of Externally Determined Resource Value: Further Comments. *Academy of Management Review*, Vol. 26, No. 1, pp. 57-66.

Provan, K. (1982), Interorganizational Linkages and Influence over Decision Making. *Academy of Management Journal*, Vol. 25, No. 2, pp. 443-451

Seristö, H. (1995), Airline Performance and Costs. An Analysis of Performance Measurement and Cost Reduction in Major Airlines. PhD Dissertation, Helsinki School of Economics and Business Administration, Finland

Sheppard, B. and Tuchinsky, M. (1996), Micro-OB and the Network Organization. In: Kramer, R. and Tyler, T. (eds): Trust in Organizations. Thousand Oaks: Sage.

Shibata, K. (2001), Motives for mega-alliance between US ex-trunk carriers and European flag carriers. *Journal of Air Transport Management*, Vol. 7, pp. 197-206

Spekman, R. and Sawhney, K. (1990), Toward a Conceptual Understanding of the Antecedents of Strategic Alliances. *Marketing Science Institute*, Report No. 90-114.

Spekman, R., Forbes, T., Isabella, L. and MacAvoy, T. (1998), Alliance Management: A view from the past and a look to the future. *Journal of Management Studies*, 35:6, pp. 747-772.

Tyler, T. and Degoey, P. (1996), Trust in Organizational Authorities. In: Kramer, R. and Tyler, T. (eds): Trust in Organizations. Thousand Oaks: Sage

Weber, M. and Dinwoodie, J. (2000), Fifth freedoms and airline alliances. The role of fifth freedom traffic in an understanding of airline alliances. *Journal of Air Transport Management*, Vol. 6, pp. 51-60.

Wernerfelt, B. (1984), A Resource-Based View of the Firm. *Strategic Management Journal*, Vol. 5, pp. 171-180.

Chapter 4

Alliancing Life: Talking to the Practitioners

In no other industry have formal, multilateral alliances been built to such an extent, and with such speed, as in the airline industry. Airline managers are pioneers of a new organisational form – which means that, as pioneers, they cannot rely very much on previous experience. It is them who have to define how to build these alliances, what they should entail, and how far they should go. Indeed, the way these cooperative groups evolve and will develop is very much dependent on the wishes, views and concerns of those who are involved in building them.

This chapter lets the main actors speak for themselves. To get an idea of the Alliance Makers' views, we talked to ten senior airline executives (Vice President up to Deputy CEO levels) involved in alliancing. We also discussed the topic with middle managers who are, or were, members of alliance task force groups, and interviewed a number of front line personnel. The formal interviews covered ten different airlines,[1] most of them Flag Carriers, all of them operating internationally, and all of them involved in some form of alliancing – be it as members of an alliance group, as being about to join, or as operating a portfolio of bilaterals strategy. In addition to this, we benefited from personal contacts in the industry, many informal discussions, and e-mail exchanges, and the monitoring of airline chat rooms on the internet.

To begin with, it was interesting to compare what the people who build the alliance had to say in our personal interviews with what is said in the official statements on alliancing that are issued on a regular basis as press releases by the carriers or the whole alliance group. We found that the statements made to the public are of relatively little informative value. Airlines include the topic of alliances in their press releases typically upon joining such an alliance, entering tighter cooperation – such as a Joint Venture – with a partner, or upon 'welcoming' a new airline to their existing alliance group. Press statements regarding a carrier joining an alliance are almost interchangeable, with little or no variation between them. They all refer to the alliance being a brand of quality, to the airline being a 'worthy' member of this group of excellence, and to passenger benefits resulting from a larger network. These statements typically read very much like this one:

> I am delighted that from 1 July, British Midland will become a member of Star Alliance, the world's largest airline network. We are already a major player in the European

market place and membership of Star Alliance allows us the opportunity to offer our customers a global network of destinations and services. With the convergence of the airline market, this is an essential element of the future growth and development of British Midland. In joining a global airline alliance, we are able to offer greater opportunities to optimise the global route network and help develop Heathrow as the airport in Europe to be the centre of two competing alliances. In addition, I am confident that Star Alliance membership will maximise growth opportunities for the airline and for our staff.

(BMI Chairman Sir Michael Bishop, bmi press release 6 June 2000)

Other alliance-related announcements refer to very specific customer-oriented features such as joint airport lounges, joint check-in facilities, or new codeshares. This could be expected, as these statements were almost exclusively directed at passengers and shareholders.

oneworld™: WHAT THE CEOs SAY

Bob Ayling, Chief Executive of British Airways, said: 'Our customers have told us they want airlines to work together to raise standards of service across the world. oneworld™ will do just that. It will bring together five leading airlines to maximise benefits for our customers, employees and shareholders.'

Don Carty, Chief Executive of American Airlines, said: 'We started this alliance effort by recognising it's all about people. We want to enhance the travel experience for our customers, improve the competitive position of our respective airlines and thus provide opportunities for our employees, as well as create value for our shareholders by building the world's premier airline network. We're prepared to set the standard for the industry by being the best and we think we have all the tools to make that happen.'

Kevin Benson, Chief Executive of Canadian Airlines, said: 'oneworld will deliver unrivalled benefits across our partner airlines, ensuring that our customers are recognised across all airlines as if they were their own.'

David Turnbull, Chief Executive of Cathay Pacific Airways, said: 'This alliance is superb news for Cathay Pacific's customers and those of our partner airlines. Customers travelling on oneworld will receive the highest levels of service and product available.'

James Strong, Chief Executive of Qantas, said: 'oneworld will provide each of us with a great opportunity to provide worldwide high quality service to our customers through airline partners acknowledged as world leaders in the aviation industry.'

(oneworld press conference, 21 September 1998)

Interestingly, these public statements very seldom refer to the implementation of the alliance; in other words, very little information concerning the set-up or organisation of an alliance group can be inferred from press releases or speeches. Whenever senior managers give press interviews or public addresses, they mostly concentrate on matters concerning their own airline – this might be chiefly due to the fact that these speeches are typically addressed directly or indirectly to shareholders and potential investors, who are more interested in matters concerning a particular airline. Indeed, after joining an alliance was announced, relatively few airline press releases and public statements continue to refer to the alliance. Supposed or real customer benefits and the quality image are instead communicated via signs at airports, in-flight magazines, and leaflets sent to members of frequent flyer programmes, i.e. at the point of immediate contact with the airline product (booking and taking a flight), rather than in corporate information about the airline and its strategy. In short, communications efforts about the alliance were directed to customers, and much less to shareholders; and they concerned mainly the benefits of a seamless route network, without discussing the internal workings of alliancing.

A reason for this might be what we call 'local rationales'. Airline managers are paid by, and responsible to, their company's shareholders, and their prime interest concerns their own company. It seems that beyond the very useful marketing tool that alliance membership represents (vastly improved reach and access to new distribution channels), their first and foremost concern is clearly with running their own airline on a daily basis.

This was confirmed in the personal talks we held. The views of those who build the alliance groups (and run their airlines at the same time) ranged from purely pragmatic acceptance of alliancing as an unavoidable fact of life, to the passionate defence of an airline's independence. We will present some of the most interesting quotes from our interviews on the following pages.

'We've got no real choice ...'

In the interviews we conducted, it was striking that a majority at all levels of the airline – from senior managers to front-line personnel – were very pragmatic about alliancing as such. The need for cooperation was no longer questioned. Alliances were seen to be inevitable, but clearly difficult and tedious to implement. It was especially employees at the front line who saw alliancing as a fact of life:

> Nowadays the system moves everyday ... of course we are worried...but business is moving on, and we have to move, too. No choice.
> (Check-In officer)

The 'no choice' attitude also prevailed at management levels. There was much allusion to the domino effect of airlines being compelled to follow their competitors' actions by establishing alliances, in order be able to offer what soon became the industry standard of seamless travel across allied airlines. This domino effect has by now created a situation where most airlines' managements feel they had no choice but to join an alliance, since their competitors were doing the same thing. In the words of one senior manager:

If there was no other alliance grouping formed, I don't think you'd need to join [alliance name]. Once other alliances form, they suck existing traffic into their network so you have to create a parallel network to make sure that you keep your traffic.

Expressions of the general inevitability of alliancing were indeed very strongly reflected in the interviews:

It's inevitable that we'll end up linking with someone at some stage, in some form.
(Senior Manager)

We found that if you didn't align yourself to one of the global groups, you were in danger of finding your interlining ability curtailed. [...] So the danger was that our ability to operate a global network would be contracted year after year. Priority would be given by the alliances to their own members and we wouldn't be able to therefore offer a global network. So that's the danger, I think, of standing alone. It's fine for point-to-point traffic, but if you have a high percentage of connecting traffic you could find your ability to offer them traffic or to get feed in to your system very much curtailed.
(Senior Manager)

These examples suggest that specific airlines are placed in a position where their strategic options may appear very limited. The question does not any more appear to be whether or not to join an alliance, but which alliance to join.

The domino effect is also visible in this press notice:

BA has followed the progress of the BMI-SAS application [for antitrust immunity] closely as it decides whether to proceed with a similar arrangement with Iberia, its main partner in the oneworld alliance.
(Airwise Online News Service, 27 February 2001)

Apart from mentioning the pure inevitability of alliance membership, a number of positive reasons for having joined were given. Most of these referred to the more defensive rationales of alliancing. Middle managers and frontline employees tended to express their appreciation of alliance membership providing them with what they perceived as a more secure operating environment:

What [alliance] brought to us – well, the most important thing is that it brings security. We can say we belong to this big alliance. We're secure. That is the most important thing.
(Middle Manager)

In several cases, the senior managers interviewed clearly stated their defensive rationale:

The form of our activities is defensive. Defend the home market. And we cannot defend the home base alone. Our [(number)] destinations cover only 60-70 per cent of our traveller's needs.
(Senior Manager)

However, the perceived security appears to be temporary; the current alliance scenario and partner constellation was assumed by more senior actors to be still quite unstable:

My own sense is that it [the current alliancing scenario] will collapse, and but it might take up to five years, six to five years [Note: This interview was conducted in 2001], but I think it will collapse. And I think when it does, everybody will re-examine their position. I think you will certainly get some consolidation; you will get consolidation in Europe ... I think something will happen, and then I think the alliances will really be up for a grab, because you will get some marriages, some consolidations, and then you're going to get a different series of alliances, but real alliances – but that's looking at the crystal ball.
(Senior Manager)

It was interesting to observe that in the interviews, criticism never touched upon the alliance as a strategic idea per se. The rationale of establishing alliances was unquestioned, and the more critical views concerning the alliances typically focused on cooperation problems; in other words, the 'how' was more of an issue than the 'why'. But the 'how' seems to be a very contentious field. Implementing the alliance – both in terms of strategic planning and in the day-to-day running of the cooperation – was seen to be hard work, and people working in airlines at all levels regularly pointed to difficulties in cooperation with their partners. In the interviews, front-line staff frequently told lengthy accounts of how coordination with a partner airline went wrong in a particular instance. Examples for this include very complex cross-alliance calculations of frequent flyer points, or recurrent departure delays due to problems with weight-and-balance calculations performed alliance-wide at a central location, remote from the airfield. Most of these accounts referred to inadequate information structure (e.g. not fully compatible IT systems and not knowing who to contact on technical issues within the partner airline) between partners.

As to management levels, in almost all interviews (and indeed across all alliance groups), senior and medium managers discussed at some length inefficient decision making processes. For example, alliance-level coordination mechanisms and meetings were very frequently perceived as tedious and inefficient, as described in the following comments:

A medium-sized airline as ours does not welcome a flood of meetings, you know that, it gets too much, and we are too small to send everybody to meetings, we are an operating

airline, we have to fly planes. So, as a smaller airline, you have this maximum level of tolerance for these meetings and coordinating stuff.
(Senior Manager)

In those [alliance coordination-] meetings, they just talk about how to cooperate. And they never agree on anything. Then there's never enough time to decide on what we should actually do together.
(Senior Manager)

In these meetings, there is a problem in that they don't decide very much. There's a lot of stuff on the table, but they cannot reach a decision.
(Middle Manager)

One airline's deputy CEO even saw this as a topic for future academic research:

It would be attractive to know what you guys might think in terms of the unmanageable size of an alliance, in other words, how many carriers can be in an alliance before it begins to be dysfunctional.

A further issue that was brought up in interviews was cultural differences. We found it very interesting to note that front-line employees were unanimously enthusiastic about the multi-cultural aspects, and saw alliance membership as uniting them, while senior managers did not mention cultural issues at all. It was the middle managers who pointed to the difficulties of working across national and corporate cultures:

Well, when you have an American and an English in one place, they cannot reach a decision.
(Middle Manager, referring to alliance coordination meetings)

More concretely, an Air France employee admits a difference in the way of working between the French and the Americans:

I have to say as someone who works with Air France, it's been difficult, from an employee standpoint. These cultural differences are a big reason for that, too. Air France's operation runs like Delta's now. [...] But their workers are not used to the 'American' way of work rules and benefits. That's been the hardest issue between Delta and Air France. Actually, the same goes for all the SkyTeam members.
(Air France employee in Airwise online discussion forum, June 2001)

An interesting question that arose from our discussions with practitioners about the tediousness of alliance implementation was whether they would like to see more centralised, and more authoritarian alliance governance as a way to increase efficiency. Probably because they are held responsible for immediate results from these meetings, it was exclusively at middle management levels that expressions of regret about a lack of a central, strong alliance authority could be found.

> Without the commitment, it doesn't happen. I think the key question is how to believe in the alliance, and how to believe in its benefits for all of us. And I think that everyone should see from our [traffic] figures that we really should think more about the alliance and the competition with other alliances. It's really too democratic, this [alliance name]. (Middle Manager)

In addition to wishing for stronger commitment by members, there were numerous calls among middle managers for strong leadership by either one lead airline, or a steering body. A middle manager with Alitalia, who had witnessed the failure of that airline's joint venture with KLM, said that

> The main problem was that before they decided how to share, they didn't talk about the leader in the Joint Venture; who should lead. I hope that in the future they first start to talk about this, and then of the integration, because it was a huge work to be one organisation.

It is interesting to note that while a call for more authority vested in the alliance itself or even calling for a dominant partner was quite common among mid-level managers as a way to smoothen and facilitate cooperation; managers that are more senior did not advocate an increase in alliance authority nearly as much. One manager, however, described the stability – and security – inherent in a tightly organised alliance group, although his statement clearly referred to more strict general rules rather than any one partner or the alliance itself clearly dominating others:

> It doesn't really have to be so extreme that there is one partner who absolutely dominates, but there must be a very clear setting of goals, and there must be very clear setting of rules of the game [...] Because otherwise, what happens is that they do not use all potential possibilities and that then, in the end, everybody loses, that means not just the customer but also the partners. And partially, well, it can happen in the extreme that partners compete with each other and go about cooperating with partners from other alliances [...] As soon as things are arranged along strict rules, these problems disappear.
> (Senior Manager)

This statement could indeed be interpreted as a plea for a superstructure in which authority is vested.

In sum, it seems that the people who build alliances are quite pragmatic in that no interview partner questioned the sense of alliancing as such, or the rationale for his airline to have established cooperative agreements with partners. Instead, alliancing was described as rational behaviour in the context of the restructuring of the airline industry. Nevertheless, the implementation of cooperation was frequently described as tedious and inefficient. It seems that airline managers have accepted and adopted the concept of alliancing as such. While the direct implementers (middle managers) frequently called for a more authoritarian alliance governance structure, this was not the case with more senior managers, who called for looser ties or a buffer from alliance influence (see below). One reason for this might be that middle managers' performance is judged by their ability to implement certain pre-agreed tasks and schemes, among them the efficient setting up of certain detail aspects of the cooperation with partner airlines. On the other hand, senior management is held accountable almost exclusively for how well they defend and extend the interests of their own firm.

'... but we try to remain as independent as possible!'

In stark contrast to the rationalisation of alliancing, and certainly to the calls for more authoritarian alliance management, was another central theme in the various interviews, namely 'independence'. This, however, is a theme that is very seldom brought up in the public statements. In fact, the only time critical voices to alliance group membership appeared in press statements, they referred to the unique national characteristics of a particular airline which they felt needed to be preserved:

> We feel it is very important to provide services which suit Japanese customers. We have to watch multilateral alliances carefully to see if they can offer service which meets Japanese travellers' needs.
> (Senior Manager, Japan Air Lines Press Release)

In a few occasions, and mostly linked to Swissair's strategy during the 1990s, national characteristics were seen as a reason for the pursuit of an independent strategy:

> The head of SAir group (Swissair), Phillippe Bruggisser, [...] is a typical Swiss: He prefers going it alone, and he prefers to gather a troupe of smaller second-league partners around his airline to joining one of the big global alliances. Because Swissair would only play second fiddle in cooperation with giants like British Airways or Lufthansa, and Zürich would be no longer a hub in its own right but rather a feeder airport for Frankfurt or London. Going it alone [...] corresponds to the Swiss national character, and this policy so far has been sanctioned by SAir's board and shareholders
> (*Frankfurter Allgemeine Zeitung*, 22 November 2000; translated)

Very interesting in this respect is that almost exactly one year later, after the demise of Swissair and during the efforts to set up a new airline on the basis of the surviving regional carrier Crossair, the CEO of Crossair referred again (or still) to nationalistic emotions as he addressed the workforce of that possible new airline:

Our government and industry have given us a job to do. They want our country to continue to have a national airline, and we want to achieve this objective together and build our common future.

(André Dosé, CEO Crossair, in a speech to Swissair/Crossair employees on 16 November 2001)

One characteristic of the airline industry is that its workers – at any level – tend to identify very much with their employer, which is often a national symbol. Working for an airline is in many respects considered an elite job, and the emotional attachment of airline employees to their carrier tends to be high. Not surprisingly, having to integrate into an alliance and thereby having to reach compromises with partners, meets with reluctance at all levels. Especially at front-line and middle management levels, the distinction between 'us and them' seemed to be very strong. For example, employees resent having to give up routes for the alliance's sake:

I think it's a shame that we had so good connections and now [with the alliance] we have cut down our route structure quite a lot. And I think that's a shame, it takes a certain edge off the business. People do remember, they say 'do you remember when we used to fly this route ourselves?' it eats into morale quite a bit.
(Middle Manager)

Another interesting comment hinting at a strong 'us and them' mentality was made by a middle manager who had been involved in the merger between KLM and Alitalia:

The problem was that we had different priorities within the firm, so the new Joint Venture had two bosses; one was green, Alitalia; and one was blue, KLM. So what happened? The boss in Alitalia asks you for something, and also the boss KLM asking you the same, or other things. So you had to decide the priority. And most of the old people, just from their point of view, they automatically decided to give priority to the 'green' order, instead of the 'blue' one, it was a really competitive environment, because there was competition between Alitalia and KLM, well, there was nothing written, but you can feel this.
(Middle Manager involved in merger coordination activities; Alitalia)

All of the senior managers interviewed discussed at some length the issue of buffering their own carrier from an overwhelming influence of the alliance, or any one partner. For example, Austrian Airline's switch from Qualiflyer to Star was attributed to the greater possibility of self-determination offered by one group as opposed to the other:

The Austrian Airlines move to Star seems to confirm that partners still value their independence. News that Austrian Airlines had chosen to forego its long-term partners

for the bright lights of Star has been accompanied by the inevitable analysis about new signs of break-up among the global alliances. On reflection, the move seems to confirm a more fundamental theme – that airlines, on the whole, are not yet ready to let go their individual identity or lose control of their key markets in pursuit of a broader alliance strategy.
(Airline Business, October 1999)

In an interview, one of Austrian's managers stated that Austrian Airlines' move toward Star was clearly triggered by Qualiflyer partner Swissair's attempt to acquire a blocking minority in that airline:

We let Swissair know that it was not in our interest that Swissair gets close to a blocking minority in Austrian. Why? Because we would like to keep ourselves as long as possible as an independent airline. That won't be possible forever, probably, but we intend to [try]. We see no reasons at the moment to ... well ... to ... let me say hastily precipitate ourselves into the financial hands of another airline.
(Senior Manager, Austrian Airlines; translated)

One further reason for this seemed to be the impression that alliances are still too unstable, too much in flux, and are therefore not worth any large, long-term investment either in monetary terms or in giving up routes. Another reason was that the drive to preserve one's own airline's independence was indeed seen by all informants as the main obstacle to tighter alliance integration:

Too often there are very ambitious [alliance] strategies being developed and when it comes to the crunch of trying to deliver it somebody hides behind, but the reason they don't want to move forward in a multilateral sense is that they don't want to give up their sovereignty and too often the decision making in this context, if it gets pushed down the food chain too much, the individuals concerned are very defensive because they see their own personal local sovereignty has been taken away from them, so, that I think is a problem that most alliances haven't yet successfully delivered on.
(Senior Manager)

Among managers from small to medium sized airlines, we could find frequent recurrence to the theme of buffering, especially from the overwhelming influence of the larger partners:

[in alliance group Z] you have the strange position where the potential two leaders can often be at odds and it allows the smaller airlines to be more influential. So from a [Alliance] point of view that's a weakness, from a small airline's point of view it is an advantage.
(Senior Manager)

One small airline's Managing Director openly admitted during the interview that he was interested in protecting his airline's freedom:

... well, it has to make sense on the [Alliance] book, but apart from that we have all the freedom, and we are protecting that, let's say [laughs].

One senior manager gave the example of Star lead airline Lufthansa as an especially 'overwhelming' partner, and offered this interpretation of his own and partner airline Finnair's decision to join oneworld. Interestingly, and somewhat contrary to calls for security being the main alliance objective, a 'healthy place' was considered one where dissent and nonconformity was allowed for even a small partner:

The way I interpret Star, and we had a lot of discussions with Lufthansa before we choose, the way I interpret it is that this alliance is driven very heavily by Lufthansa, and...like...the characteristic of Lufthansa is that they push you very hard, and [Pause]...you have to conform [laughs]. So there isn't an awful lot of room for dissent if you are a small carrier. [laughs] I think, you know, the way for our friends in Finnair is oneworld is a healthier place to be at this stage.

Some alliance groups are setting up joint management committees. When asked about those, one manager saw these committees as a way for smaller airlines to gain more negotiating clout:

Provided that the small carriers... [laughs] ... can watch this a little bit carefully, it could develop in the right direction and I think it could be the right thing.
(Senior Manager)

There was also some suspicion that partners might desert the alliance or otherwise be uncooperative:

You have to negotiate pretty smartly, I think, because you are never sure in a structure which is sub-optimal whether it is going to survive or whether it's somebody going to seek a slightly better position for themselves by changing alliances, so you've got to think in terms of – you must plan for [laughs] for the doomsday.
(Senior Manager)

Avoiding alliance membership – if possible

This theme reflects an expression of the desire to prevent the alliance from taking too much influence over one's airline. In the aftermath of the failed integration between KLM and British Airways in mid-2000, the CEO of KLM resorted to stressing his airlines capability to go it alone, thereby implicitly downplaying the absolute need for an alliance with a competitor:

During the discussions with British Airways, KLM has successfully continued to focus on the development and profitability of the company. While we continue to believe that consolidation in the European aviation industry is inevitable, we at the same time remain convinced that for the foreseeable future, KLM has bright prospects on its own.
(Leo van Wijk, Chairman KLM, in a press statement on KL-BA alliance failure; September 2000)

Frequently, the reluctance to integrate too tightly was defended with the fact that alliance membership had really nothing to offer ...

We have a good relationship with [Star members] United and Lufthansa, we codeshare with [oneworld member] British Airways. Since we have these good relationships with alliance partners, why should we join the alliance if we're doing all right?
(Senior Manager)

... or that that up to now, the alliancing scene is still considered to be too unstable ...

They [Alliance groups] have not really settled yet, there is a danger that you can spend a lot of effort, resources and money in this alliancing, and then you find out that it doesn't suit you. Or that it doesn't suit them. And then you have to separate again and that creates difficulties.
(Senior Manager)

... or, less frequently, because alliancing as such was seen as inherently detrimental to the airline:

Virgin Atlantic Boss Richard Branson has again distanced his airline from forming any alliance, claiming that such groupings 'squeeze the smaller carriers and bring no real benefits'.
(RATI online news service, 12 July 1999)

It was indeed mostly smaller carriers that openly acknowledged risks inherent in too tight integration:

As a niche National Carrier, Air Malta continued making judicious use of its limited resources to carve its place in the aviation community. It is open to commercial cooperation with other carriers, cognisant of the potential risks and opportunities encountered in developing airline alliance relationships.
(Air Malta Annual Report FY, 2000)

As to outright alliance avoidance, non-aligned carriers such as Japan Airlines and Emirates tended openly to justify their choices of avoiding alliance group membership:

Emirates Airlines says it is still reluctant to join a global alliance as its existing codeshare relationships – with both the OneWorld and the Star alliance – are providing good benefits and revenue streams. [...] [Emirates corporate treasurer] Peermohammed notes that Emirates is concerned that a global alliance strategy may conflict with the development of Dubai International Airport as an Emirates hub. He says the carrier is 'not sure that joining an alliance would make us a feeder airline for others'.
(RATI online news service, 6 April 2000)

As discussed in Chapter 3, Japan Airlines openly admits to pursuing its portfolio of bilaterals strategy and to trying to stay outside any alliance group for as long as this is feasible:

I think we have been very successful as far as our alliance strategy has been concerned, to be focused and to put the emphasis on bilateral partnerships and on specific markets. For example, in the market between France and Japan we have partnered with Air France [member of SkyTeam] and to Australia with Qantas [member of oneworld], so that makes very clear that both partners can have definite merits. Of course we are not against the idea of a multilateral alliance, and we are always studying the pros and cons of joining a global alliance. But no, we are not specifically [any closer to a decision on joining an alliance group]. We are not in a hurry.
(Isao Kaneko, President of JAL, in a press interview; *Airline Business*, April 2001)

Statements like these, which are aimed at a stakeholding public, reflect the main concern of the firm to preserve its independence as an operational (and share issuing) entity.

A note on evidence gathered after September 11, 2001

The terrorist attacks on the USA of September 11, 2001 had an immediate and profound impact on airline operations all over the world. Passenger numbers and thus revenue went down significantly, while costs to airlines remained the same or even went up due, for example, to heightened security measures and increased insurance premiums. Most airlines reacted by laying off staff and cutting routes or at least frequencies to destinations of lesser strategic importance. Interview data gathered after this date did, however, reflect the same issues as before. The main themes that were mentioned in relation to the attacks referred to the need for cost cutting in face of heightened environmental uncertainty. In some occasions, senior managers mentioned that due to the ever-increasing need for cost cutting in their airlines, many alliance coordination efforts considered as non-essential had been put on ice. A typical example was the following statement:

We've been given this mandate by [alliance group] to become the [marketing-related area of expertise] centre so to speak of [alliance]. And there was lots of money that went

into that. But now after September 11 things changed, and they looked at which cow they could kill to save money and the [area of expertise] project was one.
(Senior Manager)

Beyond these possibly temporary steps to reduce costs, there seemed to be a tendency within airlines to become even more critical of alliancing and concentrate on protecting themselves first. In the winter 2001/2002, SAS management did for the first time openly voice concerns about a possibly too tight integration with Lufthansa within the Star alliance, where Lufthansa was increasingly felt to be 'calling the shots' at SAS. In a speech to employees in November 2001, SAS President and CEO Jørgen Lindegaard said that:

It is still possible for us to avoid having our wings clipped and being reduced to a regional feeder carrier...SAS is going to remain a strong, independent, customer-oriented airline that chooses its own way.
(Source: ATW online News Service, 3 December 2001)

This fairly strong statement was in fact the only example of clear 'anti-alliance' discourse that could be retrieved from publicly available material; all other such discourse occurred exclusively during the interviews. It was especially interesting to note that interview partners from other European airlines were aware of SAS's recent openly critical stand to close cooperation with Lufthansa. One senior manager (not from SAS) interpreted the SAS statement as follows:

When times are good like they were the whole nineties, everybody was happy because the traffic was growing. But now after September 11, everything is going down the drain, and all the airlines are just thinking about themselves. So this is the time when SAS, who used to be a quite loyal partner in Star is saying, hey, are we a little bit led, you know, by a string? [laughs]. And now when everybody is looking at their own cabin [load] factors and profitability, you know, it hurts.

The events of September 11 can thus be said to confirm the assumption that an unstable environment leads to defensive measures on the part of the firm (such as cutting services considered to be 'nonessential'), and that this perceived instability can lead to increased 'fortress building' and a diminution of the commitment to alliance matters.

The institutionalisation of alliancing, or: maintaining 'loose coupling' for the time being ...

It is important to listen carefully to what the people who are engaged in running airlines have to say about alliancing because it is they who build the alliance structures of the future. Precisely because there is no blueprint for an alliance group structure, nor any recipe for how to create one, these structures are 'invented' by managers on an ongoing basis as they go about their daily business of running their airlines and participating in alliance activities.[2]

The question is, thus, what kind of an institution alliancing itself, and the airline alliance group in concrete terms, is going to become. An institution can be defined as 'web of values, norms, rules, beliefs, and taken-for-granted assumptions',[3] and as 'cultural elements [that] define the way the world is and should be'[4] Institutions influence the way people see things and the way they react on them; they are a significant part of a person's mindset, and shared institutions are one basis of culture. Institutions are ideas, concepts and issues that people have come to take for granted and no longer question. They provide guidance to managerial cognition, and, thus, action. In the airline alliance case, asking whether alliance membership has reached institutional status can shed light on the question of how, and to what extent, airline managers are willing to construct the alliance group as a joint organisation, or whether they first and foremost prefer to protect their own firm's independence.[5]

One conclusion that could be drawn from our discussions with practitioners is that clearly, the people who 'invent' and build the alliance groups still think very much in terms of their own airline first. In other words, alliance groups still seem to be evolving to a considerable extent on the basis of local (i.e. airline-based) rationales. The 'my own airline first' rationale appears to have priority over any joint alliance rationale, even though alliancing as such has been clearly understood to be an unavoidable, and necessary part of the airlines' business environment.

The 'positive' (pro-alliance) theme was almost exclusively brought up by managers talking to a stake holding public (e.g. passengers, shareholders). On the other hand, one could observe that in the interviews where they knew that neither their own nor their airline's identity would be divulged, managers resorted heavily to 'partisan' and 'independence-related' discourse; that is, they discussed issues such as coordination problems within the alliance, trying to protect one's independence from overwhelming partners, or missing the (supposedly) 'good old times' of independence. Thus, it seems that some of the strategic responses to institutional processes that have been identified in the literature[6] occur simultaneously, at least at discursive level, and during times of organisational and institutional change. In the present case, faced with the alliancing phenomenon, airline managers simultaneously acquiesce (by obeying rules and accepting norms) and avoid (openly admitting that they protect their own airline's interest first). This can be called the phenomenon of 'countervailing myths' (for an explanation of the term 'myth' in institutionalist terminology, please refer to endnote[7]). On one hand, managers gain legitimacy (in front of the public) by referring to the 'positive' myth of alliancing being good for the shareholders, and of alliancing as improving the competitive advantage of their firm. On the other hand, the very same managers gain legitimacy in front of another (e.g. company internal) constituency by referring to the myth of 'independence' with which the airline buffers itself from the alliance. In short, countervailing myths exist because of loose coupling between different managerial agendas (here: building an integrated alliance group versus protecting one's airline's independence) and different legitimacy-conferring stake holding audiences (here: passengers versus shareholders and employees).

The institutional status of 'alliancing' can be broadly classified as follows:

1. The high incidence of interviewees mentioning alliance implementation problems due to the lack of a clear decision making structure, and their frequent complaints about inefficient meetings is one indicator for the lack of a fixed recipe for cooperation, or a clear blueprint to follow when building an alliance. Hence, the alliance group itself (its shape, exact nature and extent) appears to be still a fairly vague concept in managers' minds.

2. Since managers do not question alliances as such, it can be assumed that the 'alliance environment' is an integral and no longer questioned part of their mindset. Whereas the need to cooperate, or the alliance environment itself, has been understood and accepted by managers, this does not seem to be the case with the concept of a manager's own airline as an integral part of an alliance group. In other words, alliance membership itself remains still a relatively weak institution in the sense that alliancing is considered by many to be a necessary evil, without the idea being really embraced by managers.

3. A further element of alliancing are the rules of cooperation themselves: especially in the case of tight cooperation such as in a Joint Venture, these rules are clearly spelled out, and frequently underlined by external displays of cooperation such as joint airport facilities or joint marketing efforts. However, the evidence gathered from managers who represented airlines that were tightly cooperating with a partner hinted at a prevailing 'us-and-them' mentality and thus at a strong tendency for actors to allege primarily to their own firm, not to the superstructure of cooperation. Thus, the 'rules of cooperation' can also be considered a relatively weak institution in that the rules are there to be followed, but the underlying agendas are still very much based on local rationales.

4. At the same time, the managerial discourses clearly reflected a strong institutionalisation of the concept of their own airline as an independent unit: expressions of loyalty, the high incidence of independence-related discourse and partisan themes reflect this. This institution can be assumed to be the oldest, and thus the most entrenched one. It is even more strengthened by the fact that most airlines tend to have strong corporate cultures where behavioural rules and prescriptions for the way things are done (tacit or not) are shared and supported by organisational members.

The 'Partisan' and 'Independence' themes can be seen as countervailing forces to the establishment of alliance membership and of the alliance itself as a strong institution. This is in line with previous research on organisational change,[8] where changes of interpretative schemes were found to occur in a dialectic manner in that there is interaction between old and new ways of interpreting.[9] The dialectic concept is indeed useful because it assumes a process, rather than a static perspective on institutions.[10] In addition, examining the dialectic aspect of organisational processes is helpful in investigating an organisational phenomenon where two somewhat antagonistic social structures (in this case, the individual airline and the alliance group) both claim allegiance.

However, in the present case, the question remains whether there is ever going to be an outcome of this dialectic process at all, or whether the dialectics of countervailing institutional templates is going to be an integral feature of federation between autonomous, but interdependent, firms. It appears that one of the reasons why alliancing has not (yet?) reached the status of a strong institution is that its 'cognitive pillar'[11] is missing; in other words, alliancing is not yet fully culturally supported. Whether or not alliance membership – and indeed the alliance superstructure itself – will eventually gain cultural support will, to a large extent, depend on the presence or absence of credible (i.e. legitimate and legitimacy-giving) issue sponsors. Issue Sponsors[12] are typically managers who introduce and promote (sponsor) certain ideas, concepts, ways of doing and perceiving things within an organisation. They thus aid the institutionalisation process of certain concepts.

It might be possible to predict a process in this: airline alliances seem to be a case where, in an early stage, organisational action (in this case, the building and enactment of alliances) precede a belief system.[13] In other words, managers are acting in an alliancing environment without having fully embraced the concept as such, and while still working to preserve their own airline's independence from other carriers and from the alliance group itself.

It seems that in the present case, the supposedly 'old' way of interpreting (i.e. the importance of a firm's independence and expressions of clear primary allegiance to a firm, rather than to the alliance) cannot necessarily be seen as eventually receding or fading away. Instead, it can be expected that in a continuously unstable operating environment, the requirement for a standalone capability of the airline (as discussed in Chapter 3) will indeed re-fuel this type of interpretive scheme, and provide it with continued legitimacy. Because of loose coupling between institutional allegiance and formal structure, this dialectic is likely to continue even in case of future tighter alliance integration, the acquisition of more hierarchical power by an alliance superstructure, or an increase in equity investments by larger airlines in smaller partners. One can thus say that in the case of formal multilateral alliances between autonomous firms, this type of dialectic is likely to be a permanent feature and might even prevail for some time after a firm might have formally lost its autonomy.

Chapter 9 will discuss in some depth the lines along which alliance structures might evolve, and will take up the importance of managerial perceptions on building structures.

Notes

[1] For confidentiality reasons, the identities of the persons interviewed or their companies cannot be revealed (except for a few cases).

[2] For a more in-depth study on the discursive construction of alliance strategies within airlines, see Vaara et al., 2004.

[3] Barley and Tolburt, 1997.

[4] ibid.

[5] for more in-depth discussions on institutions and institutional processes, see e.g Meyer and Rowan, 1977; DiMaggio and Powell, 1983; 1991; Meyer, 1983; Meyer and Scott, 1983; Scott, 1987; 1991; 1995; Oliver, 1988; 1991; 1992; 1997; Jepperson, 1991; Westney, 1993; Greenwood and Hinings, 1996; Selznick, 1996; Tolbert and Zucker, 1996; Osborn and Hagedorn, 1997; Kondra and Hinings, 1998; Walgenbach, 2001; Wicks, 2001; Townley, 2002.

[6] The four responses are: Acquiesce, Compromise, Avoid, Defy, Manipulate (Oliver, 1991).

[7] Meyer and Rowan (1977) introduce the concept of organisationally institutionalised techniques, policies, and programmes as *myths*. These are themes and stories assumed to be adopted and communicated primarily for ceremonial purposes, i.e. in order to gain legitimacy and not necessarily for reasons of efficiency or profitability. In fact, ceremonially adopted structures might indeed be highly inefficient. Thus, organisations and individuals alike tend to maintain a gap, or what Meyer and Rowan call *'loose coupling'*, between formal structure (i.e., the ceremonially adopted structure of a n organisation, or the face an organisation or an individual person turns to the outside world), and actual activities.

[8] Bartunek, 1984.

[9] Johnson et al., 2001 call this 'competing institutional templates'.

[10] This concept also implies that institutionalisation is not seen as a dichotomous variable but rather that there are different institutions which represent continua (degrees of institutionalisation) and which coexist and compete for the allegiance of a person or a group.

[11] Scott, 1995.

[12] Dutton, 1993.

[13] E.g. Björkman, 1989.

References

Barley, S. and Tolbert, P. (1997), Institutionalization and structuration: Studying the links between action and institution. *Organization Studies*, Vol. 18, No. 1, pp. 93-117.

Bartunek, J. (1984), Changing Interpretive Schemes and Organizational Restructuring: The Example of a Religious Order. *Administrative Science Quarterly*, Vol. 29. pp. 355-372.

Björkman, I. (1989), Factors Influencing Processes of Radical Change in Organizational Belief Systems. *Scandinavian Journal of Management*, Vol. 5, No. 4, pp. 251-271.

DiMaggio, P. (1998), The New Institutionalisms: Avenues of Collaboration. *Journal of Institutional and Theoretical Economics*, Vol. 4, pp. 696-795.

DiMaggio, P. and Powell, W. (1983), The Iron Cage revisited: Institutional Isomorphism and Collective Rationality in Organizational Fields. *American Sociological Review*, Vol 48 (April), pp. 147-160.

DiMaggio, P. and Powell, W. (1991), Introduction. In: Powell, W. and DiMaggio, P. (eds.): The New Institutionalism in Organisational Analysis. Chicago, Ill.: University of Chicago Press.

Dutton, J. (1993), The Making of Organizational Opportunities: An Interpretive Pathway to Organizational Change. *Research in Organizational Behaviour*, Vol. 15, pp. 195-226.

Greenwood, R. and Hinings, C.R. (1996), Understanding radical organizational change. Bringing together the old and the new institutionalism. *Academy of Management Review*, Vol. 21, No. 4, pp. 1022-1054.

Jepperson, R. (1991), Institutions, Institutional Effects, and Institutionalism. In: Powell, W. and DiMaggio, P. (eds.): The New Institutionalism in Organisational Analysis. Chicago, Ill.: University of Chicago Press.

Johnson, G., et al. (2000), Microprocesses of institutional change in the context of privatisation. *The Academy of Management Review*, Vol. 25, No. 3, p. 572.

Kondra, A. and Hinings, C. (1998), Organizational Diversity and Change in Institutional Theory. *Organization Studies*, Vol. 19, No. 5, pp. 743-767.

Meyer, J. (1983), Institutionalization and the Rationality of Formal Organizational Structure. In: Meyer, J. and Scott, W.R. (eds.), Organizational Environments: Ritual and Rationality. London: Sage, 1986.

Meyer, J. and Rowan, B. (1977), Institutionalised Organisations: Formal Structure as Myth and Ceremony. *American Journal of Sociology*, Vol. 83, No. 2, pp. 340-363.

Meyer, J. and Scott, R. (1983), Organisational Environments: Ritual and Rationality. London: Sage.

Oliver, Chr. (1988), The Collective Strategy Framework: An Application to Competing Predictions of Isomorphism. *Administrative Science Quarterly*, Vol. 33, pp. 543-561.

Oliver, Chr. (1991), Strategic Responses to Institutional Processes. *Academy of Management Review*, Vol. 16, No. 1, pp. 145-179.

Oliver, Chr. (1992), The Antecedents of Deinstitutionalization. *Organization Studies*, Vol. 13, No. 4, pp. 563-588.

Oliver, Chr. (1997), Sustainable Competitive Advantage: Combining Institutional and Resource- Based Views. *Strategic Management Journal*, Vol. 18, No 9, pp. 697-713.

Osborn, R. and Hagedorn, J. (1997), The Institutionalization and Evolutionary Dynamics of Interorganizational Alliances and Networks. *Academy of Management Journal*, Vol. 40, No. 2, pp. 261-278.

Scott, W.R. (1987), The Adolescence of Institutional Theory. *Administrative Science Quarterly*, Vol. 32, pp. 93-511.

Scott, W.R. (1991), Unpacking Institutional Arguments. In: Powell, W. and DiMaggio, P. (eds.): The New Institutionalism in Organisational Analysis. Chicago, Ill.: University of Chicago Press.

Scott, W.R. (1995), Institutions and Organizations. Thousand Oaks: Sage.

Selznick, P. (1996), Institutionalism 'Old' and 'New'. *Administrative Science Quarterly*, 41, pp. 579-604.

Tolbert, P. and Zucker, L. (1996):, The Institutionalization of Institutional Theory. In: Clegg, S. and Hardy, C. (eds.), Studying Organization - Theory & Method. London 1999: Sage.

Townley, B. (2002), The Role of Competing Rationalities in Institutional Change. *Academy of Management Journal*, Vol. 45, No. 1, pp. 163-169.

Vaara, E., Kleymann, B. and Seristö, H. (2004), Strategies as Discursive Constructions: The Case of Airline Alliances. *Journal of Management Studies*, Vol. 41, No. 1, pp. 1-35.

Walgenbach, P. (2001), The Production of Distrust by Means of Producing Trust. *Organization Studies*, Vol. 22, No. 4, pp. 693-714.

Westney, D.E. (1993), Institutionalization Theory and the MNC. In: Ghoshal, S. and Westney, D.E. (eds.): Organisation Theory and the Multinational Corporation. New York: St Martin's Press.

Wicks, D. (2001), Institutionalized Mindsets of Invulnerability: Differentiated Institutional Fields and the Antecedents of Organisational Crisis. *Organization Studies*, Vol. 22, No. 4, pp. 659-692.

Chapter 5

Competing with the Alliance: Strategy Options of Independents

Changes in competitive arena due to alliance formation

An independent carrier pondering its strategic options in competition against alliance groups must analyse, first, the industry in which it operates and, second, the competitors it has to face. The airline industry is best analysed through structural analysis, which means identifying the underlying characteristics of the industry in terms of its economics and technology that form the framework for competitive strategies. Competitor analysis includes determining the objectives of the allied airlines in addition to their strengths and weaknesses (for example resources, skills, political aspects). As most of the world's 40 largest airlines are members in some alliance groups, the discussion on independent carriers' strategic options is bound to concern mainly medium-sized and small airlines. For the sake of clarity, by independents we mean airlines that are not allied with other carriers to any significant degree.

It is notable, though, that during the last few years some of the independent low-cost carriers have grown into the big league or will do so in the near future. Here one should remember that the new breed of independents, i.e. the low-cost carriers such as EasyJet, Ryanair or Southwest Airlines, have started with a clean sheet and therefore have an advantage compared to many older independents that carry the burden of history in their cost base. So, aggressive low-costs are special species, but an airline has to be born a low-cost airline, one cannot easily transform into one.

Research has addressed airline competition extensively, and there may be valuable lessons for independent carriers of today in selected studies of the past. Chen's (1988) study of competitive interaction as an aspect of strategic airline management focused on 'actions' and 'responses' of airlines. The study showed that the more active and responsive the companies were in competition, the better their performance. For the independent carriers of today, this would suggest that in the ever-increasing competitive pressure from the alliance groups, flexibility and the ability to react quickly to changes in the competitive environment are essential survival skills. Alamdari's (1989) study on the rivalry of airlines in a deregulated environment, and particularly on interactions between fare and service frequency in different competitive environments concluded that despite having the lower resource cost, the airlines with some initial disadvantage, such as poor location or smaller scale of operations always performed financially poorer compared with their larger counterparts in the market. Therefore, it would be recommendable for such smaller airlines to merge into or to cooperate with larger carriers. For independent carriers, which are often smaller-scale operators and are disadvantaged by having limited access to the larger hubs like London-Heathrow or Frankfurt, the findings would suggest that staying completely independent and being successful may possibly be a difficult combination. Interestingly, in her study, Alamdari also indirectly suggested that in order to have a well-functioning airline industry, small carriers should be allowed to merge, but such mergers should be prohibited from larger carriers, so as to prevent them from forming large, dominating carriers. As it appears in 2004 that pressure is mounting for authorities to allow more cross-border mergers and acquisitions of airlines, the premises for independent carriers to survive and prosper may be getting more difficult.

Sorenson's (1990) study on the linkage of airline competitive strategies and network patterns attempted to uncover groups of airlines with similar network characteristics and similar strategies, grouping these airlines into the same competitive group. The study suggested three major competitive strategies:

- the most common course of action for airlines is their service differentiation, which sometimes is associated with the creation of large networks including numerous destinations, and other times it means concentration on particular niche markets;
- the second most common approach was area monopoly: this means that an airline assumes a dominant position, controlling various strategic airports;
- the least common strategic approach was that of cost leadership: as the competition heightens, airlines start to cut costs as best they can, and therefore it may not be possible to attain a sustainable advantage through the mere low-cost approach.

For independent carriers, the first strategy suggested by the study, differentiation through the creation of a large network, is seldom feasible. Differentiation through concentration on a niche market would appear possible, as would the area monopoly in smaller or secondary markets. Finally, the cost leadership approach may be feasible for some independent carriers that enjoy lower operating costs rather than the larger established carriers, which for instance in Europe have typically been national flag carriers that have to bear the ballooned costs for personnel. Of course, the last few years have witnessed the rather phenomenal growth and success of low-cost carriers – including EasyJet, Ryanair, JetBlue and Southwest; an indication of the growth is, for instance, the fact that Ryanair opened more than forty new routes during the first five months of 2003. So the competitive environment has changed significantly from the days of Sorenson's study, especially in Europe.

Kling's (1989) study focused on competition at airports where one airline has a dominant position. The relevance of the study for our discussion is that, even outside the North American market, the alliance grouping of today may well lead to situations where one group clearly dominates a key airport. Kling's research suggests that there are possibilities for challenger airlines even at hubs with one dominant airline. Often the challenger has no competition from the dominating firm on certain niche routes, and these routes often proved quite profitable, too. In other words, being selective could offer opportunities for an independent carrier that challenges an alliance group or groups at major hubs.

Leigh's (1988) study on the impact of United States deregulation on the marketing strategies of domestic United States airlines suggested, not surprisingly, that an airline should concentrate on routes that are either not very competitive or which provide good inter-connections with the rest of the airline's system. However, rather worrying from the independent carriers' perspective was the finding that there appears to be great competitive value in dominating hubs rather than merely using them.

To summarise the key message of the discussion above, it appears that it has always been rather challenging for small airlines to compete with larger ones. As the alliance groups get their strategies and operations better integrated, the competitive position of independent airlines does not become any easier, but they have to face coalitions that are more powerful competitors in comparison with the largest independent competitors of the past. In light of recent experiences within the airline industry and the pressure for authorities to allow restructuring in this industry, the choice to remain an independent airline appears a very brave one. Then again, Ryanair and Southwest have shown very brave moves and even questioned conventional wisdom in the industry and have been very successful.

However, for further discussion it must be remembered that dependence versus independence is not necessarily dichotomous, but there may be varying degrees of dependence. In the following discussion on whether an airline should join an alliance group or not, the emphasis will be on carriers that are not typical regional airlines, but are closer to the traditional medium- and long-haul carriers. However, as some 50 per cent of regional carriers' aircraft are already jets, some with capacities of more than 100 seats – instead of smallish jet-props – the line between regional and regular carriers is blurring.

To join or not to join an alliance

There are many factors that make growth a desirable object for airlines: potential economies of scale in many functions, economies of densities on routes, the value of significant market presence, or the prestige of a larger and perhaps geographically more widely operating company. As internal growth is typically either slow or risky, external growth through mergers, acquisitions or contractual coalitions becomes more appealing. However, as authorities are still restrictive on M&As and government-owners appear reluctant to sell flag carrier assets, the obvious avenue for growth is alliance formation. As 2003 recorded more than 500 alliance agreements within the airline industry, involving more than 200 airlines, there must indeed be strong arguments for joining an alliance. Staying independent of alliances in today's airline business would mean going against the mainstream.

The benefits of joining an alliance are thoroughly discussed elsewhere in this book and therefore we shall focus our discussions on the risks of joining an alliance, particularly from the point of view of a present-day independent carrier. The risks associated with membership in an alliance would appear to increase as the degree of integration in the alliance and the degree of involvement by a member increases. The risks in alliance membership include the loss of sovereignty, loss of flexibility and harm to an airline's brand. Loss of sovereignty would be relevant particularly in decision-making concerning routes to be served and capacity offered; larger carriers have an advantage over smaller carriers due to sheer bargaining power. To use an old phrase, in theory and in principle alliance members may be equal, but when conflicts of interest arise, bigger members may be more equal than smaller ones. The loss of flexibility means that, in the future, a membership in one alliance is bound to restrict co-operation possibilities with airlines of other alliances or with independent airlines. Also the sunk costs in an alliance membership through investments in, for instance, training, IT systems and promotion, and the cost of leaving or changing alliances reduces an airline's flexibility.

In a competitive setting where an independent carrier has to face increasingly large and more tightly integrated alliance groups, vulnerability deserves a brief mention; vulnerability refers to a firm's capability to defend its position against the attacks of competitors. Vulnerability of an airline can be based on the same factors as success; cost structure and route network are of particular significance. A simple example to illustrate this vulnerability could be the comparison between a medium-sized independent European carrier and a very large US-European alliance group in the North Atlantic market. Even if predatory pricing is forbidden, but hard to prove, the alliance group could take one particular area at a time and try to drive out the smaller European carrier from the market. The alliance might offer flights with fares even below cost for many months; even so it would not significantly affect the group's total financial position. As such, the independent carrier with a large proportion of its total long-haul traffic in that particular market would either lose a significant portion of its long-haul traffic, or, through matching the low fares, would incur such losses that would seriously damage the company's financial position. Eventually, the smaller European carrier might be forced to withdraw from the market. Having established its position in the first area, the group could target some other geographic area and other carriers. In this example, the vulnerability of the smaller carrier is due to features which are quite typical in independent airlines: sparse network of long-haul routes – where it is economically feasible to use wide-body aircraft – as well as the thinness of those routes, in other words, only a few flights per week.

As more and more airlines join alliance groups, the position of those that stay independent gets more difficult because there are likely to be fewer airlines willing to code share with independent carriers. As the alliance groups get more integrated, they may become more restrictive as to how they would allow members to code share with non-member carriers. This has been brought up, for instance, by Alex Grant, Director of Strategy at British Midland.[1] So far, however, groups have been very tolerant concerning code sharing outside one's own group.

The issue of whether to join or not to join an alliance must obviously be approached differently in different parts of the world. It appears that it is easier to find room to operate as an independent carrier in markets that are well developed, where the economy and infrastructure are well developed and where purchasing power is high – North America and Western Europe are such examples. However, in economies that are not that well developed yet, such as in South America, it may be difficult to compete with the alliance groups. This has been echoed by Juan Posada, CEO of ACES, a Colombian carrier affiliated with Continental Airlines of the United States, which eventually faced serious problems in the autumn 2003.

Finally, the issue of independence versus cooperation can be broadened to include potential partners other than just the airlines. It appears that there is room for innovation in developing seamless transportation services that include both air and land travel components. For independent carriers, co-operation with rail and bus operators, for instance, could provide interesting opportunities that would enhance their competitiveness against allied carriers, which may be slower and somewhat more cautious in pursuing such link-ups. Figure 5.1 summarises factors that need to be assessed when an independent airline considers whether to stay independent or to join an alliance group.

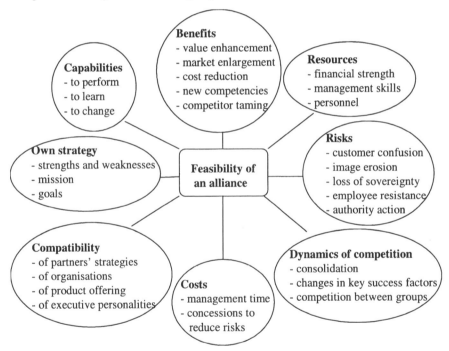

Figure 5.1   Assessing the feasibility of alliance membership

Evaluation of the basic strategy options

So, the assessment of strategy options should first ask whether the independent airline should stay independent, or seek some sort of cooperation with an alliance group or individual member airlines in a group. For instance, Japan Airlines and Emirates have been, at least publicly, long against joining an alliance group, but seem to have changed their views, perhaps recognising the inevitable restructuring that is currently sweeping the industry. British Midland, which has long been a key challenger of British Airways in the United Kingdom market, opted for a membership in Star Alliance at the end of 1999, evidently much due to its ambition to grow from an intra-European into a trans-Atlantic operator. Virgin Atlantic, having been the arch-opponent of the BA-AA link and against alliancing in general, has been since 1999 owned 49 per cent by Singapore Airlines, and has codeshared with carriers such as Continental. Moreover, Spanair, a carrier when judged by its history would look like one wanting to stay independent, is since 2000 associated with the Star Alliance.

One basic option is to decide to join an alliance. If an independent wants to join an alliance at some stage, its competitive strategy should aim at increasing its value as a partner in the alliance. Here, it is worthwhile noting a trivial point – joining an alliance is by no means up to the candidate airline only, as it may even be difficult to find an alliance group willing to accept the airline as an alliance partner. The ideal number of members in the two largest groups may be reaching the upper limits. Moreover, it is not just about joining any alliance group, as it is also highly relevant to decide on which particular group to join. The roles of existing members in an alliance, power positions and existing member route structures should be considered, as these have significant bearing on the choice of the most suitable alliance group.

The independent airlines' strategic approaches can be assessed by using three logics for strategy research, proposed by Lengnick-Hall and Wolff (1999). The first logic, capability logic, suggests that a firm can out-perform another if it has a superior ability to develop, use, and protect elemental, platform competencies and resources. The second, guerrilla logic, suggests that all competitive advantages are transitory and a firm will outperform another if it is more adept at rapidly and repeatedly disrupting the current situation to create an unprecedented and unconventional basis for competing. The third, complexity logic, suggests that strategic success would be a function of a firm's talent for thriving in dynamic nonlinear systems that rely on network feedback and emergent relationships. Interestingly for the airline industry application, none of these logics would promise long-term success if firms simply extrapolate from the past success or try to maintain the present competitive situation. Also, all three logics recognise that success requires a variety of, at least temporary, alliances or exchanges beyond firms' traditional boundaries. This would suggest that some loose coupling with other airlines is needed even for carriers that wish to stay independent of alliance groups.

As the alliances are in the long term also bringing resource utilisation benefits to the members, undermining the favourable cost position of many independent carriers, it is doubtful if capability logic alone is a good strategic approach for an independent airline. Considering the turbulent nature of the airline industry, it would appear that the guerrilla logic or complexity logic, both associated with hypercompetitive and volatile industry characteristics are the more promising strategic approaches for independent airlines. It has been suggested by Lengnick-Hall and Wolff (1999) that Southwest Airlines has followed the complexity logic in its successful battle against large carriers.

As mentioned earlier in this chapter, there may by degrees of independence and dependence. It may be possible to build some sort of symbiosis with an alliance group or groups without really being a member in any of them. The point is then to seek such a position that the alliance group or large members in those groups do not see the independent carrier challenging them, and would rather be willing to leave part of the business to the independent carrier. For an independent carrier this would mean not having to bear the risks of joining an alliance (nor having a chance to benefit from the advantages of a membership either) and at the same time avoiding the threat of retaliation from the alliance groups. A special case of a symbiosis, very close to membership in an alliance group, is that of operating a franchised service. British Airways had already in 1998 a network of nine regional franchises, some of them very small companies, like Loganair, which operated mainly 8-seater aircraft in Scottish routes. Lufthansa has had franchising arrangement with small airlines that operate under the Team Lufthansa brand. So far, franchising has been used mainly in regional services. However, it would be surprising if it did not become more widely used in longer-haul services in the future.

If the independent airline is determined to remain independent, then an effective competitive strategy takes either offensive or defensive action in order to create a defendable position against large alliance groups. First, the strategy should position the independent airline so that its capabilities – whether they are based on production efficiency or ability to provide superior service – provide the best defence against the competition from alliances. Naturally, the independent's strategy should be built on real, sustainable competencies which might be derived from a superior understanding of consumer behaviour, superior training methods, or just the geographic location, to name a few examples. Lessons from history suggest that it is important to stick to the original strategies and competencies, and resist extending itself into a game where the original strengths may not provide a competitive advantage. An example of such uncontrolled growth, among other difficulties, was provided by the case of PeoplExpress in the 1980s. In addition, it seems that the likelihood of success is higher if the independent aims at stimulating new demand, either through offering low-cost or differentiated service, rather than trying to carve market share from the allied carriers. Again, notable here is the recent success of European low-costs EasyJet and Ryanair. Moreover, an independent's strategy should anticipate shifts in the factors underlying the competitive forces – for example, changes in the legislative framework and actions by competition authorities – and respond to these shifts before alliance groups fully recognise them and act accordingly. Figure 5.2 illustrates the strategy framework for independent carriers, including such changes in the industry that have an impact on the strategy choice and the key objectives of carriers.

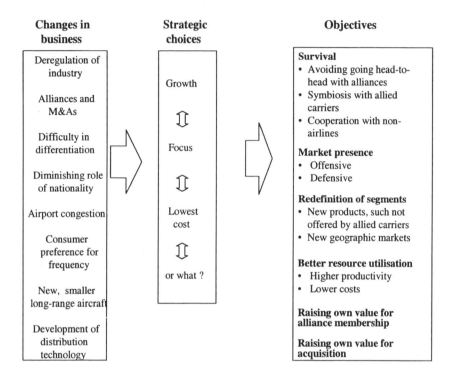

Figure 5.2   Strategy framework for independent airlines in competition with alliances

One of the basic strategic options for an independent carrier is to aim at being the lowest cost operator. As the low-cost option is today the primary approach of smaller carriers in challenging larger airlines, relatively much of the following discussion on the strategic options of independents centres around that approach.[2]

There are two ways to gain cost advantage: to control cost drivers, or to reconfigure the value chain. In the control of cost drivers it is mainly the cost of personnel that is relevant. They make overall some 30 per cent of total operating costs, but there is wide variance in costs between countries and airlines. For other major cost items, no airline really has a superior control; fuel, traffic charges and capital costs are fairly similar to all carriers. A prerequisite for the growth of low-cost operators has been and will be the fact that there are lightly utilised secondary airports – where landing charges are significantly lower – located conveniently close to major cities.

In the United States, Southwest Airlines is a prime example of how cost leadership strategy can lead to success. However, it is very important to remember that most of the other carriers that have emulated this strategy have either gone bankrupt or been acquired. Southwest Airlines has not prospered due to its lowest cost strategy only, but thanks is owed to the skilful combination of geographic focus and differentiated service, in addition to very low costs. However, the very high productivity, thanks to motivated and hard working personnel, is undeniably a key success factor. In Europe also the large market share of non-scheduled carriers in tourist traffic proves that cost leadership strategy is a viable strategic approach. All in all, the experience in the United States and elsewhere suggests that the lowest cost strategy alone may not provide sustainable competitive advantage to an airline, and therefore – without a unique source of cost advantage – it probably is the most demanding strategy.

As to the value chain reconfiguration, the possibilities are numerous. Many non-scheduled carriers, mainly from Europe, have built their successes on the reconfiguration of the value chain, and Southwest Airlines is a prime example of a scheduled airline that has used value chain reconfiguration very successfully. As an example of reconfiguration, reservations can be done through an airline's website only, instead of traditional travel agencies or own call centres. The cost savings potential is substantial, as studies have suggested that the cost of a traditional travel agency booking was USD 23, through an on-line agency (for example Travelocity) USD 20, through direct reservation to an airline's own call centre USD 13 and only USD 6 through an airline's own website.[3] In 2003, some 95 per cent of the seat reservations at EasyJet and Ryanair were reported to have been made on websites. The corresponding figure for Southwest appears to be between 40-50 per cent, whereas American and United sell only about five per cent of their tickets on their websites. Remembering that allied carriers are building internet market places, and that the distribution sector, primarily travel agencies, is consolidating and thus perhaps enhancing their bargaining power against airlines, any independent airline should seriously consider selling tickets primarily through the web.

Many of today's independent carriers in Europe and the United States are pursuing the lowest cost approach. This is very much understandable because, due to the shorter history, they have significantly lower personnel costs than the established large carriers. Personnel are often younger and have earned fewer seniority related salary raises, and scales of salaries and wages are lower overall because unions do not possess the power that they have in larger airlines. The low-cost carriers have been able to create a new leisure travelling segment of the market, but have also been able to attract a number of business travellers from higher-fare operators. For instance, Frontier Airlines, established in 1994 and based in Denver, has been present very much in the same geographical markets as United Airlines. However, Frontier has found its niche in tourist traffic and in small and medium-sized company business travellers who perhaps do not travel that much.

The success of the lowest-cost approach in the United States is proved by the fact that some 25 per cent of all domestic air traffic in the U.S. already in 1998 was on low-cost carriers. In Europe, where the corresponding figure is just below ten per cent but rising, excluding non-scheduled traffic, EasyJet, Ryanair, and Virgin Express are good examples of successes utilising the low-cost approach. In Europe, the numerous non-scheduled or charter carriers use the low-cost approach, and the volumes, too, speak for the rationale of this approach; nearly 40 per cent of traffic in Europe has been operated by non-scheduled carriers. It has been forecasted, for instance, by Mercer Management Consulting that the market share of low-cost airlines in Europe could reach 25 per cent by 2010.

The fact that so many of the European low-cost, and at the same time low-frills or no-frills airlines, are based in the United Kingdom proves that personnel costs are a crucial factor in attaining a low cost position; particularly in air transport, the United Kingdom is clearly the low-labour-cost country of Western Europe. In addition, the labour laws in the United Kingdom allow for very flexible hiring and firing of personnel, adding to the overall advantages in terms of personnel costs. In addition to direct costs, it is of utmost importance that the personnel in a low-cost airline are willing to perform tasks traditionally not in the sphere of their jobs; one example might be having to alleviate peak-hour work loads at the ramp or gates.

An area which needs clarification is cost-leadership in serving particular market segments. As originally suggested, a cost-leader airline would gain superior profits through combining lowest costs with average fares. However, as the products can be segmented along the lines of their prices, the question which arises is whether the airline is the lowest-cost producer serving its particular target segment – as opposed to being the lowest-cost producer of all the airlines. In other words, the point of reference ought to be other carriers serving the same particular segment. The distinction between scheduled and non-scheduled airlines has therefore been crucial. Until now, the two have served different market segments, but the borders between those segments are rapidly eroding, something that has a bearing on the roles those independent airlines could adopt. As the trend in leisure travel appears to be towards more individual travel, instead of the usual package tours, the future for scheduled low-cost carriers in Europe would look promising. However, the non-scheduled business still has massive volumes in Europe and it seems that the charter carriers will have a key role in servicing the tourist segment as long into the future as we can see.

Another issue in need of clarification is that of confusing inputs with outputs. It has rightly been proposed that competitive strategy should primarily be concerned with the positioning of a firm's outputs, not of inputs.[4] The lowest-cost strategy is invisible to the customer (in other words as output), if the airline has lowest costs but charges average fares for average products. In order to produce a difference in the output – in other words, to gain larger market share, which is often required in order to achieve a low overall cost position – the company has either to lower its fares or differentiate its product; the mere lowest cost will not suffice. For instance, Ryanair's low fares are certainly visible to the consumer; in 2003 it offered for instance a return fare of 20 euros between Tampere, Finland and Stockholm in Sweden. Competing airlines' fares were typically ten times as much, often twenty times the fare charged by Ryanair. Here one has to be reminded, though, that Ryanair decided to discontinue the route in late 2003, as it evidently was not viable with such low fares.

Concerning differentiation as a strategic option for an independent airline, it must first be accepted that an airline product is difficult to differentiate in a sustainable way.

The core of the service, transportation from the origin to the destination, is almost the same for every airline. Differences in flight time are very small as all airlines tend to use aircraft that are very much alike. Scheduling, however, can be a key form of product differentiation. Pricing has become one way of differentiating an airline product as the regulation has been eased. However, at least in the short term, pricing is easy to imitate but will only lead to deterioration of profits. The differentiation must then be done in the reservation services, check-in, in-flight services, route selection and different types of marketing components (advertising, bonus-programs, etc.). Shearman (1992) talks of tangible and intangible ways of differentiating an airline product. The challenge is that tangible improvements in airline product are easy to imitate, whereas the intangible improvements (for instance corporate image, in-flight service atmosphere) are difficult to sustain. Shearman classifies three methods of differentiating an airline product:

- value-added (tangible)
- standards of service (intangible)
- economic (discounting).

Differentiation has been used successfully by some airlines in the past. Examples are Singapore Airlines' high quality approach and American Airlines' introduction of a frequent flyer program. However, it appears that differentiation for a wide market, in other words, without limited focus, has become more and more difficult to sustain. Also, as differentiation is built on the recognition of brands, and as brands in the airline industry may be in turmoil due to alliances and potential mergers, it appears that differentiation alone is a very challenging competitive strategy.

So, differentiation in air transports is not easy, and it is also somewhat arguable as to what constitutes a differentiated service. For instance, on-board service can be a differentiating factor, but it is to some extent a matter of taste whether it really differentiates. Also, one should remember that there is differentiation between airlines but also within an airline – service in a first class cabin is very much different from that in tourist class. History suggests that the results of differentiation on an airline level seem to be mostly larger market share, rather than premium pricing. This would apply, for instance, to Singapore Airlines and Virgin Atlantic. There are few convincing cases in the airline industry where differentiation would have allowed sustainable premium pricing on a large scale; Concorde services are perhaps the best cases. Other cases of luxury services are, or have been, either very small-scale, short-lived or both. However, new companies do try this approach every once in a while. An example of such a differentiating carrier, Legend Airlines, based at Dallas' secondary airport Love Field, was convinced that its concept of providing luxurious first-class-only long-haul service from Dallas to a few major United States cities would attract sufficient clientele. Legend Airlines' services included valet parking for passengers, oversized seats (only 56 seats in a DC-9), and gourmet meals. The question was whether there would be sufficient volume to fill the planes; Legend ceased operations in December 2000.

Another way to differentiate is to position the carrier against its main rival. It would appear fair to say that British Midland and Braathens SAFE of Norway have both purposefully positioned themselves in promotion and communications as the challenger carrier of the big, dominant airline, that is, British Airways and SAS, respectively. As David won sympathy for fighting Goliath, so have these carriers won loyal customers for providing an alternative. However, it appears that this kind of underdog positioning approach alone leaves the carrier quite vulnerable when fighting against larger flag carriers or alliance groups; sympathy may turn into pity.

Route networks are a factor in differentiating airlines. To characterise the importance of route networks, it has been said that the network of an airline is a production element, a distribution element, and a marketing element. Also, in Reynolds' terms, the network is the physical manifestation of an airline's production plan.[5] This multiple role of network makes it a key strategic and competitive variable for airlines. The size of an airline's route network is a competitive variable. If one city-pair is regarded as one product of an airline, then, the larger the network the airline has, the larger is its range of products. As travellers, according to most surveys, prefer flying on-line as opposed to making interline transfers, airlines with more extensive networks have an advantage over their smaller rivals. However, here one should remember that travellers also prefer direct flights to non-direct flights, if there is no significant difference in fares. In addition, particularly in business travel, customers do value frequent flights; in other words, perhaps three departures a day to choose from rather than just one. The experience from EasyJet – concentrating on fewer markets but with more flights – would suggest to independent carriers that entering new routes with high frequency from the very beginning enhances the value of the new service considerably. Southwest Airlines with its average of more than 40 daily departures per city provides a benchmark. Naturally it is not only the size of the route network of an airline that matters to a traveller, but also the selection of particular city-pairs.

A point for independent airlines not to miss is that through tighter integration of alliance groups, the roles of members in these groups are likely to change. One outcome of this change may be that many carriers must focus their operations. For instance, there is pressure for medium-sized alliance group members to give up intercontinental traffic and concentrate on, say, intra-European traffic. As this is bound to enhance efficiency of many allied carriers, it is even more important that the independent carriers determine their geographical scope of operations carefully. Related to route network based differentiation is market power; research has shown that airlines which dominate certain airports are able to charge a premium in fares. Also, it has been suggested that the sheer dominant size of an airline at a certain airport, or on a certain route gives it a market power advantage. For independent carriers this would underline the importance of concentration and focus in building the route network.

An independent airline can use the focus approach basically in two ways. First, it can focus on a particular buyer segment, such as business travellers or leisure travellers. Second, it can focus on a particular geographic market such as the southern Europe to South America market. In the buyer-segment based focus, airlines have not so far been very adventurous, but rather conservative and cautious. There are carriers that have emphasised business travellers as their target and there have been attempts to operate small-scale services targeted at the very wealthy travellers. On the other hand, low-cost airlines provide no-frills services which are targeted to the most cost-conscious travellers. So, the bottom line remains that focusing has been based either on the ability or willingness to pay, or the valuation of time by the customer. It would seem that there are many more bases to focus than only these two. Creativity by independent carriers in re-segmenting the market and developing appropriate products and marketing concepts for these segments is called for. Figure 5.3 summarises the basic strategic options for independent airlines.

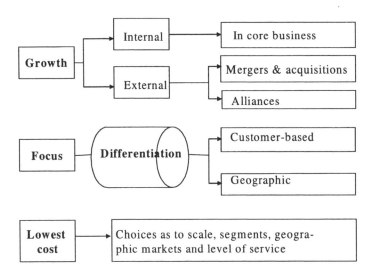

Figure 5.3   Strategic options for independent airlines

Leading us to a brief discussion on the objectives of independent airlines, it is worthwhile taking the allied carrier perspective on the competition against independent airlines. Applying the suggestions of Barkin et al. (1995) concerning traditional airlines' strategies against low-cost challengers, it appears that the allied carriers have basically four strategies to adopt: to withdraw from markets where an independent carrier is strong and to transfer resources to more profitable routes; to go into the head-on competition using aggressive marketing and pricing; to seek co-existence through dividing the market; or to join forces with an independent through limited marketing or service agreement.

Past research on multi-market rivalry in the airline industry has suggested that attacks, particularly on an airline's important markets, are more likely to cause response, are associated with more intense retaliation, and are more likely to lead to counterattacks in other markets, rather than defence of the market.[6] So, an independent carrier should carefully assess its overall vulnerability to retaliation should it decide to challenge allied carriers in some particular markets; the point to remember is that, the larger the alliance groups, the more retaliation opportunities they possess.

Objectives of independents in the new competition

It appears that the power of airline alliance groups will be such that independent carriers need to be very innovative and skilful in order to prosper in tomorrow's competition. One should remember that it is not only tougher competition from other airlines, but also intensive development of very rapid train services and advancing distribution channel consolidation that will pose a challenge for independent carriers in the future. In fact, it may be right to say that the primary objective of an independent carrier is to survive in the hardening battle. Again, here it is worthwhile reminding that the new low-cost carriers are a different breed from most other independents.

Taking a 'distant' corporate strategy perspective on the matter, one objective of independent carriers – often relatively small carriers – could be to grow big and attractive enough to be acquired by a larger airline. This would apply particularly to small carriers which are owned by entrepreneurs themselves or by private investors and to whom the sale of the company is the ultimate way to make money from their investment of capital and effort. Perhaps the sale of CityFlyer Express to British Airways in 1999 and the sale of Regional Airlines to Air France in 2000 are good examples of this. It would seem likely that, in the future, even in Europe, large airlines will acquire or at least invest in carriers that provide feed traffic for their networks, something for small independent carriers to take into account early enough in their strategic planning.

Going beyond mere survival and onto a more operational level, a key objective for independents is to find such areas of the market where they do not go head-on with allied airlines. It is essential to find areas of the market where they can play according to their rules instead of the rules set by the larger groups. Independents should seek areas of competition where the drivers for alliancing are not valid or at least not very strong. This may mean, for instance, finding small markets which may prove unattractive for the alliance groups, markets where flight connections are not key factors of success, markets where certain special differentiation is valued by customers, markets where customers are not interested in loyalty programs, or even markets where strong presence in the reservation system is deemed unnecessary.

There are airlines that have challenged bigger players head-to-head, and many of them have perished, but many have flourished, too. In Spain, Iberia had long been the monopoly operator on the busy Madrid-Barcelona routes, until in 1994 the privately owned Air Europa challenged Iberia by cutting fares by one-third. Soon after, Spanair also followed suit and came into the market by offering fares half the original Iberia prices. Interestingly, Spanair later joined the Star Alliance group and Air Europa was associated with the Wings alliance. An example in the

United States market has been American Trans Air (ATA), an Indianapolis-based low-frills carrier, which in 1998 challenged United Airlines on the Chicago-Denver route, and American Airlines on the Dallas-Chicago route. ATA's rationale apparently was to enter with low fares such routes that have very high fare levels due to airport capacity constraints, believing that it can find its niche of low-fare passengers without causing retaliation from the dominant, larger carriers. However, the reaction from both American and United through fare cuts and added services was immediate and strong, suggesting that larger players and thus also alliance groups would be unlikely to leave 'free' niches easily for smaller, independent carriers.

In the light of intense competition it seems that no matter how the independents plan to avoid head-on confrontation with the allied carriers, they need to pursue low operating costs. If there is a market that can sustain high fares and inefficient operations, it is only a matter of time before the larger allied carriers are tempted to enter that particular market. The challenge for the independents would then be to strike a balance between attaining large enough scale to enable profitable operations, but avoid growing too large or into the markets of allied carriers, in order to preclude retaliation from them.

Summary of strategies for independent carriers

Survival and securing market presence can be considered the primary objectives of airlines, be they independent or allied. For the independent carriers, this means finding a delicate balance between defensive and offensive strategy. The basic strategies for independent carriers can be derived from the discussion on generic strategies above. So, there appears to be three feasible strategies:

- growth strategy
- focus strategy
- lowest cost strategy.

These strategy options for independent carriers are summarised below with selected propositions.

Growth strategy

- Base growth on core competence; do not grow beyond skills.
- Seek growth only in the core business.
- Keep low profile, in other words do not challenge the larger competitors in their terms.
- Seek symbiosis with allied carriers in order to reduce costs.
- Position your company as the 'good competitor'; it is possible.
- Strive constantly for lower overall costs.

Economies often speak for larger volumes, but the threat of retaliation from the larger, allied carriers would suggest a rather low profile in growth. Nevertheless, growth in some ways can be seen as one basic strategy. One point of view of the matter is for an independent carrier to grow big enough to become an attractive partner for an alliance. The fundamental thing to remember is that it is not only up to the applicant carrier to decide its membership in an alliance, but the decision to accept a new member is made by existing member airlines too.

Growth can be sought internally, as done by American Airlines earlier in the United States. Quite interestingly, as an answer to the question of how long American Airlines can continue to stand by itself, without partners, company Executive Vice President Carty replied in 1992: 'Forever. We do not need anyone else'. Times have changed, indeed, proved by the American membership in the oneworld alliance group. Internal growth may be slow, but nevertheless it may be a feasible option for an independent carrier.

Lowest-cost strategy

- Strive constantly for lower overall costs.
- Make use of differences in factor costs between countries or cities.
- Focus on segments that may seem less tempting for larger airlines.
- Focus on markets where conventional marketing power is less decisive.
- Stick to your own strengths and resist the temptation of growing too rapidly.

Pursuing the strategy of lowest cost requires tight cost control in all areas of operation. It may even require some up-front investment so that efficient scale is achieved. In airline operations, the lowest-cost strategy has so far been associated with differentiation in the sense that most low-cost carriers have provided services that are very basic. The deals negotiated by low-cost carriers in Europe, particularly Ryanair, with secondary airports or regional authorities – resulting in very low charges and ground-handling costs – are good examples of utilising differences in factor costs.

Focus strategy

Broad differentiation without focus may be difficult to sustain. Should an airline choose focus as its basic strategy, it should target segments that are perhaps too small for allied carriers or which have been forgotten or neglected by other carriers for whatever reasons. Also, it would be an advantage if those segments are such that it can be reached in an innovative way, not relying on massive, broad marketing, and which do not value extensive FFPs.

Focus based on customer segment

- Innovate in defining new segments in market.
- Focus on segments that are neglected by the allied carriers.
- Focus on segments that are willing to pay premium for the differentiated product.

- Strive constantly for being the leader in differentiation and invest accordingly.
- Stay loyal to the original segment.

Combining focus with fresh differentiation would appear to provide a lot of opportunities for ambitious independent carriers. We have seen earlier that the level of differentiation in air transport services is in fact rather low. As an analogy, there is a much broader variety of restaurants and clubs than merely cheap and expensive ones. There are various ethnic restaurants, clubs and bars for different culture, lifestyle, music or whatever preferences. So, perhaps in the future there is an opportunity for focused airlines serving the travel needs of ladies, students, music lovers, health fanatics, food-connoisseurs, senior citizens and so on.

Focus based on geography

- Find markets where larger competitors are not present.
- Strive for domination in your region.
- Enter new routes selectively but with sufficient capacity from the start.

It appears that focus strategy based on geography requires some sort of a competitive advantage as a starting point. The self-evident case is mere geographic location; i.e., if the carrier is based in Italy, it has opportunities to develop traffic between southern Europe and northern Africa. The base could also be the heritage or image of the carrier. An example could be SAS, albeit a member in an alliance, being associated with the image of Scandinavia very strongly and therefore, having the upper hand in serving the Scandinavian market.

Notes

[1] *Air Transport World*, April 1999.
[2] The premises for the discussion here on strategic approaches, generic strategies, etc. can be found in the writings of Porter.
[3] Flint, 1999.
[4] See e.g. Faulkner and Johnson, 1992
[5] Sorenson, 1990.
[6] See Gimeno, 1999, 124.

References

Alamdari, F. (1989), *Airline Deregulation: an Analysis under different Regulatory and Operating Environments*, Doctorate thesis to the Cranfield Institute of Technology.

Barkin, T., Hertzell, S. and Young, S. (1995), 'Facing Low-cost Competitors: Lessons from US Airlines', *The McKinsey Quarterly*, no. 4, pp. 86-99.

Chen, M. (1988), *Competitive Strategic Interaction: a Study of Competitive Actions and Responses*, Doctorate dissertation to the University of Maryland.

Flint, P. (1999), 'Alliance paradox', *Air Transport World*, April 1999, pp. 33-36.

Gimeno, J. (1999), 'Reciprocal Threats in Multimarket Rivalry: Staking out 'Spheres of Influence in the U.S. Airline Industry', *Strategic Management Journal*, vol. 20, pp. 101-128.

Kling, J. (1989), *Competition at Airports Dominated by One Airline: an Empirical Analysis of Challenging Airlines' Strategies*, Doctorate dissertation to the University of Maryland.

Leigh, L. (1988), *Competitive Airline Strategy in Deregulated Markets*, Doctorate dissertation to the University of North Carolina at Chapel Hill.

Lengnick-Hall, C. and Wolff, J. (1999), Similarities and Contradictions in the Core Logic of Three Strategy Research Streams, *Strategic Management Journal*, Vol. 20, pp. 1109-1132.

Shearman, P. (1992), *Air Transport: Strategic Issues in Planning and Development*, Pitman Publishing, London.

Sorenson, N. (1990), *Airline Competitive Strategy: a Spatial Perspective*, Doctorate dissertation to the University of Washington.

Chapter 6

Marketing Airline Alliances: The Branded Alliance

Introduction

Extensive market presence plays an essential role in major airlines' plans for survival and prosperity – having global reach appears to be a must in most major airlines' strategic plans. Most airline executives would also agree that, at least until now, it is the enhanced revenues rather than lowered costs that have rewarded most of the benefits from alliance arrangements: 'The biggest opportunity is not in the cost line, it is in the revenue line' said American Airlines chief executive Carty in 1998.[1] However, as discussed elsewhere in the book, the focus is shifting more into the cost side.

So the marketing function of an airline is at the core of alliance arrangements. This is suggested also by past research which has found that most of the co-operative arrangements have been related to marketing and improvement of product offering, rather than enhancing efficiency or reducing costs in production. For instance, Bruce Harris, director at United Airlines, characterised Star Alliance in 1997 as a relationship of marketing partners.[2] One could even say that the existing airline alliance arrangements of today still are, in fact, strategic marketing alliances. So marketing is an area where an alliance arrangement may create most of the value-added. However, it is also an area where there are many difficult, sensitive, and risky issues that have to be resolved between alliance members. As Doz and Hamel (1998, xi) have characterised alliances, the manner in which value is created is not preordained, the relationships between partners evolve in ways that are hard to predict, and the playing field is very unstable or turbulent – today's partner may be tomorrow's rival; these are very challenging premises for the marketing function in strategic airline alliances. This chapter will address such marketing-related issues as marketing-driven motives for alliances, roles of alliance groups in the new structure of air transport marketing channels of the future, alliance brand management, as well as risks and problems related to joint marketing efforts.

Marketing-driven objectives for alliances

In Chapter 2 we discussed the objectives of alliancing. It is worth recapitulating that discussion to provide background for addressing the challenges in alliance marketing. Earlier research on strategic alliances – concerning mostly manufacturing industries – has pointed to two primary categories of objectives in alliance arrangements: namely product objectives and knowledge objectives. In the area of product objectives there have been two primary goals: either the enhancement of product offering or the reduction of production costs. As to knowledge objectives, the goal has typically been to learn a new technology or process from a partner; the goals of knowledge transfer have often been rather specific and particular. Also, partly corresponding to the findings of Lorange et al. (1992), and Murray and Mahon (1993), the objectives for airlines in alliance arrangements can be divided into three categories: market-defensive, market-offensive and efficiency-seeking objectives.

A key objective for airlines joining alliances is to enhance the value of service offering in the eyes of the customer, and this value enhancement can be done for either defensive or offensive purposes. So far it appears that for the larger airlines, like American, British Airways, Delta, and Lufthansa, the purpose has mainly been offensive; larger airlines seek market power and consequently enhanced value for customers by pursuing larger network coverage, higher frequencies, more extensive loyalty programs and dominance of hub airports. For medium-sized and small carriers, for instance Aer Lingus, Austrian, Finnair, and Lan Chile, the purpose appears to have been mostly defensive; they appear to have been more interested in market coverage rather than outright market power in responding to the challenge by expanding larger airlines. Smaller carriers also seem to consider participation in alliances essential in trying to avoid shrinking into mere regional operators. Overall, the primary motivation for international alliances has so far been the need to secure an extensive catchment area or a larger onward connection network. However, for the market presence objective it is necessary to distinguish between global level and specific market level sub-objectives, which may require arrangements of seemingly conflicting nature.

Past research on airline alliances has split value enhancement into more specific objectives, which can be tactical or strategic in nature and are mostly product objectives. They comprise, for example, access to a larger route network, higher load factors, larger market share, joint fare setting and sales efforts, and shared loyalty programmes. Partly following the division by Rhoades and Lush (1997) marketing-related alliance arrangements can be split into three types: 1. Code-sharing and schedule co-ordination; 2. Joint frequent-flyer programmes and facility sharing (e.g. airport lounges); 3. Broad marketing co-operation.

Providing a larger network for own 'traditional' passengers, on one hand, and tapping into a larger market, on the other hand, have been key objectives from the very early days of modern alliance arrangements between airlines. SAS's CEO Carlzon wrote in 1987:

We base our efforts on two main strategies: broadening our passenger base through co-operation in Europe, and establishing new gateways on other continents. By establishing alliances with local airlines in these foreign locations, we can extend our fully integrated system to our passengers in their continued travel.

As presented in Chapter 1, Kleymann (1999) has distinguished between three different types of internationally operating airlines: Local Champion, Long-haul Operator, and Global Connector. Local Champions operate typically short- and medium-haul routes, and include carriers such as Austrian Airlines and Finnair. Long-haul Operators are in many ways like local champions, but a large share of their operations are on intercontinental routes. These carriers include Air New Zealand and South African Airways. Global Connectors aim to serve the world-wide market and comprise large carriers such as American Airlines and Lufthansa. The objectives for alliances by different carriers can be assessed using these classifications, as shown in Chapter 2.

Alliance groups prefer not to talk of tiers in alliance arrangements. However, if we see alliances composed of *de facto* tiers of members with different status within the alliance, a particularly interesting issue is that of getting the third-tier carriers – in the future, more and more regional type of carriers – under the brand umbrella of the alliance group. Is the format of American Eagle or Team Lufthansa right? Or should these feeder carriers fly the colours of the alliance instead of an individual larger airline? There obviously is a need for new ideas and innovation, for instance through franchising arrangements for these types of carriers.

Turbulence in marketing channels

There are great changes taking place in the travel and tourism industry, and particularly the changes in the travel agency sector are very relevant to the airline alliances. The pressure to redefine the marketing and sales channel is building. The well-known factors contributing to this pressure are, first, the need for airlines to cut costs in the face of hardening competition, and second, the rapid advances in information technology, particularly in internet technology and in mobile communications. Moreover, the evolving customer needs, particularly due to globalisation, add pressure to reconfiguring marketing and sales practices.

Airlines have had and will have great difficulties in cutting personnel costs, the major cost item, mainly due to strong unions both in the flying personnel and maintenance personnel sectors. The other important cost items, fuel costs and traffic charges, practically are beyond the control of airlines. Consequently, airlines have realised that there is cost reduction potential in the sales channel margins. Research by McKinsey & Co.[3] showed that some 18 per cent of the price of an airline ticket is accrued by outside stakeholders between the airline and customer. Cost reduction has been introduced, for instance, by cutting the commissions paid to travel agents – traditionally at nine per cent – down to 0-5 per cent. Also, airlines have increased sales through internet-based agencies, which are content with smaller commissions, and have established their own websites where customers can be make purchases. The cost reduction potential is significant; studies have suggested that a typical air ticket purchase transaction through a traditional travel agency costs USD 26, whereas a transaction directly from an airline's website costs only USD 6.

Also, consolidation in the travel agency sector similar to that of the airline industry is likely to happen – perhaps more on national levels rather than on a global level. Consequently, the balance between airlines and travel agencies is changing; it seems that the airline alliance formation has put airlines in a more powerful position in relation to travel agencies. However, the consolidation expected among the travel agency sector may restore or even turn around the balance. The outcome of this restructuring is yet to be seen, but it seems likely that some sort of coalitions will be formed by airline alliance groups and consolidated travel agency groups. This could mean, for instance, that Star Alliance would sell in a certain market primarily through a selected group of travel agencies – and focus its marketing support measures to that group of travel agencies only – while strongly developing direct online sales through its own Star website.

It was estimated in the late 1990s that online sales of airline tickets would reach some ten billion US dollars by 2003.[4] In fact, the sales turned out to be some USD 17 billion in 2002 and about USD 20 billion in 2003. Strong growth in online sales is expected in the coming years; annual growth figures are in the magnitude of 15 per cent. The success of online travel service companies such as Cheap Tickets, Expedia, Priceline and Travelocity has challenged traditional travel agencies and airlines. It seems that the large online travel sites have an edge over the websites by airlines in the sense that they can provide a broader selection of travel-related services, especially accommodation and car rentals. Recently some airlines have refused to pay the fees that travel sites have demanded, and have pulled their products off these sites. Also, there are some airlines, like the low-costs JetBlue and Southwest, which have not offered their fares on sites other than their own. Southwest apparently sold some 40 per cent of tickets through its own website in 2002, whereas for American Airlines and United Airlines the corresponding figure was some five per cent.[5]

The message for alliance groups is that there is an open window of opportunity. Today, individual airlines provide online services with purchasing possibilities over the Web, but in the future the systems would need to be developed into tools for powerful relationship marketing. In the internet presence continuum we can see four stages: broadcast publishing, dialogue service, commerce, and enterprise integration. Today's airlines are on stage three, in other words, providing sales opportunities of services. However, it appears that airlines must rapidly advance to stage four, which means that Web technology is integrated with back-office systems together with the systems of third party vendors or service providers. For many individual airlines this would be a mighty task, but with a concerted effort by an alliance group it would be manageable. The joint effort by five leading United States airlines (American, Continental, Delta, Northwest and United) setting up Orbitz.com in 2001 has been a move into this direction. Orbitz provides today a wide spectrum of travel services. There is an increasing order for alliances to start acting as travel infomediaries or aggregators, drawing in partners from outside the airline industry. The biggest challenge seems to be getting member airlines working together in developing powerful online applications. The ever more challenging thing is the fact that airlines are on different levels in terms of online service capabilities. Generally speaking it seems that the North American carriers are most advanced in developing online services, followed by the European carriers, with Asian carriers being somewhat late in development. As IT technology is increasingly being shared in alliances, for instance through the Starnet within Star alliance, the shared alliance-wide online marketing and distribution systems should and will most likely be given top priority.

Overall, given the strength of the largest travel websites, and the relatively high fees that the sites have started to charge, the alliance groups obviously need to build comprehensive travel service sites. Recent studies suggest that consumers prefer getting the whole travel package from one website, as opposed to going to an airline's site for flights, a car-rental company site for a car, a hotel chain's site for accommodation, etc. The next few years will evidently witness a fierce competition between general travel services sites and individual airlines' own websites. Interestingly, as travel sites will remain a key distribution channel, it will be ever more difficult to say who is a partner and who is a competitor.

Changes to airline marketing

The changes in information and communications technology makes it necessary for airlines to segment markets differently from the old days. Looking at the markets in terms of geography is perhaps becoming less important, but they should be viewed more and more in terms of reason for travel, demographic features, and travel purchase patterns. These factors have a bearing on how airlines can reach customers with information, and how these customers like to make reservations and purchases. There are two ever more important dimensions in segmenting the market; one is the value of time to the potential customer, the other is the relative complexity of the travel service to be bought. As the less complex, more routine type of purchases is done increasingly through the internet, it is likely that travel agencies will develop into more consultant type actors, which typically look for the best complete solutions of rather complex travel services. This would imply, too, that the roles of travel agencies change, becoming more consultants and actors for customers, rather than being solely agents selling for airlines. The change in the roles may seem subtle but can nevertheless have a profound impact on the relationships between airlines, airline alliances and travel agencies in the future.

Alliances have implications for member carriers' marketing organisations. For a single airline it is not so important anymore to have an extensive presence in terms of geographical markets with one's own marketing, sales and handling organisation. Airlines can, in terms of physical presence, de-internationalise, or replace international presence with that of virtual presence through alliances. As an airline's employee abroad may cost some USD 200,000 per year, it is easy to see that there are significant cost savings to be reaped through this deinternationalisation. Another very relevant point to consider from the organisational perspective is that new information and telecommunication technology combined with alliancing offers opportunities to reduce the number of personnel in the sales function.

Determinants of alliance image

In the marketing of services like air transport, images in the eyes of customers and identities – as seen by the organisations themselves – are of utmost importance. For the sake of clarity, we use these terms in the following way: image means how one appears to others, whereas identity means what one is in reality. In addition to transportation from point A to point B at a certain time, customers are buying other dimensions of services, too: quality, dependability, punctuality, attention, friendliness, safety, life-style, nationality, prestige, etc., and these are the dimensions which make the image of an airline. Interestingly the images of airlines, particularly in Europe, are very much linked to the image of countries. For instance, Lufthansa is often seen as punctual, clean, efficient, of high technical quality and perhaps a bit formal in terms of service; in other words attributes quite typically associated with German goods and German people. These images are typically formed over long periods of time and are very difficult to change. On the other hand, the image of the quality of service on Alitalia flights in many consumers' eyes has traditionally been that there is substantial room for improvement, and no matter what Alitalia does in terms of improving its service this image is stuck with it for years.

As to brand identity, it can be seen from four perspectives: brand as a product, organisation, person, or symbol.[6] Historically, airline brand identities have always been closely associated with national cultures, symbols of nations and personalities of executives, and the starting point for creating a successful alliance brand to replace member carrier brands is not an easy one. Another challenge is to position an alliance brand against other alliance brands. Single carrier brands have at least their national backgrounds as premises, but how should Star really be made different from oneworld?

Brand image represents the perceived values that make up the brand existence; these values are evaluated positively or negatively by potential customers and others in the market. Brand image is a perception, not necessarily a fact.[7] Brand image also reflects customer expectations. Research has shown that in service marketing the danger of creating expectations that are difficult to fulfil is a real danger indeed. Brand image also has an impact on the company internally, mainly through employee motivation, thus affecting productivity and the quality of service.

It is important to remember that branding and brand strategy concerns a wide spectrum of issues, it is not only about advertising and logos. The components of brand strategy implementation comprise such areas as distribution channel policy, design of retail (sales offices, ticket encounters), customer interface (for instance personal vs. automated), product design (aircraft cabins, meals, entertainment, service quality), pricing, advertising, corporate communications and corporate action, and public relations.

Brand equity is a set of brand assets and liabilities linked to a brand, its name and symbol that add to or subtract from the value provided by a service to a firm and to its customers.[8] It represents a financial concept associated with the valuation of the brand; it stems from brand loyalty by customers, name awareness, perceived quality, brand associations and other assets, such as channel relationships. If airlines are to change the brand name from old carrier names to alliance group names, the old brand equity might be affected or even lost. Holt (2002) divided brand value into four components: reputation value, relationship value, experimental value and symbolic value. Applying these components of brand value into the airline industry, we could suggest, for instance, that customers are willing to pay a little bit more for a Lufthansa flight because they want to reduce risks and Lufthansa has a very dependable reputation. As to symbolic value, perhaps Virgin Atlantic's success owes partly to the fact that Virgin and its founder Richard Branson became symbols for the different, non-conservative or even rebellious values in the 1990s.

Airlines typically have monolithic brands, in other words, there is only one brand which is the same as the company name. Airline brands are often very well recognised and highly appreciated brands, at least within their home countries. Even if a new, original image is sought for an alliance, the old images of member airlines bring much of the brand equity to the alliance. The investments required for building a strong global alliance brand are naturally significant. For instance, it has been estimated that Wings Alliance was spending in the range of USD 50 million for its 1999 campaign to position the alliance as a customer-friendly travel network.[9] Because alliances cannot invest limitless amounts of money into building their brand, at least in the first few years the image builds on the inherited images of its members.

Stronger roles of alliances in marketing can be seen as a sociological issue, too. If alliances are replacing individual airlines as brands, a sort of new patria is created. Until today, airline personnel and customers have associated a particular airline with a particular country that has a certain history. An alliance, on the other hand, may not really have a home country, its history is short, and its 'personality' or character is only developing. Also, if the alliance group is to have a centralised governing body, the choice of the leading executives in that body has a reflection on the identity of the group. In fact, one of the key issues keeping airlines from going into more tightly integrated, if not virtually merged, alliance arrangements may be the choice of executives for the larger unit. Somebody has to be 'the boss', and the difficult question is which partner 'the boss' should come from; this perhaps cannot be solved without exhausting power struggles.

It has been assured by many airline executives that members in alliances will retain their own identities. However, it appears that alliance groups in their own right are taking a more important role in the marketing of alliance carriers' services. The outcome may be that, in the future, services are marketed primarily as alliance services and only secondarily as member carriers' services. For instance, services between Chicago and Oslo would be marketed as Star service rather than as flights by United Airlines and SAS. However, so far alliances have been very careful not to interfere with the marketing and brands of member airlines. 'We are not planning an airline called oneworld. Individual airline brands will continue to exist as before', said John McCullogh, managing director of oneworld, in October 2003.[10]

Problems may arise from the fact that airlines can have very different images. What then determines the image of an alliance? It might be possible to create an image for an alliance that is different from any of the member airlines' images. However, a more likely answer is that the image of an alliance will be some sort of compromise between the different images of its dominant members. For instance, oneworld image would thus be close to that of American Airlines or British Airways. This means that there may be a difference between the original image of a member, particularly a smaller airline, and the image of its alliance group, which in turn would suggest that the small airline would need to adapt itself to the new alliance image. This could mean improvement in certain dimensions of image, but it also could mean losing in some dimensions of image. To make a point, it is difficult to imagine how any alliance association could improve the quality dimension image of Singapore Airlines.

A relevant issue from the image perspective is the alliance structure. If there is a tiering system in use, in other words there are core members, second-tier members and perhaps third-tier members, maintaining a coherent alliance brand image will be challenging. The tiering can be straightforward and clear for member airlines, but for customers it could be very confusing. Again, knowing that there are different levels of memberships in the alliance group, a customer would not always feel that he will get the same level of commitment and service from all the alliance partners; this would prove to be not very assuring nor beneficial from the alliance marketing perspective.

The value of established brand names is shown by the case of KLM and Northwest alliance. The two airlines have in the past combined much of their marketing and sales efforts in the United States and the Netherlands. Already in 1996, KLM took over all advertising for Northwest in Europe and Northwest started to handle KLM advertising in North America. In 1998 Northwest closed its Amsterdam office and transferred all marketing and sales for Europe to KLM; similarly KLM closed its New York office.[11] However, the companies did not touch the brand names and company logos, even if they have appeared as a combination. It will be most interesting to see the impact of the Air France – KLM deal in 2003 on the close marketing relationship between KLM and Northwest.

In addition to sales offices, alliance members would often like to show joint presence at airport terminals. There undoubtedly are functional and image-related benefits to reap through coordinated presence. However, this is often easier said than done as terminals seldom have spare capacity, and moving individual airline offices and desks from one location to another may be opposed by airport management and other carriers.

Finally, planning for the intended image of alliance brands, it is worthwhile taking into consideration the broader turmoil in the travel industry. Perhaps in the near future, alliances or conglomerates merged from alliance members will develop into providers of total travel services. These conglomerates may include many partners other than airlines only (such as travel agents and land transport providers). In that case brand image cannot be the typical and traditional airline image but rather something new. Most airlines' and airline alliance images have been aircraft driven, but the image of a broader travel service provider would need to be more human driven. An example of alliance image building has been the ad campaign by oneworld, where people orientation was introduced through the 'oneworld revolves around you' theme.

Benefits, challenges and costs of alliance brand association

Obviously different kinds of alliance members enjoy the benefits of the common alliance brand differently. As discussed above, the image of a member could benefit from a joint alliance brand, depending of course on the original independent image of the airline. For a small carrier like Austrian Airlines, attachment to the alliance brand gives more visibility than what the carrier alone has been able to create. Also, being part of joint promotion of such scale and quality that would be unattainable for a single small airline is obviously a benefit. The benefit of being under the umbrella of an alliance brand would seem to be a function of distance: in the home markets of a particular member the benefits would be very limited, but in the far away markets the benefits can be significant. In other words, Austrian Airlines is likely to benefit most from the Star Alliance brand in the remote markets, such as South America and Asia Pacific, where as a small carrier it is not well known. As Dr. Bammer of Austrian Airlines put it, 'if passengers do not find you, they will not fly you'.[12]

There are challenges, costs and potential risks in being associated with an alliance brand. First, confusion over brand is possible as code-sharing is typically used in alliances: for instance, a customer may book on Lufthansa flights from Stockholm via Frankfurt to Hong Kong, but will never actually sit on a Lufthansa aircraft nor enjoy Lufthansa service in any way. There have been numerous cases where passengers have been deeply upset when they have found out that they are not flying the carrier they thought they would. In fact, an IATA survey among 1000 travellers in 1998 found that one-third had found themselves flying with a different airline from the one they expected.[13] However, later research, by IATA for instance, suggests that consumers are rather quick in accepting the code-sharing practice and do not mind the fact that one does not always get what one has bought. Nevertheless, the confusion risk remains, and it has to be addressed properly; it would not be easily accepted to be accommodated in some 'partner hotel of Sheraton' if one has booked a room in a real Sheraton hotel. This is especially relevant if there are differences in the quality of service.

There are cases in the airline industry where a code-sharing airline's quality has not been sufficient: it has been suggested that Emirates cancelled its code-share with Cyprus Airways after there had been complaints that the Cypriot carrier's business class was not on par with that of Emirates. The short-lived co-operation between TWA and Malev is perhaps another example.

The alliance brand such as Star may challenge individual member airline brands. Also, an airline's investments in concerted marketing operations and joint brand advertising within an alliance may turn out to be wasted if the alliance dissolves or the airline decides, or is forced, to move into another alliance. Moreover, if the airline changes – typically through significant investments – its own brand image in order to align it with that of the alliance group, and then for some reason leaves this alliance, adopting the old image or a third image may prove difficult and costly. An interesting hypothetical example is British Midland, today known as bmi, UK's second largest full-service airline which has long been a challenger to British Airways, operating only within Europe and targeting mainly business travellers, but which has joined Star Alliance and become a transatlantic operator. Stepping into a bigger league may require that the brand image be rethought; it might mean changing the very name of the airline, changing the colours, reconfiguring service classes aboard aircraft, changing the advertising and other communication messages, etc. This is very costly but all very fine, provided the airline is successful and satisfied with its new role. However, if life among the 'Establishment' carriers fails to satisfy the airline and a new role needs to be adopted, then the brand image repositioning exercise might need to be done again. Playing with company and brand image too frequently in a service industry has often spelt trouble.

There is value in airline names being associated closely with countries, and it would be risky to abandon old established names completely. A case supporting this is British Airways replacing the Union Jack with different ethnic liveries in the tails of its aircraft in the late 1990s: apparently a majority of the British and foreigners alike preferred the Union Jack and BA had to return to the traditional style. The risk of losing home market customers may be biggest for small carriers from smaller countries such as Austria, Finland or Portugal; in those countries the national flag carriers have benefited from the fact that the one national flag carrier is an important icon of national identity.

An airline may also have such a special image that it would lose much of its value if it were put under a joint alliance brand. An example of this would be Virgin, which in the eyes of consumers has always been an innovative challenger, an alternative to the established and perhaps boring national flag carriers and other large carriers. Joining an alliance and going under a joint alliance brand would undoubtedly mean that part of this image would be compromised. In fact, the need to control the brand has apparently been in the past the factor that has prevented Virgin from tying partnerships in the United States for the purpose of operating intra-United States Virgin services.

Much related to the image is the issue of classes of service. Even if the trend seems to be towards abandoning first class and upgrading business class instead, members in alliances still have somewhat different class categories. To make things even more complicated, classes in most airlines are marketed as brands; some of the biggest marketing campaigns in the industry include BA's Club World and Club Europe branding campaigns. Ideally, from the alliance image and marketing point of view, the aim should be to have at least a rather uniform offering in terms of classes, meaning that if a customer books on Singapore

Airlines business class but ends up on a code-shared flight by United, he should not experience poorer service than he is used to. The problem is that for airlines the classes are one of the few ways to differentiate their product – there still is competition even between members in an alliance – and the premium classes particularly are key means in creating the image of quality in an airline.

Another challenge is the volatility in the alliance game; making changes to an airline's class policies is risky in the sense that, first, policies in the alliance may change, and second, an airline may find itself in a new alliance group where the policies are different. Commonality of classes is possible, as shown by the case of KLM and Northwest. The two carriers have had since the mid-1990s a joint intercontinental business class, where the seat comfort, pitch, food and in-flight entertainment are to the same standard. However, doing the same with ten partners is a task of different calibre. Nevertheless, if we see alliances as a transitory phase in the development towards mergers and acquisitions, then investments in commonality of classes are better justified. Cathay Pacific CEO Turnbull said of the oneworld alliance in 1998 that 'the idea is not to have one uniform service, but different services to a single standard'.[14] Understandably, service standards between alliance member carriers differ. It is also quite understandable that services will remain different in the sense that each carrier will have its own flavour, but the levels – however that is measured – should not differ too much within an alliance group. If airlines are able to improve services through alliancing – as the purpose is – the challenge then is to convince the customers that this has indeed happened, also in the carriers of poorer service image.

An important but little publicised dimension of image is safety and security. This has, of course, become very much of a concern to passengers since September 11th 2001. The major carriers that are members in alliance groups today all have good safety records, but the images do not necessarily reflect the statistical reality. The issue may become more of a concern when carriers from less well-known, perhaps more 'exotic' countries join alliance groups. These carriers may in reality actually have poor safety records, at least a poorer safety image than that of the most well-known carriers. In the eyes of consumers it is somewhat disturbing that one cannot be exactly sure which carrier operates a flight and what is the safety standard of that carrier. Perhaps the lamentable accidents and consequent doubts over safety standards of Korean Air Lines in the late 1990s are an example where the safety image of a carrier may have an impact on alliance arrangements; Delta Air Lines postponed code-sharing with KAL apparently due to the string of accidents of KAL aircraft. Other safety-related issues may arise, too; Delta Air Lines was sued by the survivors of the Delta ticket holders who were aboard Swissair flight 111 which crashed off the coast of Nova Scotia in 1998. The claim was that Delta was responsible for those passengers as they had bought Delta tickets, even if the flight was operated as a code-share by Swissair.

Recent research has suggested that since the terrorist activity in 2001 airline passengers have felt more stress about flying than earlier. Consequently, it has been suggested that airlines should emphasise care and the very human factors in marketing in order to make people less stressed about air travel. Professor Jonathan Bricker from the University of Washington has suggested that airlines could emphasise the opportunity for people to visit friends and relatives in their seeking support in these stressing post-September 11th times.[15] Building a caring 'family' atmosphere into an individual airline's marketing and product offering is a challenge. Given the different national and corporate cultures, competitive pressures, etc., it may be too much of a challenge for a multi-partner alliance group.

Frequent flyer programmes have been central tools in all alliance arrangements from the very beginning. The alliance benefits come not only from the ease of collecting and redeeming points but also through the better visibility of the alliance FFP brand. Experiences from alliances have so far proved that there is great power in multilateral FFPs; the leverage of adding partners into a multi-partner FFP is significant in enhancing the marketing power of the FFP. This would suggest that, in an alliance, the member airlines are better able to sell the points or miles to non-airline companies such as credit card companies, insurance companies, ferry operators, holiday resorts, store chains, and so on. A point, or mile, from a major United States carrier costs some two cents, but it may be possible for a strong alliance group to charge more for its mile.

FFP cooperation between airlines crosses alliance group boundaries to some extent, due to the rapidly changing compilation of groups. However, it would seem logical for FFPs to evolve from being single airlines centred towards being truly alliance group level programmes. In this evolution phase, the management of FFPs will indeed be very challenging. Especially in the early phases of alliance cooperation or when airlines switch from one group to another, it is quite a task to manage the transitions of FFPs. For instance, how long should it be possible to redeem points? This might be less of a problem in the future as airlines are becoming more lax about time limits within their own programmes. Also, what should the exchange rate of points be, how should the non-airline partners in loyalty programmes be taken into account, and so on, are not simple issues. Moreover, most carriers have bilateral FFP relationships with airlines outside their alliance group, and these relationships might not always be looked upon favourably by alliance group partners. The potential risk in all this is the confusion and irritation among customers that may follow, should an airline decide to leave a particular alliance group.

An interesting component in airline alliance marketing is pricing. Airlines, individually, step up aggressive pricing when the demand is weak – very much understandably. In tougher economic climate, like post-September 11th, pricing is also emphasised in airline advertising. On the other hand, when the demand is strong, airlines underline the quality of service, comfort, etc. in advertising. The eternal challenge in airline marketing and particularly advertising is striking a balance between building a quality image and conveying the message of low prices: too much emphasis on low prices in ads may hurt an airline's brand and quality image, but a failure to inform consumers about low prices may result in lost traffic. In alliances, there are limitations to concerted pricing. But even acknowledging the fact that alliance groups, for instance, cannot offer fully coordinated price campaigns without raising the interest and attention of competition authorities, it is noteworthy that alliance advertising is practically silent about prices. As the low-cost carriers are really challenging the established carriers in terms of pricing – and making it more and more difficult for the established carriers to justify the higher fares – it appears that alliances, too, have to address the pricing issue more vigorously in their future advertising – provided that it is allowed by the regulators. Of course, individual airlines are responding to the price challenge of low-costs, but if alliances are completely inactive in this area, they may risk developing an image of high prices and disinterest in customers.

Regarding the challenging price-quality balance, for instance Ryanair has chosen the very aggressive pricing strategy and does not appear to worry that much about its image in terms of quality. However, as the prices are so low, the product experience typically exceeds expectations. In the regular carriers today, it is often the case that the high expectations are often not met – due to traditional advertising promoting the quality of air travel and to relatively high fares. So, the established carriers indeed have a communication challenge, as they try to convince consumers that, for instance, the lunch included and flexibility in the ticket is worth the extra thousand euros in intra-European travel. True, airlines know the rationale behind the price differences, but many consumers fail to understand, or at least accept, the high prices charged.

Marketing and information

A crucial facet in the marketing of any services is that of information flow. Customer surveys by airlines repeatedly tell that belated information, wrong information or the lack of information are serious causes for dissatisfaction among passengers. On the other hand, marketing is the interface through which a company gets its ideas and views for directing strategies, product development and so on. In fact, a study by Ernst & Young on knowledge management in corporations found that 77 per cent of respondents identified knowledge about customers as the most critical knowledge.[16]

Customers often require information that is specific to the airline (for example the type of seats in the business class, availability of electricity outlets onboard for portable PC), its home country or base station/airport. This information may not be readily available from the personnel of a partner airline, who in all fairness cannot be expected to know so well another company and its home country. Alliances have set up training programmes, special help desks and information sites in the computer systems and trained partner carrier specialists to address the issue, but the challenge is not easily equalled. Another set of information flow, feedback from customers to the company, poses challenges, too. It is quite unlikely that feedback from the market would flow between alliance members as well as it does within one airline. For instance, it is only human for an SAS check-in person to have less incentive to forward valuable feedback from a customer to Lufthansa management than to the management of her own organisation, SAS. In fact, as the flow of customer feedback within a company is a problem in many airlines, one can imagine that on an alliance level the problems will be even larger.

A related issue is the loyalty of marketing and sales personnel, and also of personnel in the frontline, in other words check-in personnel, cabin personnel, and so on. As research on alliances in manufacturing has many times implied, it is quite understandable that personnel are likely to favour their own employer, for instance, when giving recommendations to customers, even if this from the alliance perspective would be sub-optimising. While the purpose of alliances is not to eliminate competition between member carriers, this form of loyalty to one's own airline may seriously work against the purpose set for alliance marketing.

Evidence from other industries also suggests that in order to respond to the challenge of information provision, gathering, and conveying, and also of knowledge transfer, airlines need to invest heavily in staff training. However, research in other industries[17] suggests that codification of marketing know-how is often very difficult and costly, and there are no real substitutes for learning-by-doing in the presence of partners that have better knowledge or more developed practices. This is done in some alliances, but findings from airlines suggest that there is still a lot of work to be done. Training should include rotation of staff within a firm, and more important, swapping of staff between partner airlines to provide a holistic picture of the alliance cooperation and to give opportunities to thoroughly learn the practices of other member carriers. The magnitude of training programs is quite significant; if there is a quarter of a million staff in Star alliance, one can estimate that the number of people to be trained is in the range of tens of thousands within one alliance alone. Looking further into the future, rotating and swapping personnel between alliance group members would nicely pave the way for smoother management of mergers and acquisitions in the industry – if those are ever allowed by authorities. Apart from training, to illustrate the magnitude of information-related investments is the fact that apparently more than half of the Star Alliance budget in the first years was allocated to developing information technology solutions.

In conclusion

Alliances between airlines still today are primarily marketing alliances. Airlines have invested significant amounts of money into making alliance groups known and in coordinating marketing efforts of members. However, the lives of alliances are still very unpredictable and unstable. Consequently, the investments that airlines make in alliances can be considered very risky, but in today's competitive circumstances it would be even riskier to stay out of the alliancing game.

It seems that the international airline industry is experiencing the first phases of its evolution from a very fragmented structure towards a consolidated industry of truly multinational players; first, through marketing alliances and then through 'real', strategic alliances covering a broad range of activities. The last phase – consolidation through cross-border mergers and acquisitions – may have started in 2003 and the scene is quite turbulent. Therefore, airlines might be wise to be at least careful in investing in alliance-specific marketing. More importantly, it seems essential not to neglect or compromise the own company marketing in general and brand management in particular, for the brand equity of the own firm to a large extent determines the ability of the firm to stand alone in case it decides to leave or is left out of alliances. Moreover, this single company brand equity might prove a key asset if the mergers and acquisitions game really gains momentum.

Notes

[1] *Aviation Week & Space Technology*, 28, September 1998.
[2] Phillips, 1997.
[3] Grant, 1996.
[4] O'Toole, 1999.
[5] *WSJ*, 18 June 2002
[6] Aaker, 1991, 5.
[7] See e.g. Hague and Jackson, 1994.
[8] Aaker, 1991.
[9] *Advertising Age*, 12 July 1999.
[10] STT, 2003.
[11] Flint, 1999.
[12] *Avmark Aviation Economist*, May 2000.
[13] Skapinker, 1998.
[14] *Aviation Week & Space Technology*, 28 September 1998.
[15] *Air Transport World*, 2003.
[16] Moran, 1997.
[17] See e.g. Simonin, 1999.

References

Aaker, D. (1991), *Managing Brand Equity. Capitalizing on the Value of a Brand Name,* The Free Press, New York.
Advertising Age, 12 July 1999.
Air Transport World, September 2003, vol. 40, issue 9, p. 61.
Aviation Week & Space Technology, 28 September 1998.
Avmark Aviation Economist, May 2000.
Flint, P. (1999), *Air Transport World*, April 1999, pp. 33-36.
Grant, B. (1996), 'Trends in U.S. Airline Ticket Distribution', *The McKinsey Quarterly*, 4.
Hague, P. and Jackson, P. (1994), 'The Power of Industrial Brands: an Effective Route to Competitive Advantage', McGraw-Hill Books Co. Europe.
Kleymann, B. (1999), 'Future Developments in the Structure of Airline Alliance Networks', Conference proceedings of the 1999 Air Transport Research Group of the WCTR Society, Hong Kong.
Lorange, P., Roos, J. and Simcic Bronn, P. (1992), 'Building Successful Strategic Alliances', *Long Range Planning*, vol. 25, no. 6, pp. 10-17.
Moran, N. (1997), 'Knowledge management', *Financial Times*, January 10, p. 8.
Murray, E. and Mahon, J. (1993), 'Strategic Alliances: Gateway to the New Europe?', *Long Range Planning*, vol. 26, no. 4, pp. 102-111.
O'Toole, K. (1999), 'IT Trends Survey', *Airline Business*, August.
Phillips, E. (1997), *Aviation Week & Space Technology*, 17 November 1997, pp. 65-69.

Rhoades, D. and Lush, (1997), 'A Typology of Strategic Alliances in the Airline Industry: Propositions for Stability and Duration', Conference Proceedings of the 1997 Air Transport Research Group of the WCTR Society, vol. 1, no. 1, University of Nebraska at Omaha.
Simonin, B. (1999), 'Transfer of Marketing Know-How in International Strategic Alliances', *Journal of International Business Studies,* vol. 30, no. 3, pp. 463-490.
Skapinker, M. (1998), *Financial Times,* 10 January 1998.
STT (Finnish News Agency), October 18, 2003.

Chapter 7

The Effect of Strategic Alliances
on Performance

Introduction

Since airlines have historically shown poor financial performance, it has been suggested that airline business is not cyclical business but bad business. Indeed, the combined net profit margins of United States airlines, for instance, have typically been only about half of the Standard and Poor's 500 list of industrial, utility and transportation companies' net profit margins. An average airline loses money in the long run; between 1982 and 2002 IATA airlines, representing 280 airlines that carry 98 per cent of the world's scheduled passenger traffic, had revenues of two trillion USD and cumulative losses of five billion USD. Of course, due to terrorism, the global airline losses in 2001-2002 combined were truly exceptional, nearly USD 25 billion. For some twenty years, the airline industry has been very turbulent and has been through financial ups and downs. Alliances in the industry can partly be seen as a response to the uncertainty and risks associated with industry turbulence, in other words, alliances are seen as a way of improving performance in times of hardening competition. Knowing the performance implications will be increasingly important in the future, especially in large alliance groupings, firstly, for the group to monitor overall progress in the alliance, and secondly, for individual members to see and understand all the benefits and costs related to an alliance membership.

There are some fundamental questions concerning the evaluation of the performance impact of alliances. First, it needs to be specified from which company's perspective the performance is evaluated; as airlines have different premises and objectives for alliances, they would then also evaluate outcomes differently. Secondly, what is the time span of the assessment? It may be that an alliance has difficult first three years, but after that the effects on performance may be very positive. On the other hand, it may happen that an alliance has a promising start, but results later in separation, lost investments, and thus poor performance. Finally, the assessment of the impact on performance is difficult, because most often we do not know the alternate reality, in other words, what might have happened if there had not been an alliance. Perhaps an alliance's impact on an airline's performance is insignificant when compared to the history of performance in that airline, but at the same time the alternative of not having an alliance might have lead to a worse outcome.

Moreover, assessing the performance of an alliance proves difficult as many of the objectives of alliances are very general and thus tricky to measure. Some of them are listed below:

- add value to an airline's product line
- reduce competitive pressure
- provide access to new capabilities
- share and decrease risks.

Past research suggests that companies do a rather poor job in assessing the performance of alliances. Bamford and Ernst (2002) found out that amongst the more than 500 companies studied, there were three major problems in terms of alliance performance measurement: 1. failure to measure performance of individual alliances rigorously, 2. failure to recognise performance patterns across alliance portfolios, 3. failure by alliance portfolio managers to know whether the portfolio really supports the overall corporate strategy.

This chapter attempts to present views that are relevant in performance assessment of an alliance. As research-based evidence of performance implications of alliancing is still scarce, we raise issues and relevant questions rather than try to provide answers.

Performance measurement in airlines

Before going into the performance impact of alliances, it is worthwhile taking a look at how airline performance has been measured in general. Of course, financial performance of airlines is measured like in any other industry, using indicators such as net profit margin, return on equity and investment, and cash flow measures. However, as these indicators are familiar to all business managers and observers, we will in this chapter skip the general financial measures and concentrate on measures that are more specific to the airline industry, in other words, airline operational performance measures.

Operational performance of an airline is often referred to as productivity. Two main categories of productivity concept exist: gross (non-parametric) measures of productivity and shift (parametric) measures of technical change.[1] Within these categories there are many different ways to measure productivity. The choice of measurement depends on the purpose of the measurement. Productivity can be measured either in partial or comprehensive terms. Partial measures are often very simple to use, but as the name implies, they provide only a partial measurement of productivity. Comprehensive measures compare total outputs to total inputs; such measures are generally known as Total Factor Productivity (TFP). For TFP, overall input and output indices are created by weighting individual inputs by their share of total (or variable) costs and individual outputs by their share of total revenue for the firm.[2] For assessing performance implications of alliances from an airline management perspective the partial measures appear much more applicable.

Very widely used partial measures are those related to the use of labour; often this means that some output measure is expressed on a per-employee basis. As Windle and Dresner (1992) pointed out, a major disadvantage of these labour productivity measures is that they do not account for possible trade-offs between labour and other inputs, typically capital in the form of machines. In other words, an airline with a high capital-to-labour input mix may show high labour productivity but not necessarily high overall (or total factor) productivity. It would be better to use labour costs in monetary terms, rather than simply the number of employees, as the denominator in the measures. This would also take into account the differences in wages and social payments in different countries, a key factor in capital versus labour investment decisions. Another weakness of labour productivity measures is that they often treat all labour categories uniformly; a senior vice-president of marketing, a pilot and a baggage handler all count as one employee, but clearly they each have different output and cost effects.

Of the partial labour-related measures, available tonne-kilometres (ATK) per employee may be the simplest one; a comparable measure is the revenue ton-kilometres (RTK) per employee. Both measures are quite limited in value, but may be good additions in productivity assessment. ATK and RTK do not differentiate between different types of payload but treat both first-class passengers and bulk freight only on a weight basis. This clearly makes inter-airline comparisons – and even comparisons over time – difficult, because airlines have different payload profiles.

More specific labour-related measures are, for instance, flight-crew flight hours per certain time period. Like all partial measures, these should not be used without consideration of other measures. For instance, short routes with frequent stops would imply lower flight hours than long-haul routes. On the other hand, even if long-haul flights can imply very high daily flight hours at times, due to the typical lower frequencies they also imply rather long stop-overs and thus non-productive days while the crew is away from their home base. However, as one of the main factors affecting this measure is company policies concerning workloads for crews, and as the route lengths and frequencies are not a given factor but something that airline management can affect, these two crew utilisation measures appear to be quite good for comparative purposes.

Another category of productivity measure is related to the utilisation of aircraft; a widely used measure is load factor, which can be applied to passenger seats or to the overall payload. In the application of load factor measures it is important to take into account yield measures, too; attaining high load factors through very low fares does not necessarily maximise revenues. An aircraft utilisation measure based on daily flight hours per aircraft is widely used. Just as with ATK or RTK measures, this measure should not be used in isolation from route length considerations. Aircraft that operate very short route sectors have difficulties in obtaining high daily flight-hour measures.

As to how past research has analysed airline performance, a couple of examples can be presented. Bruning (1991) assessed relative efficiencies of internationally operating airlines through a stochastic frontier production methodology. Building on a log-linear cost function, the analysis included the following variables: total operating costs, total revenue tonne-kilometres, price of capital services, price of labour services, price of fuel, measure of the degree of competition facing an airline, percentage of government ownership, and dummy variables indicating liberal versus non-liberal bilateral agreements and the scope of an airline's operations. It was concluded that cost disadvantages may be overcome by increasing traffic density.

Schefczyk (1993) analysed the operational performance of airlines through the Data Envelopment Analysis (DEA) technique. The study used the following inputs: available tonne-kilometres, operating costs, and non-flight assets. The outputs measured were revenue passenger-kilometres and non-passenger revenue. Regression analysis was used to determine the relationship between profitability and performance, and the influence of structural characteristics on both performance and profitability. As to the conclusions of the study, not surprisingly, high operational performance appeared to be a key factor of high profitability.

In performance assessment one needs to bear in mind that there are two sides to a coin: revenue side and cost side. As to cost side, it is important to clarify the cost areas that are most important in airline operations and which may offer the most potential for cost reduction and consequent performance improvement. Cost sources in the airline business can be categorised as follows – in a descending order of typical significance:

- labour
- fuel
- charges for landing, en-route navigation, etc.
- aircraft (depreciation)
- other materials
- ground equipment and property (depreciation)
- outside services expenses (ground handling, etc.)
- financial expenses
- other expenses.

Labour costs in total account on average for about one-third of airlines' costs, being the largest item. In the largest United States airlines, labour's share is now more than 40 per cent, in low-cost airlines it can be only 25 per cent. Also, labour costs are among the few cost items that really are controllable by airlines; most other items like fuel and airport charges must be taken as given. Therefore, discussion on cost reduction potential often centres on the utilisation of labour force, productivity of labour force, and their remuneration.

Measuring the performance impact of alliances

There are numerous views on how performance of alliances can be measured, but there is no consensus as to what the correct way would be or what the best determinants of performance would be. Research has concluded that traditional financial measures that build on the accounting systems are inadequate and that new forward-looking measures ought to be developed. It appears somewhat problematic that the assessment of alliance performance uses mostly financial feedback, which is backward looking in nature and may fail to anticipate future possibilities and challenges for alliances. In addition, it has been suggested[3] that financial measures ignore many issues relevant to management and are solely based on historical costs providing little basis for judgement on the effectiveness of processes like personnel relation systems. Moreover, it seems that these 'soft' resources, which are difficult to measure, are today's drivers of company success and are valued now more than ever. An interesting comparison is that to the bio-technology firms, some of which have market capitalisation larger than major airlines, but whose assets really are only promising ideas and concepts; many of those companies have never shown good performance when assessed by conventional financial measures.

Traditionally strategic alliance performance has been measured, first, in terms of survival or duration, stability in the case of multi-partner arrangements, and stock market reactions to alliance announcements. Secondly, such measures as profitability, cost position and growth rates have been used. A third category of measures is the opinion of managers concerning performance. Discussion on criteria used in alliance performance measurement can be found for example in Dussauge and Garrette (1995). For airline alliances in particular, it appears that performance has been measured mostly by using market share and sales volumes as proxies for performance. Research has shown that results from alliances are monitored much on a route level, comparing mostly to budgets based on market development estimates, to estimates of results if there had not been an alliance, or to results from previous years.

A factor that makes performance measurement in alliances difficult, as opposed to that of individual airlines, is the fact that organisational politics are much more complex in alliances. Often organisational politics translate into the issues of control, either through financial or non-financial mechanisms. The control-performance relationship is evidently important, but so far research has not been able to conclude satisfactorily how much and through which mechanism control impacts alliance performance. Also, the more extensive the alliance, the more difficult it typically is to measure its impact on performance from an individual airline's perspective. For instance, it is rather easy to monitor performance effects of a simple codesharing arrangement on a few routes. However, if the arrangement comprises codesharing on several routes, shared marketing efforts, division of work in maintenance, co-operation in flight and handling operations and perhaps joint sourcing activities, the assessment is much more complicated. In other words, on a route level the performance assessment is manageable but on a system-wide level it may be extremely difficult.

Performance assessment has to take into account the company's internal and external factors. Performance assessment is also contingent on the actions by authorities concerning the limitations on alliances and the alternative ways to improve competitiveness or otherwise reach for the desired benefits, for instance, through mergers or acquisitions. An overall framework for alliance performance assessment from an individual member airline perspective is suggested in Figure 7.1.

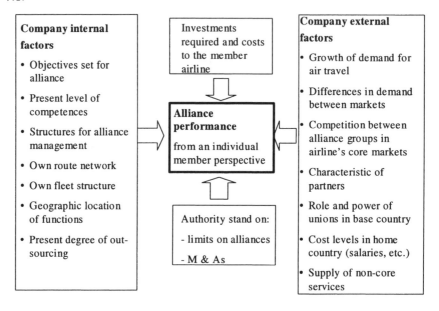

Figure 7.1   Framework for alliance performance assessment

Time continuum in performance assessment

It has been suggested by Dresdner Kleinwort Benson that during the first couple of years, the benefits from an alliance are accrued almost solely from the enhanced revenues. In about seven years the share of benefits should be a 50:50 split between enhanced revenues and reduced costs, and from ten years into alliancing more than two-thirds of the benefits should be attained from the costs side.[4] Experiences by airlines up till 2004 appear to support this view.

At the end of the day alliance performance is assessed through profit rates and cash flow – naturally the ultimate goal of an alliance venture is to enhance or maximise these. However, if performance is monitored only by looking at these indicators the view is only partial and too short-termed. If the alliance is seen as a continuum of inputs and outputs, we can distinguish several variables that can be assessed for performance monitoring purposes.[5] At the input end there are such factors as financial resources, productivity and innovativeness of partners and at the output end these factors are as profit and cash flow. The performance should be assessed by monitoring variables through the continuum, not only the factors at the output end. The output end variables should measure short term performance, but the input end variables should communicate the condition of the alliance in order for the partners to produce high performance in the long term. Figure 7.2 illustrates this continuum of input and outputs.

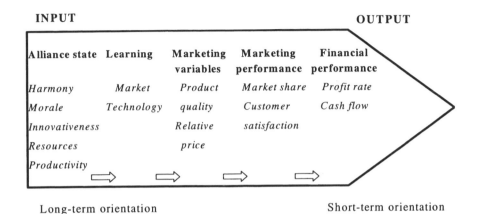

Figure 7.2   Input–output continuum in alliances
Source: Adapted from Anderson (1990, 19–30).

Whether one should use more of the input or output end variables in the assessment of alliance performance depends on how well the results can be measured and how well the transformation process of inputs into outputs is understood; a thorough discussion can be found in Saramaa (1998). Our experience is that airlines rely too much on measuring the operational indicators such as cost savings in a certain function, but suffer from the shortage of appropriate metrics for the assessment of the strategic value of an alliance arrangement. There is a need to develop suitable measures for the performance in terms of the 'soft' input end or the mid-process variables, such as brand image or organisational learning and flexibility.

Concerning the time continuum in an alliance, it is important to remember that survival of an alliance is not a goal in itself. In other words, alliances do not need to survive; they need to reach their objectives. Sometimes an alliance can reach its objectives and serve its purpose in a short time and is no loss when dissolved. However, experience in the industry suggests that many alliances disintegrate prematurely. Research by Segil suggested that 55 per cent of alliances disintegrate within the first three years; interestingly, three airlines out of four attributed the failure to incompatibility of corporate cultures or personalities.[6] A study by the Boston Consulting Group indicated that the overall survival rate for airline alliances between 1992 and 1995 was 38 per cent, but between 1995 and 1998 it was up to 68 per cent. Equity-based alliances have survived better than non-equity alliances and domestic alliances better than regional or intercontinental alliances.[7]

Traffic and revenue enhancement

Many executives of major airlines have emphasised that the success of large, established network carriers depends on their ability to reduce operating costs. It is widely accepted that in the revenue side there is no return to the good old days, transparency of prices due to the Internet and the aggressive growth of low cost carriers makes it unlikely that airlines could raise their yields markedly from today's levels. So, perhaps the discussion on the revenue enhancement through alliances in many airlines should be seen in a 'defensive' spirit, i.e. with the aim of not necessarily raising revenues but keeping them from falling.

It has been suggested that during the first years of alliances, the majority of benefits come from enhanced revenues. Indeed, already in 1995 the General Accounting Office of the USA suggested that international alliances have generated large gains for the partners in terms of passengers and revenues. Some experiences on traffic and revenue enhancement reported by airlines are presented below, although the numeric estimates must be read with caution – airlines present figures that understandably may be more or less sophisticated guesses. These examples are from the time before autumn of 2001, as the September 11th events caused such turbulence in demand that the alliance effect assessment is even more difficult than in normal times.

United Airlines' average number of passengers on its Chicago-Frankfurt flights increased from 110 passengers to 212 passengers after linking with Lufthansa. For Lufthansa flights, the average boardings per flight rose from 134 to 186. It was also suggested that these increases owed wholly to capturing Frankfurt and Chicago beyond traffic, Chicago-Frankfurt O&D traffic remaining flat. Delta Air Lines reported in spring 2000 that as a result of its alliance agreements, some 2000 additional passengers are being fed onto its routes daily. In order not to forget the cargo's role, it is worthwhile noting that Morrell and Pilon (1999) studied the impact of passenger traffic alliance on the cargo service characteristics, using KLM-Northwest alliance as a case. The study concluded that the connecting cargo services went up and cargo layover times were reduced significantly along the years of allied operations.

Revenue enhancement is discussed more in detail in Chapter 8, so it suffices to note that, for instance, the larger carriers have expected the alliances to bring additional annual revenue in the magnitude of USD 200 million.

Costs

One objective of alliances is to reduce costs, primarily through economies of scale or scope from joint operations. In addition, alliances may provide opportunities for individual members to use the alliance as a means to internationalise cost structures, in other words, relocate some functions in lower cost countries. The key areas for cost reduction through alliances appear to be labour, aircraft, material, ground equipment and property, and third-party service expenses.

Based on past research it is possible to suggest areas where performance improvement through cost reduction is most likely to occur. Figure 7.3 highlights areas of the airline business system that can offer significant cost reduction opportunities through alliancing.

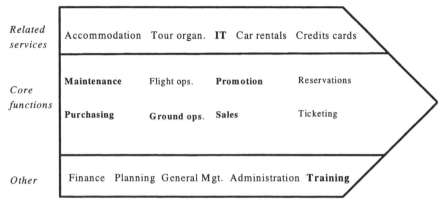

Related services	Accommodation Tour organ. **IT** Car rentals Credits cards
Core functions	**Maintenance** Flight ops. **Promotion** Reservations **Purchasing** **Ground ops.** **Sales** Ticketing
Other	Finance Planning General Mgt. Administration **Training**

Functions in bold present clear cost reduction opportunities in alliance arrangements

Figure 7.3   Cost reduction opportunities in airline business system

It was estimated back in the early 1990s that if the sales operations of British Airways and USAir were merged in New York, that alone would result in annual savings of one million USD. On the other hand, the extensive KLM-Alitalia venture, which never materialised, was expected to reduce the combined annual operating costs of the partners by some USD 400 million.

Cost reduction potential is significant in the area of sourcing. One of the early arrangements where these savings were reached – DSS World Sourcing AG established by Delta Air Lines, Singapore Airlines and Swissair in 1995 – started through the procurement of small items for cabin service and achieved marked cost savings from the very beginning. Joint sourcing of fuel, spare parts, information technology and eventually aircraft is likely to be part of alliance arrangements in the future. As to aircraft spare parts, there has long been pooling between carriers, but there appears to be room for further rationalisation of inventory. It has been suggested that joint aircraft purchasing could produce discounts of some ten per cent off the normal cost for the participating airlines.

A significant cost item to airlines is payments for the use of Computer Reservation Systems (CRSs). Even if airlines have vested interest in CRS providers through investments, it would seem likely that an alliance group could use its enhanced bargaining power towards CRS vendors to press for lower prices. Similarly, telecommunication services, including intra-firm telecommunication and data communications, mobile phones, satellite communications, toll-free services to customers and so on, should be a likely area for cost reduction, as an alliance group has more bargaining power than a single airline in dealing with telecommunication service providers. Perhaps alliance groups will set up joint telecommunication subsidiaries to take advantage of the status of a telecom service carrier, which in some markets gives an opportunity to negotiate unpublished rates with large telecom service providers.

Even if there is significant cost reduction potential through swapping flight crew and/or maintenance capacity with other alliance carriers, this might prove an arduous task due to the conservative attitude of the unions towards alliances. The emergence of Star Solidarity Alliance gives reason to believe that global co-operation between unions may increase in the future, making alliance-wide re-organising difficult. Past disputes concerning two-tier salary schemes and the use of outsourced pilots support this argument rather strongly. The reluctance of pilot unions within an alliance to approve cost reduction measures concerning flight crew labour is evident in, for instance, the case where Northwest Airlines pilots refused to fly Northwest aircraft which were to replace KLM flights if KLM pilots went on strike.

Figure 7.4 suggests some areas of activity where there is significant and realistic potential for cost reduction through alliances.

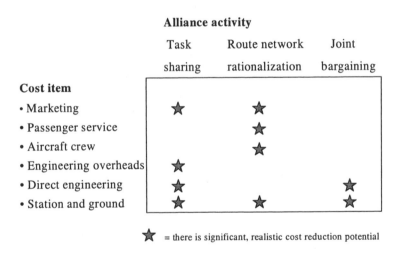

= there is significant, realistic cost reduction potential

Figure 7.4   Cost reduction potential through alliances

Productivity

Oum et al. (2000) studied the productivity implications of alliancing using data for 22 airlines and 108 alliances between 1985 and 1996. Their study suggested that a new alliance contributed to improving the participating airlines' productivity by an average of 1.7 per cent. It was also found that airlines achieve greater productivity gains when the scope of the cooperation increased; productivity gains from major alliances were greater than from minor alliances. Productivity gains from major alliances were on average about five per cent, whereas the gains from minor alliances were rather insignificant. Even this very thorough study did not reveal which input factors (for example material, labour, capital) contribute most to the overall improvement in productivity.

In 1998, Lufthansa and SAS projected productivity increases of four to five per cent thanks to the Star Alliance.[8] This was a typical estimate of overall productivity improvement thanks to an extensive alliance. So far it has been almost impossible to find compelling case evidence on the overall productivity effects of alliances. Even in the future it will be difficult to say which proportion of productivity improvement is actually from the alliances and which is owing to other factors.

Airlines are rather reluctant to talk about labour restructuring following the alliances, perhaps due to union opposition. As mentioned earlier, estimates on the labour force reduction effect of alliances range widely; some say there will only be insignificant effect, others have forecasted at least 30 per cent decrease in the world wide airline workforce due to alliancing.

A challenge in pursuing higher labour productivity through shared operations is that of loyalty. When everything runs according to schedule, let us say in ground handling or line maintenance, shared operations may work fine and every airline is treated equally. However, if for some reason there is an overload of work, employees will need to decide on either which carrier to serve first or whether they can compromise quality. In the first case it is likely that loyalty towards the own company takes precedence; therefore it is one's own carrier that is handled or serviced first, leaving the partner carrier at the bottom of the priority list. In the latter case, both carriers may suffer if employees decide to opt for lower quality in order to simultaneously serve both airlines as scheduled.

Alliances may provide an opportunity to rationalise fleet structures within alliance members and thus reach higher aircraft productivity. Fleet rationalisation typically requires changes in the route structures; this might mean, for instance, that a smaller partner concentrates on operating within a continent, gives up intercontinental traffic and thus has a chance to dispose of its wide-body fleet. However, estimating aircraft productivity improvement thanks to route or fleet changes in monetary terms is very difficult. Guidance can be sought in past research, which has suggested that if a medium-sized European carrier can reduce the number of aircraft types in the fleet from five to two, this reduction would offer cost reduction similar to a six to seven per cent cut in employee salaries or an increase of 1.3 percentage points in load factors.[9]

A prerequisite for many areas of productivity improvement is that information systems of alliance members are compatible. This will enhance flow of information and will thus result in the ultimate goal of seamless service. But it is questionable whether compatible information systems would necessarily lead to higher efficiency and lower costs in short-to-medium term. It appears that information systems of airlines are so extensively customised that making them compatible will take years and substantial amounts of money. An example of that is given by

KLM, which set a five-year time frame for achieving common use of IT resources between Alitalia, Northwest Airlines, and itself.

Building on past research of airline productivity and performance[10] we can propose a framework for assessing the overall benefits of alliances, including the cost and revenue impacts (Figure 7.5). As this framework presents the accrued benefits, one must remember that performance assessment should take into account all the alliance-related costs, too. These costs include direct investments in new information systems and equipment, but more important is the time that the company management spends on alliance issues, and this should be honestly allocated to the cost side of alliance assessment.

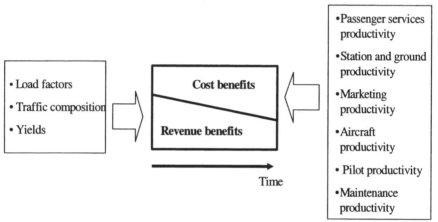

Figure 7.5   Alliance benefit framework for performance assessment

Profitability

So, at the end of the day, airlines aim at improving their financial performance through alliances. Along with enhanced revenues and better productivity, the profitability of allied airlines is expected to rise. But again, it is very difficult to find evidence on the cause-and-effect relationship between a particular form of co-operation in an alliance and profit improvement. Research by Oum et al. (2000), building on data from 1985-96, suggested that forming an alliance enabled partner airlines to improve profitability by an average of 0.3 per cent. Just as with productivity, discussed above, the study found out that profitability gains from major alliances were clearly greater than from minor alliances, and concluded that profitability gains were mostly resulting from improved productivity.

It is difficult to put any figures on profit improvement through a particular measure or function in an alliance. What makes this assessment difficult is the fact that airlines have, up to now, experienced mostly revenue-related improvements in profitability, and the cost-related benefits are only gradually showing. At this still early stage of development in alliances, the best source of information may only be the estimates given by airlines; however, it is wise to examine these numbers carefully, as will be discussed in Chapter 8.

The challenge for airlines and industry observers now lies in developing metrics that can be used in assessing the performance implications of alliances. Particularly difficult is the assessment of the forward-looking, strategic variables and their value in alliances. Further, if one includes inherent risks of alliances in the analysis and tries to give them some sort of a quantified value, developing appropriate metrics becomes a mighty task, indeed. Overall it seems that analysing the performance, and the eventual financial impact of alliances for airlines, may prove significantly more complicated than in the case of alliances in most manufacturing industries.

Notes

[1] Oum et al., 1992, 493.
[2] Windle and Dresner, 1992.
[3] See Atkinson et al., 1997.
[4] *Air Transport World*, February 1999.
[5] See Anderson, 1990.
[6] *Aviation Week & Space Technology*, 17 November 1997.
[7] *Avmark Aviation Economist*, May 1999.
[8] Collet, 1998.
[9] Seristö, 1995, 201.
[10] See e.g. Seristö, 1995.

References

Air Transport World, February 1999.
Anderson, E. (1990), 'Two Firms, One Frontier: on Assessing Joint Venture Performance', *Sloan Management Review*, vol. 31, no. 2, pp. 19-30.
Atkinson, A., Fleenor, C. and Toh, R. (1997), 'A Stakeholder Approach to Strategic Performance Measurement', *Sloan Management Review*, vol. 38, no. 3, pp. 25-37.
Aviation Week & Space Technology, 17 November, 1997.
Avmark Aviation Economist, May 1999.
Bamford, J. and Ernst, D. (2002), *Managing an Alliance Portfolio, The McKinsey Quarterly*, 3/2002, pp. 28-39.
Bruning, (1991), 'Operating Efficiency in International Airline Industry', *International Journal of Transport Economics*, October 1991.
Collett, N. (1998), *Airfinance Journal*, April 1998, pp. 38-41.
Dussauge, P. and Garrette, B. (1995), 'Determinants of Success in International Strategic Alliances: Evidence from the Global Aerospace Industry', *Journal of International Business*, 3rd Quarter, pp. 505-530.
Morrell, P. and Pilon, R. (1999), 'KLM and Northwest: a Survey of the Impact of a Passenger Alliance on Cargo Service Characteristics', *Journal of Air Transport Management*, no. 5, pp. 153-160.

Oum, T., Park, J.-H. and Zhang, A. (2000), *Globalization and Strategic Alliances: the Case of the Airline Industry*, Pergamon, Elsevier Science, Kidlington.

Oum, T., Tretheway, M. and Waters, W. (1992), 'Concepts, Methods and Purposes of Productivity Measurement in Transportation', *Transportation Research*, no. 6 (1992).

Saramaa, T. (1998), *Strategic Alliance Performance Measurement*, Helsinki School of Economics and Business Administration Press, Helsinki.

Schefczyk, M. (1993), 'Operational Performance of Airlines: an Extension of Traditional Measurement Paradigms', *Strategic Management Journal*, vol. 14, pp. 301-317.

Seristö, H. (1995), *Airline Performance and Costs: an Analysis of Performance Measurement and Cost Reduction in Major Airlines*, Helsinki School of Economics Press, Helsinki.

Chapter 8

Extraction of Financial Benefits by Alliance Partners

Introduction

The ultimate goal for most airlines in joining alliances is to improve financial performance. Intermediate objectives can be numerous, the most obvious being survival, increase in market share, increase in yields, or reduction in operating costs. The airline industry is such a complex business, though not necessarily very much different from most of the fast-cycle businesses of today, comprising so many interdependent variables that have an effect on the financial performance of companies, that it is not easy to extract the exact cause for fluctuation in financial performance. Factors that make the airline business unique include the fact that operations are still regulated extensively, for example in the area of safety, and the fact that infrastructure is congested in some markets. Also, all operators use the same airports and aircraft types, making it very difficult to differentiate within this business; moreover, cost levels vary significantly from country to country for historical reasons.

Airline alliances are still continuously evolving, and we have not yet seen all the financial benefits that are to be reaped. Evidently, the structure of an alliance has an impact on the financial benefits to be gained. It may be rather easy to determine benefits in a simple code-share arrangement between two carriers, but it is very difficult to quantify the benefits in a versatile multipartner arrangement where codesharing, joint purchasing, shared use of ground facilities, etc. are involved. It has been suggested that in the first phase, most of the financial benefits are accrued from the revenue side, thanks to increased volumes and perhaps increased yields, too. It appears that the financial benefits from the cost side are to be gained at a later stage: in other words, improved productivity and thus lower operating costs, and lower prices in purchasing material and services. The issue of financial benefits is tightly linked to the issue of performance in airlines, which was discussed in more detail in the previous chapter. This chapter is therefore rather brief, focusing narrowly on the financial benefits.

In the discussion on financial benefits one must remember that the times after September 11th, and SARS in 2003, have been very testing for airlines, and they airlines have been very much occupied with internal cost reduction campaigns, apparently having less energy and time for joint initiatives with partner airlines. It appears that particularly multi-partner efforts to create alliance-wide common platforms for IT services have been put on hold, and airlines have rather worked more on a bilateral basis with selected partners.

Sources of financial benefits

Oneworld's managing partner, Peter Buecking, estimated in November 2002 that the linkages to eight airlines bring about benefits of nearly one billion US dollars by generating revenue and reducing costs. As to cost reduction, it was estimated that by the end of 2002 the initiatives at oneworld would have produced cost reduction in the 'hundreds of millions of dollars'.[1] In summer 2003, Lufthansa CEO Jürgen Weber saw that at least 50 per cent of the alliance benefits are now on the cost side.[2] Naturally, the division of benefits, that is, enhanced revenues versus reduced costs, may vary from one airline to another. Petri Pentti, CFO at Finnair, characterised the benefits from the oneworld membership in spring 2003 as 'it's very much focused on the revenue side'.[3]

The sources of benefits from alliances can be put into three categories:

- market-presence related benefit;
- resource-utilisation related benefit;
- learning of new and improved practices.

Learning of better practices is, in a way, an indirect source of benefit as it would eventually lead to financial benefits, either through better utilisation of revenues, in other words, better productivity, or through higher revenues.

As to market-presence related benefits, it is the enhanced revenues that are the ultimate objective. This may be attained through a larger catchment area for a carrier's route network, something that may result in higher load factors and can be gained by code-sharing with a large partner. Revenues may be enhanced through higher yields, too, and this is possible in two ways; either the mix of passengers shifts towards high-yield business-class passengers, or the overall level of fares can be raised. It has been suggested that there is potential for two to five per cent revenue enhancement through alliancing in a typical scheduled service airline. How much revenue enhancement potential there is depends partly on whether there is room to grow at major partners' key hub airports. If the availability of slots is very much restricted, much of the revenue increase potential may be impossible to realise.

Resource utilisation benefits can be accrued, for instance, from higher labour or aircraft productivity and from lower costs of procured goods and services. Most of the cost reduction potential is in labour costs, whether the labour is in marketing, maintenance, ground handling or flight operations. Other avenues for cost reduction are in equipment and property costs, capital costs for aircraft, and expenses paid for third party services such as ground handling. Within marketing, the payments for the distribution channel, in other words CRSs and travel agencies, offer a potential for cost reduction. In fact, there appear to be quite many cost cutting possibilities if airline alliance groups got together to start bargaining strongly for lower commissions and fees for CRS services.

Salomon Smith Barney estimated in 1998 that the operating profit improvement at British Airways, thanks to the alliance with American Airlines, would in the first phase come almost entirely from enhanced revenues, but would eventually materialise from cost savings, so that in four years cost savings would make up nearly half the profit improvement figures.[4]

Even if it is very difficult to get exact figures on enhanced revenues and reduced costs from airlines, in early 2004 it is possible to estimate that during the first few years of alliance group activity the benefits indeed came mostly from the revenue side. It has taken longer than expected to gain significant cost reduction benefits but it appears that the great potential in the future is in the cost reduction side, and cost reduction is where the airlines now focus on.

In the following we shall briefly discuss the particular sources of financial benefits through cost reduction and try to give some rough estimates on the magnitude of benefits. As many airline costs are in fact fixed, we have a basis for quantifying such estimates. However, estimates on revenue enhancement are significantly more difficult to quantify as there are so many uncontrollable variables affecting demand and revenues. In the discussion, it is assumed that the alliance does not make radical changes in the route network of a member airline; if that was to happen, then the changes on the cost side – and of course revenue – can be significant.

Labour cost reduction

Restructuring labour-intensive functions will inevitably mean that part of the workforce will have to go. Radical views have suggested that, worldwide, the airline workforce will be reduced by a minimum of 30 per cent from the levels prior to September 11th. It has been suggested that the order in which labour costs are targeted in different functions of airlines will be as follows:

* sales offices
* maintenance
* passenger services
* cabin crew.

Joining forces in international marketing and sales provides considerable opportunities for reduction of personnel costs. The magnitude is easily estimated as we know that the overall cost of one marketing person in a foreign location in Western Europe and North America is roughly USD 100,000 per year. Marketing and sales function rationalisation may be relatively easy to amalgamate, but welding maintenance or information technology departments together is a much more demanding and costly exercise. Therefore the cost reduction potential, for instance, in maintenance has to be approached with a long-term view. Nevertheless, a large scale in maintenance is likely to bring cost savings; a study by Booz-Allen & Hamilton (1994) has suggested that airframe shops that employ at least 2.5 million man-hours per year enjoy an 18 per cent cost advantage over shops that are half their size.

In case the alliance allows for fleet structure rationalisation, the savings in cabin and cockpit personnel costs through better utilisation of crews may be substantial. For instance, if the number of pilot crews per aircraft could be reduced from six to five, in a mid-sized carrier this could mean that there is a need for 200 fewer pilots, resulting in an annual saving of, say, USD 25-30 million. However, in the short term it is unlikely that such cost reductions from flying personnel are possible, because it is not expected that the unions would easily allow a reduction in the number of pilots or cabin attendants.

Concerning passenger services other than cabin services, there is potential for more cost savings in the airport functions of airlines. This is also proved by the extent that airlines have started to outsource services at airports. The mechanism to realise cost savings is that partner carriers share tasks in check-in, baggage handling and other ground handling. Just to give an idea of the magnitude of potential savings, and to reflect them against the savings figures given by airlines, it can be estimated that if a medium-sized European carrier is able to reduce by only 20 per cent its airport workforce at a major hub airport in Europe, it can save some ten million US dollars annually.

Cost reduction in sourcing

If alliance group members are jointly able to bargain for even slightly lower prices of goods and services in their sourcing, the savings may be quite considerable. Savings potential has been estimated to be up to 25 per cent. The volume and value of sourcing are significant: the purchasing organisation of Star Alliance spent, in the late 1990s, some nine billion US dollars annually on outside purchases, excluding fuel and new transports; purchases including fuel were in the region of USD 15 billion.[5] Star Alliance worked, in 2000, on an internet-based technical parts and services exchange; Air Canada expected to save five to ten per cent in annual purchases thanks to this venture, resulting in an annual saving of some USD 200 million.[6] A competing exchange or e-commerce portal called aviationX claimed that conducting sourcing transactions over the network would cut costs by 15 per cent and would potentially bring savings of USD 300 million per year to the commercial aviation industry.[7] Another such venture, Sabre's e-Marketplace, estimated that savings in purchasing would be in the magnitude of 10-15 per cent.

Oneworld spends more than five billion US dollars on engineering, without staff costs, and the group has formed a special task force comprising the heads of maintenance from each member airline to develop joint engineering and maintenance specifications across all the members.[8]

An area where there may be great potential for cost reduction is aircraft purchasing, but it appears that, so far, airlines have not been able to coordinate their action in fleet planning and aircraft configuration. The challenge in fleet planning, of course, is the fact that airlines have the historical 'burden' of an existing fleet structure, which is not easy to change in a short time. Also, the aircraft interior configuration is one of the few measures available to differentiate the product offering, and carriers seem willing to specify the interiors to their very needs and tastes, thus making it difficult to reach full commonality advantages. Moreover, flight crews are used to certain layouts in the cabin, galleys and cockpits, so changes in the layouts are not necessarily welcomed. One of the most notable joint aircraft acquisition programs is that of Star, or rather Austrian Airlines, Lufthansa, SAS and Air Canada, to purchase regional jets – the number of aircraft discussed has been between 100 and 200. Austrian's CEO, Sörensen, said in summer 2003 that one of the greatest benefits in the joint purchase of similar aircraft would be the ability to easily lease jets to each other.[9]

An interesting example of the challenges in joint sourcing is provided by Star, which started in 1997 exploring savings opportunities by setting up a committee to look at joint purchasing for in-cabin products. Standardising something as basic as plastic cups for the economy class proved difficult, because the member carriers could not agree on where to put their logos and how big the brim should be – United States airlines prefer a wide top for lots of ice, while Europeans use fewer ice cubes.[10]

Concerning aircraft purchasing, there have been estimates that a large alliance group could get discounts in the magnitude of ten per cent off the 'normal' prices. However, it is not self-evident what a normal price is, since there has always been room for price negotiations in large aircraft orders. Nevertheless, even relatively small discounts would be welcomed, as airlines in major alliance groups have acquired new aircraft worth some USD 20 billion annually, except for the disastrous years right after September 11th.

Airlines increasingly source handling, including catering, from non-airline firms; the number of handling companies in the world has roughly quadrupled during the last decade. Also, there is a developing trend of handling companies internationalising, which may in the future provide more opportunities for large alliance-wide accounts with handling service providers.

Airlines have long outsourced a large part of their sales and distribution function through travel agents and CRSs. Some airlines see CRS costs as one object for cost reduction through alliances. Strong alliance groups may be able to bypass CRSs and go directly to the travel agents or even to the consumers. One measure which has already been used by airlines is the reduction of commissions to travel agents. With the increased bargaining power of large consortiums such efforts might be easier to realise in the future.

Making financial benefits come true

There will be difficulties in driving through the changes that are needed for realising the potential benefits discussed above. First of all, organisations in general are often rather rigid and resist major changes in practices. Airlines may represent the type of companies that are not the most flexible of organisations; the history of particularly larger European carriers is rather bureaucratic, and there is still an older generation of employees who might not be easily motivated into new ways of operating. Also, the unions in air transport are very strong and seem to have taken a rather cautious view on alliances. It is expected that any measures which result in the reduction of personnel will create opposition from the unions.

Changing and streamlining operations within alliances naturally require investments. For instance, Star Alliance has had a five-year budget of more than USD 100 million for operational activities. This sum is provided by member carriers according to their size and the benefits they reap in certain markets.[11] Airlines are quite willing to publicise their revenue enhancement and cost savings, which they eventually expect to get from these improved practices, but are somewhat reluctant to talk about the investments required to realise these savings. As an example of the magnitude of investments, KLM reportedly invested some USD 100 million in the collapsed Alitalia alliance through the Malpensa airport development alone.

Another question is how the authorities would view the increasing integration in alliances. It may be that stricter limitations will be imposed on alliances, if they lead to de facto merged functions among partners. This would make the realisation of financial benefits difficult. On the other hand, pressure appears to be mounting for competition authorities to allow the airline industry develop into a true MNE industry, in other words, an industry where there are large, globally operating market-driven firms which are truly multinational enterprises. The recent cases of Air France and KLM, and British Airways and Iberia, give a reason to believe that true consolidation will be allowed by the authorities.

Airline views on financial benefits

A rather wide spectrum of numbers has been presented about the financial benefits from alliances. Of course, to a large extent, these numbers are at this stage of alliance evolution mostly estimates. However, it is interesting to compile the views of the airlines and consultants on what financial benefits the airlines can expect; first, from the enhanced traffic and revenues, and second, from reduced costs. In the following, we summarise the estimates of the industry from recent years.

Traffic increase

Experiences have been rather compelling: Austrian Airlines experienced a dramatic increase in the number of boardings on its transatlantic routes since joining the Atlantic Excellence Alliance. The emplanements rose from 150,000 in 1995 to some 265,000 in 1998.[12] Of course, the question that arises is how much of that is actually from joining the alliance. As Austrian Airlines joined Star Alliance in 2000, it expected overall synergy benefits worth USD 23 million per year.[13]

United Airlines' average number of passengers on its Chicago-Frankfurt flights increased from 110 passengers to 212 passengers after linking with Lufthansa. For Lufthansa flights, the average boardings per flight rose from 134 to 186. Also, it was estimated that the Atlantic Excellence Alliance achieved passenger demand growth of 23.5 per cent per annum, compared with overall demand growth of 9.7 per cent on North Atlantic routes during the first ten months of its existence.[14]

Revenue enhancement

United Airlines executives expected the Star alliance to contribute an extra USD 200 million to revenues annually. SAS CEO Stenberg forecasted in 1997 that the Star Alliance would add some USD 250 million to the company's operating revenues within some three years.[15] Elsewhere, SAS forecasted that the Star Alliance will contribute at least five per cent of its revenue at the turn of the millennium.[16] It has also been suggested that SAS's contribution to income from the Star Alliance cooperation was USD 40 million in 1997, USD 60 million in 1998 and USD 100 million in 1999.[17] Air Canada claimed that it was getting USD 270 million in additional revenues annually thanks to Star Alliance.[18]

It was estimated that the marketing and code-sharing arrangement between Continental and America West would give some USD 40 million in additional revenues.[19] All Nippon Airways has estimated that it benefits some USD 100 million in additional revenues thanks to Star Alliance, a five per cent boost to international services revenue.[20] It was estimated that Qantas would enjoy a revenue increase of USD 25 million per year, owing to its code sharing agreement with British Airways.[21] Delta Air Lines estimated in the spring 2000 that the Delta and Air France led alliance will bring Delta some USD 400 million in extra revenue in 2000.[22] In 2003 the so-called alliance gross revenue for Delta was some USD 600 million, representing about five per cent of Delta's overall revenues.[23] In 2003, Air France CEO Spinetta said that closer ties amongst the SkyTeam members in the area of scheduling, marketing and sales are expected to produce up to USD 100 million in additional revenues in the following three years.[24]

Cost reduction

Lufthansa and SAS have expected (labour) productivity increases between four and five per cent thanks to the Star alliance arrangements.[25] Lufthansa estimated that the cost reduction programs within the Star Alliance will bring the airline savings of some USD 200 million.

Alitalia and KLM expected in 1999 to cut combined annual operating costs by an estimated USD 400 million, and expected the savings to increase significantly over the years.[26] It was further estimated that most of the cost savings would come from merging sales and marketing operations; each partner was to be responsible for sales and marketing in its home market, but in third markets the partners would have shown a combined presence.[27] On the other side of the Atlantic, it was estimated in 1999 that the marketing and code-sharing arrangement between Continental and America West would accumulate some ten million US dollars in cost savings for Continental annually.[28]

As to more concrete cost savings, SkyTeam members launched combined tenders for fuel and were able to reduce ground handling costs by some 20-40 per cent at five South American airports.[29] In December 2003, Star Alliance founded Star Alliance FuelCo which is starting operations as an American-based company in 2004. In another concrete example of savings reached, the eight airlines of oneworld saved some ten million US dollars in 2002 through concerted purchases of headsets only.

Going beyond alliance, the Air France-KLM merger was justified through significant cost savings. Air France estimated in the autumn 2003 that the merger would reduce costs by some 75 million euros in the first year and between 400 and 500 million euros within five years.[30] This may seems massive, but in fact represents only about a two to three per cent reduction in the companies' combined cost base. Even this level of cost reduction was deemed unrealistic by some observers, as they believed that the relatively belligerent unions would not tolerate the means to such savings.

Profit improvement

It was estimated in the mid-1990s that the KLM-Northwest alliance yielded USD 200 million a year in operating profits.[31] Code-sharing between United Airlines and Lufthansa reportedly added USD 100 million to United's profits.[32] United Airlines estimated that Star alliance accounted for some ten per cent of the airline's profits in 1998. Air Canada and Lufthansa have given estimates of the same magnitude. In 1999, Lufthansa claimed to have made a profit of some USD 200 million thanks to Star in 1998, and estimated that the figure for 1999 is more than USD 250 million.[33] Ansett had estimated the profit improvement, thanks to Star, to be at least ten per cent. Air France expected in 1999 that it experiences a profit improvement of some USD 165 million annually through the scale economies and enhanced revenues thanks to its alliance with Delta Air Lines; Delta has expected similar benefits from the alliance.[34]

In conclusion

Gemini Consulting has suggested that in a typical mid-sized flag carrier, a loose marketing alliance could bring about cost savings of some two per cent; but if the alliance is a more integrated and unified structure, the benefits could be in the range of more than ten per cent.[35] Summarising the above-presented estimates by airlines concerning the enhancement of revenues, reduction in costs and improvement in profits thanks to alliances – compared with the time before alliance, in other words, not compounding annually when in the alliance – we can recapitulate the following:

- in broad alliance arrangements revenue enhancement varied between one and seven per cent;
- cost reduction expected was typically between one and two per cent;
- profit improvement expected was typically in the region of ten per cent.

Interestingly, research by Oum et al. (2000) found out that between 1985-96 the profit improvement in a sample of 22 airlines thanks to alliances was only 0.3 per cent on average; improvements of profitability in major alliances (typically broader alliances) were 1.4 per cent. Based on the research one might suggest that airlines are today overly optimistic about the profit enhancement potential in alliancing; however, the alliances of today are more extensive and more tightly integrated than the alliances in the late 1980s and early 1990s, so the optimism is perhaps warranted.

It is important to remember that airlines have very different objectives for alliances and have also very different cost bases. Therefore, it is rather useless to try to give any guidelines on what kind of revenue enhancement or cost reduction targets alliance members should aim at. Moreover, there are numerous obstacles in the way of making financial benefits a reality. Perhaps the safest conclusion is that there are significant financial benefits to be reaped through alliances, but these benefits are not easily realised.

Another way to look at the financial effects of alliancing is to take the customer view. Brueckner (2003) studied the impact of airline cooperation on the level of interline fares paid by international passengers, focusing on three measures of cooperation: alliance membership, code-sharing and antitrust immunity. The conclusion of the study was that these three cooperative forms jointly lead to a 27 per cent reduction in interline fares; the immunity enjoyed by Star alliance partners generated in 1999 an aggregate benefit of some USD 80 million for interline passengers. However, Brueckner and other observers have noted that for nonstop trips between international gateway airports, such as Chicago and Frankfurt, on a single partner airline the fares may indeed rise, partly offsetting the gains enjoyed by interline passengers – in this case cooperation could be anticompetitive.

Finally, just to give an alternative perspective to the presented profit-and-loss-account perspective of financial benefits, let us have a few words on alliances and airline share prices. Park and Zhang (1998) studied the impact of the announcement of alliances on the share prices of both the involved partner airlines and their key rivals. The study concluded that announcements which increased the probability that a strategic alliance will be implemented were perceived as good news and raised the share prices of the partner airlines. On the other hand, announcements that changed the probability of a successful alliance affected rival firms' values negatively. In other words, investors considered complementary strategic alliances to be valuable activities which make the partners more competitive. The conclusion of that study could be that it pays to be publicly optimistic and ambitious concerning one's own airline alliance plans. Undoubtedly management in most airlines would welcome higher prices for their stocks.

Notes

1 *AWST*, 18 November 2002.
2 *AWST*, 9 June 2003.
3 *Aircraft Economics*, May 2003.
4 *Airline Business*, April 1998.

5   Proctor, 1999; Tarry, 1999.
6   *ATI*, 14 April 2000.
7   *ATI*, 5 April, 2000.
8   *Airfinance Journal*, March 2003.
9   *AWST*, 9 June, 2003.
10 *Wall Street Journal*, 20 May 2003.
11 Knibb, 1999.
12 Flint, 1998.
13 Solon, 2000.
14 *Air Transport Week*, April 1999.
15 Taverna, 1997.
16 *Airfinance Journal*, June 1997.
17 *Avmark Aviation Economist*, April 2000.
18 McMillan, 1999.
19 *Avmark Aviation Economist*, April 1999.
20 *Airline Business*, February 2000.
21 Collett, 1998.
22 *ATI*, 3 April 2000.
23 Paul Matsen, Delta SVP, in SkyTeam Steering Committee Roundtable, Dallas, July 2003.
24 *AWST*, 18 August 2003.
25 *Airfinance Journal*, April 1998.
26 Sparaco, 1999.
27 Gill, 1999.
28 *Avmark Aviation Economist*, April 1999.
29 *AWST*, 7 October 2002.
30 *WSJ*, 30 September 2003.
31 Tully, 1996.
32 Phillips, 1997.
33 Zehle, 1999; *Air Transport World*, December 1999.
34 *Aviation Week & Space Technology*, 28 June 1999.
35 *Airline Business*, November 1999.

References

Baker, C. (2003), *Airline Business*, November 2003, pp. 30-32.

Bennett, B. (1999), *Airline Business*, October 1999, p. 9.

Booz-Allen & Hamilton (1994), A Survey of Airline Maintenance Benchmarks, San Francisco.

Brueckner, J. (2003), The Benefits of Codesharing and Antitrust Immunity for International Passengers, with an Application to the Star Alliance. *Journal of Air Transport Management*, vol. 9, issue 2, pp. 83-89.

Collett, N. (1998), *Airfinance Journal*, April 1998, pp. 38-41.
Feldman, J. (2002), *Air Transport World*, vol. 39, no. 11, pp. 56-57.
Flint, P. (19998), *Air Transport World*, April 1998.
Flottau, J. (2002), *Aviation Week and Space Technology*, 7 October, 2002, p. 50.
Flottau, J. (2003), *Aviation Week and Space Technology*, 9 June, 2003, p. 24.
Gill, T. (1999), *Airline Business*, January 1999, p. 31.
Johnson, K. and Gauthier-Villars, D. (2003), *Wall Street Journal*, September 30, 2003, p. A2.
Knibb, D. (1999), *Airline Business*, July 1999.
McMillan, B. (1999), *Airline Business*, November 1999, p. 9.
Michaels, D. and Lunsford, J.L. (2003), *Wall Street Journal*, 20 May, 2003, p. A3.
Oum, T., Park, J.-H. and Zhang, A. (2000), *Globalization and Strategic Alliances: the Case of the Airline Industry,* Pergamon, Elsevier Science, Kidlington.
Ott, J. (2002), *Aviation Week and Space Technology*, 18 November, 2002, p. 65.
Park, J. and Zhang, A. (1998), 'Strategic Alliance and Firm Value – a Case Study of the British Airways / USAir Alliance', paper presented at the 1998 Air Transport Research Group of the WCTR Society Conference.
Phillips, E. (1997), *Aviation Week and Space Technology*, 17 November, 1997, p. 67.
Proctor, P. (1998), *Aviation Week & Space Technology*, 5 July, 1999.
SkyTeam Steering Committee Roundtable meeting, Dallas, Texas, July 17th 2003.
Solon, D. (2000), *Avmark Aviation Economist*, May 2000, pp. 12-13.
Sparaco, P. (1999), *Aviation Week and Space Technology*, 9 August, 1999, p. 34.
Sparaco, P. (2003), *Aviation Week and Space Technology*, 18 August, 2003, p. 36.
Tarry, C. (1999), *Airline Business*, June 1999, pp. 90-92.
Taverna, M. (1997), *Aviation Week and Space Technology*, 27 October, 1997, p. 37.
Tully, S. (1996), *Fortune*, 24 June, 1996, pp. 64-71.
Zehle, S. (1999), *Manager Magazine*, 12/1999, pp. 134-164.

Chapter 9

Challenges to Federation Governance

Airline alliances have become much more than just a collection of codeshares and mutually recognised Frequent Flyer Programmes between several partners. They increasingly take on some characteristics of organisations in their own right. In some cases, alliance group governance structures (such as Star's 'AMT' – Alliance Management Team – and oneworld's Management Company) are set up. These groups can take a variety of governance structures. One important characteristic of a governance structure is the number and type of member airlines, and how they are linked to each other. For example, they can be a community of equals, where each member has the same weight in deciding alliance matters. Or they consist of a very heterogeneous membership, where two or three lead airlines are often surrounded by smaller partners that provide them with feed. As the number (and diversity) of alliance group members increases, so will its complexity. Growing complexity in a system of relatively independent units means that at some point, coordination between the units becomes so difficult that there will be a need for some structural governance. It is at this point that the alliance becomes an organisation in its own right. Eventually, this organisation acquires some degree of authority over member airlines, and members are deeply embedded in the group structure so as to make it fairly difficult for them to leave.

There are three main rationales behind the formation of alliance group governance structures: the first is the provision of a forum for discussion (and consensus-seeking) for managers of member airlines. Thus, the governance structure serves as a coordinator for meetings, and as a steering mechanism for the numerous working groups and committees that are set up often at middle management levels between participating airlines. The second rationale is somewhat more authoritarian and refers to the speeding up of decision-making processes. As the governance structure itself acquires some authority over members, the often very slow democratic decision making process should not have to be gone through in certain routine issues. Thus, decisions which are considered to be routine are taken by the alliance governance body, on behalf of members. The third rationale is that the existence of such an alliance management company sends a signal to the outside world that the alliance group is indeed an arrangement to which members are dedicated. It thus has a certain role of communicating and reinforcing the alliance brand identity.

The reasons for setting up such a governance structure are fairly straightforward, but the exact details of how to set it up, how much authority it should be given, and what exactly its job would be, have yet to be decided upon in each airline alliance case. Indeed, it appears that, beyond a certain basic structure, airlines themselves are still very much experimenting with which structure – and, most importantly, what degree of leverage over their own strategy – they want to give these governance bodies.

The basic setup of alliance governance bodies is common to each alliance group: at the top of the structure sits what is often called an alliance management 'company', which typically consists of relatively few fixed staff. These alliance managers can either be former employees of member airlines (or on secondment), or they are hired from the outside. It is their role to arrange, preside over, and coordinate meetings between alliance committees. These committees, in turn, consist of managers from member airlines, who often meet regularly to discuss specific issues. The member airlines' CEOs meet each other on a certain schedule, as do the managerial levels below. There are different committees according to functional areas (e.g. Marketing, IT, Flight Operations, Sales, etc), geographic regions, and also according to hierarchy. Interestingly, different hierarchy levels operate according to a different logic: at middle management levels, the committees are really task forces. The task force members are expected to fulfil a certain technical or administrative function, or to accomplish a clearly defined project or task – such as, to take up a previous example, to harmonise IT based departure control systems across members. People are in the task force to complete a certain joint project, and even though they are employed by, and responsible to, one specific airline, they are rewarded for how well they accomplish their task force jobs. In other words, it is often the middle managers that first get confronted with acting truly *on behalf of the collaboration itself*, of the alliance as a joint venture (in the sense of the word). At senior management levels, however, the brief of committee members is often that of establishing consensus between members, or just 'sounding out' other parties. The members of these committees *clearly pursue the agendas of their respective airlines*. A senior manager is responsible to (and employed by) his airline's owners. His actions are likely to reflect this, even (or especially) in alliance steering group meetings.

It is here that one of the principal challenges to alliance group governance can be found: while integration and consolidation of an alliance governance structure is worked towards in some areas, the main rationale underlying senior managers' actions is still very much oriented toward a single firm, not so much the alliance group itself. This chapter will discuss the challenging task of alliance group building and governance in view of these countervailing forces.

The structure of airline alliance groups

In general management literature, quite a lot has been written about alliances and Joint Ventures between two or sometimes three partners. Literature dealing with multilateral alliances, however, is still relatively scarce. One reason for this is that multilateral alliances, or formal networks between firms, are still a fairly recent phenomenon. Multilateral alliances have been called 'constellations', 'blocks', even 'cliques', but these labels refer more often than not to inter-firm networks that are based on rather informal ties (such as social contacts between managers), short-term contracts, or contractual links that only concern a part, but not the whole operation, of a firm. Very little is known about formal, long-term ties between entire firms, and about the challenges inherent in trying to organise, let alone govern, such a fairly complex arrangement.

An airline alliance group can be described as a multilateral, formal network of airlines that have formed sets of bilateral strategic alliances with each other, or with the alliance group itself. It is possible to distinguish four basic structural types of alliance groups:

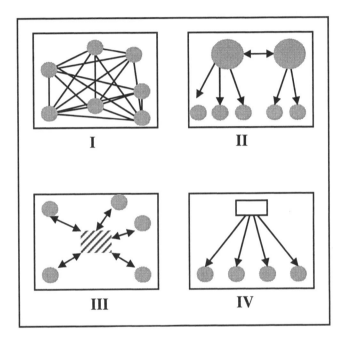

Figure 9.1   Four basic types of multilateral alliances

Type I can be considered to be a true multilateral network. Every firm in the group has some sort of alliance agreement with every other firm. In this type of multilateral alliance, there is no locus of decision-making (or alliance authority) outside any member firm. Cooperative decisions are mainly taken on the level of bi- or trilateral negotiation between members. This is potentially time-consuming and inefficient, but has the advantage of leaving issues open to re-negotiation at certain intervals. A further advantage is that this type of structure carries a low requirement for an institutionalisation of the alliance group itself; the 'alliance' comprises a brand and possibly a linkage of Frequent Flyer Programmes, but it does not require members to submit to any decisions taken at alliance level. Members retain a maximum of organisational autonomy. This type of structure also facilitates the building of parallel alliances, e.g. cooperative networks in areas such as procurement, e-sales or cargo, which comprise carriers that do not necessarily codeshare or otherwise cooperate on the marketing side.

One important characteristic of such a structure is the relatively high within-competition; at every round of negotiation, each firm would seek to maximise its own advantage; there is relatively little incentive to create, and sustain, structures that are alliance group related. The high within-competition also implies a relatively unstable immediate task environment for each member firm, making specialisation a riskier strategy. Hence, while members in this configuration would retain a maximum of independence, they would also have to face the inefficiencies of operating in an unstable environment, and although costs sunk into alliance membership would be relatively low, they would need to face relatively higher recurring coordination costs in order to reap at least some benefits from alliancing. This type of structure would be appropriate for airlines who primarily seek to extend their scope, by cooperating with one or two key partners, and who feel capable of maintaining their standalone capability (see Chapter 3). An example for a Type I alliance group was the early Star alliance. It is likely that a Type I alliance is a temporary stage toward a more centralised, or dominated, alliance type, especially if there is growth in membership.

Type II is a 'dominated network' in that there are lead, or hub firms, which maintain hierarchical links with firms within their own networks, such as two airlines cooperating with each other, while both are fed by local smaller carriers. An early example for a pure Type II alliance is the early KLM-Northwest alliance, where each of the partners is fed by regional partners (CityHopper and Northwest Airlink respectively). A variant of Type II would be a single-leader alliance group, such as the (now defunct) Qualiflyer group, where each of the members had a strong and hierarchical link to the lead airline, Swissair.

Type III is an alliance group that already has a structure which belongs to the group, but to no one member alone. This organisational type can be called a confederation. The confederation has been defined as 'an alliance of independent, sovereign states in a union of common norms and rules in which the operations are defined and carried out by each state'.[1] This can be transferred quite easily to the air transport context by replacing 'state' with 'airline'. Note that in this cooperative form, bi- or trilateral negotiations between partners are still frequent, but, in addition to these, there is a formal structure that facilitates group-wide discussion. Hence, the individual airline in this type of alliance has two types of relationships to manage: one is still the relationships with other airlines. The second type of relationship is that with the alliance group itself. This structure can also be likened to the idealised state organisation of the 'polis' in ancient Greece, where all full citizens of a city state convened to establish policy consensus. The creation and maintenance of a 'forum for democracy' will require a medium level of costs sunk into the alliance; in other words, members invest in the alliance itself. The effectiveness of this forum concept would still depend strongly on member consensus. This consensus, in turn, can be reached easier if membership to the forum is limited in numbers and relatively homogeneous (but with non-overlapping route systems in the airline case). An early example of this form of alliance is the current oneworld set-up: alliance members have created a oneworld management company that currently serves as a forum provider and decision-making facilitator for fairly democratic decision-making, and which is widely expected to take on more formal authority in the future.

The more heterogeneous the members of such a 'polis' are, the more one can expect that some of them will form within-groups, or clusters, that comprise a small number of members that agree on certain issues and press ahead with their implementation without waiting for alliance-wide consensus to be established. An airline alliance group where clustering can be currently observed is the Star alliance: Lufthansa is building clusters in IT systems with its neighbours SAS and Austrian, and traffic joint ventures with SAS, Austrian, British Midland and United. Clusters can be considered to be alliances within the alliance, and they could be a sign of a Type III alliance moving toward a more hierarchical form – either a Type II 'Empire' (as some industry observers would interpret Lufthansa's moves), or toward a Type IV alliance with a governance superstructure (see below).

Type IV is the most hierarchical alliance in that here members relinquish a significant degree of authority to the alliance group itself. The appropriate analogy would be that of a Federation: 'In contrast to the confederation, the federation has a strong central power, and the individual states have much less authority'.[2] Here, many issues of network management, branding, marketing, procurement and some aspects of sales (such as FFP) are determined at the level of the superstructure – the alliance management organisation. An important characteristic of an alliance group is its exclusivity,[3] or the degree to which an alliance is insulated from other alliances. This constitutes the outside boundary of the alliance. Type IV is the most exclusive type of alliance, where the presence of a clear hierarchy requires the definition of boundaries. Even if individual members do maintain ties with contributors from outside the alliance, the nature and degree of these links is likely to be influenced by the focal airline's membership in the hierarchical Type IV organisation. It is at the level of a Type IV alliance that an alliance group starts to behave much like a diversified firm, and no longer as a coalition of independent actors. There are several advantages to such a highly hierarchical alliance structure. First, the cooperative decisions taken by fiat by the alliance superstructure provide for efficient and fast decision-making because member consensus has been given 'ex-ante' (by investing the superstructure with power and authority). Second, because authority rests with the superstructure and not with any one airline, this structure can possibly mitigate power asymmetries between larger and smaller airlines. Another advantage, especially for smaller airlines, is that a Type IV

structure will display very little within-competition, and thus relatively high stability and an opportunity for specialisation. Third, this type of alliance binds its members much more to it, which implies a more stable immediate operating environment for the individual airline. Related to this is, fourth, the increased possibility for reaping some scale economies, e.g. in joint procurement, but also in areas such as joint flight training. Scale economies could be reaped at lower integration levels, too, but would be somewhat reduced by higher negotiation costs (i.e. the costs of negotiating a consensus between partners), and some scale economies can only be reaped if partners are bound together in the longer term.

There are, however, some characteristics to this type of alliance group structure that are disadvantageous to individual members, and could render the whole structure quite unfeasible. For one, membership to such an 'authoritarian' alliance implies a high loss of operational and even strategic autonomy for the individual airline. In addition, the high level of alliance-related sunk costs makes it very difficult to leave this type of alliance (but see Chapter 3 for a discussion of the advantages and disadvantages of costs sunk into alliancing). Thirdly, building this type of alliance is especially difficult, because of differing member agendas. These points will be taken up below.

A Type IV structure is currently emerging with a holding company being formed as a superstructure to the KLM–Air France Duo. This is still a very simple Type IV structure in that it entails only two members (possibly a third in the future with Alitalia). At this point, KLM and Air France are supposed to continue as separate operational entities, and even though some scale economies will be reaped through joint procurement, there are still considerable obstacles in e.g. legal requirements for operating under two national flags (to retain Flag Carrier status of France and the Netherlands, respectively), and the fact that both airlines will continue to pursue their alliance strategy outside the Tandem, with KLM partner Northwest effectively competing with Air France and their US partner Delta on North Atlantic and domestic US routes.

The main characteristics of the different alliance types can be depicted in the following table:

Table 9.1 Characteristics of different alliance types

	Type I	Type II	Type III	Type IV
Locus of authority	individual airline	lead airline(s)	individual airline, consensus sought	superstructure (ratification by individual airlines)
Locus of alliance decision-making	individual airline, some bilateral or cluster consensus	lead airline(s), ratified by 'junior members'	multilateral consensus, sometimes in clusters	superstructure
Decision-making efficiency	very low	high	medium to low	high
Exclusivity	none	possible	little	very likely
Costs sunk into alliance	low	medium to high, often equity (top-down)	medium to high	very high; possibly equity investment in alliance governance structure
Within competition	high	very low	medium	low
Stability	very low	high	low to medium	high
Specialisation of individual airline	too risky	possible	relatively risky	possible
Reaping of scale economies	almost none	yes	limited, possible at 'cluster' level	yes

An interesting point is that of 'specialisation of individual airline'. This refers to assumptions by organisation ecologists (see Chapter 3) that in a federated environment, firms can afford to specialise (and be therefore more efficient), without falling prey to environmental shifts, because in a tight enough federation, parts of it will be capable of operating well, no matter what state the environment is in. In other words, whatever the environmental state, the units that are more fit, i.e. specialised to operate in a specific context, will subsidise those that are less so, knowing that they in turn will be subsidised if the environment changes to yet another state.

In practice, specialisation is only possible if the airline is bound to the alliance in a formal way, which will mean through equity. Thus, a regional subsidiary of a large carrier can afford to be a specialist on a limited set of routes, and operate ideally a single-type fleet, because it is 'subsidised' by its parent – these 'subsidies' can take the form of guaranteed traffic feed, help with procurement and infrastructure, flight and cabin crew and mechanic training etc. It can also take the form of financial subsidies. But for most alliance members (who are by default specialised in a certain region, but mostly also operate in several markets beyond their core region), true federation-based specialisation, or giving up some routes for the sake of a partner, is still too risky a strategy. Giving or expecting subsidies is out of the question. Thus, as alliances stand nowadays (as mostly Type I and III), they cannot yet yield the full benefits of a secure, stable, and sheltered operating environment.

A second important issue is that in some Type III airline alliance groups, the locus of alliance *decision making* moves further up to the newly created hierarchical level of the alliance group management organisation, while the locus of *authority* [4] is likely to remain for some time primarily or possibly exclusively, at unit level. In cases where the locus of decision making and of final authority is not the same, the commitment to an independent firm (i.e. the 'unit') can then be countervailing to the (supposed) commitment to the superstructure. Unless the locus of final authority is clearly moved up, this conflict can only be mitigated through the institutionalisation of the superstructure to such an extent that key managerial actors consider submission to it – or at least close coordination with it – as normative. Unless such a norm is established, any superstructure is likely to be considered by participants as a 'battlefield' for the pursuit of their own interest rather than a coordinating body for the pursuit of a common good.

The alliance as an organisation in its own right

In many cases, management literature dealing with alliances focuses on mostly dyadic inter-firm cooperation in a specific field (such as a joint product), for a specific purpose (such as R&D cooperation), or a specific geographical market. The main issues dealt with typically relate to process optimisation in the widest sense. It is assumed that the individual firm manages, and has continuous control over, at least its share of the alliance, or of the joint venture.

However, a somewhat different picture emerges when the alliance itself takes the form of an organisation in its own right. Several firms (not just two) working together to create a cooperative structure implies that the individual firm – while still investing in the alliance itself – will have relatively less control over the way the cooperative structure evolves. In such a scenario, it becomes increasingly important to examine the impact of alliance integration on the individual firm (and especially on that firm's autonomy).

Most airline alliance groups are currently still in the making; new members are admitted, constellations change, and there have also been some demises. There are no existing blueprints on how to construct a functioning airline alliance group, and examples for multilateral alliances from other industries – from which airline managers could learn – are very scarce. The air transport industry is really pioneering multilateral alliancing. In a way, airline managers are constructing, or rather 'inventing' these alliance groups as they go along in the daily business of establishing and managing cooperation, of finding consensus, of agreeing on compromises on one side, and protecting their own airline's vital interests on the other. Here again, we have the conflict of individual managers' accountability to their own firms, and the requirement to build an alliance governance structure that could eventually take away some organisational autonomy from these firms.

To obtain a more systematic understanding of the new organisational phenomenon of multilateral alliancing, the following sections will briefly discuss airline alliances in the language of four (interrelated) perspectives from organisation theory, namely those of (1) hybrid organisations, (2) industrial networks, (3) multinational corporations, and (4) federations. Each of these perspectives focuses on slightly different aspects of inter-firm cooperation and points to different problem areas; together, they provide quite a useful conceptual overview of what alliance building in the airline industry might entail.

Perspective 1: The airline alliance group as a hybrid organisation

An interesting organisational structure that extant academic literature has been discussing is the so-called 'hybrid organisation'. It is worthwhile to examine the characteristics of hybrid organisations in a little more detail, since many of their features do indeed apply to airline alliance groups, and these features point to some problems inherent in alliance governance.

First, hybrids are said to exist where 'two or more sovereign organisations combine to pursue common interests'.[5] In its broadness, this definition leads to some interesting questions, such as how sovereign, if at all, the organisations are *after* they are 'combined', and in how far the pursuit of common interests is indeed a prerequisite for a hybrid to exist. In fact, organisations can federate, or 'combine', while maintaining their own agenda, or seeking different kinds of benefits from the federation (for example, one partner requires resource access, another technical know-how; a third seeks sheltering from competition etc). Thus, it might very well be that organisations might federate due to interdependencies, but not necessarily to pursue a common interest. This will create a certain tension in the alliance in that firms that are highly interdependent and interconnected pursue different, sometimes possibly conflicting, agendas.

Even if they can be assumed to pursue a 'common goal' (such as alliance prosperity), the specific *objectives* of hybrid membership, and the individual contributions to the hybrid, can indeed vary considerably between parties that make up a hybrid. This is because each (airline-) party is different in terms of size, route system and alliancing objectives. Within the hybrid organisation of an airline alliance group, one can thus observe a certain degree of power asymmetries. These power asymmetries can be expected to significantly influence the way the alliance superstructure (i.e. the governance mechanism) is being constructed. Clearly, some positions within an alliance group provide more leverage over fellow members (and/or the alliance governance body itself) than others.

A further definition of hybrid organisations is that 'Hybrids are organisational arrangements that use resources and/or governance structures from more than one existing organisation'.[6] This takes the perspective of the hybrid as an organisation in its own right, while leaving open the issue of the goals, and objectives, involved in creating and maintaining the hybrid. It focuses mainly on what was described as a Type IV alliance above; in other words, an alliance group that goes beyond being a purely multilateral network to having already some kind of governance superstructure in place. The interesting issue here is that attention is directed to the governance of the hybrid itself: how can 'governance structures from more than one existing organisations' be effectively combined – especially if these organisations are sovereign? As we shall see, the issue of just how much sovereignty the individual alliance member can or should relinquish to the alliance superstructure is one of the key questions shaping the structural development of airline alliance groups.

Perspective 2: The airline alliance group as an industrial network

Research on strategic management provides us with another interesting concept, namely that of 'industrial networks'. The focus of industrial network research is on how firms manage their relationships with customers, suppliers, competitors, regulators and other entities with whom they have formal or informal contact. Each firm is considered to be embedded in a network of relationships, and this embeddedness[7] – the overall number, strength and kind of ties it maintains with other entities – can help explain its strategic positioning in the future, and the degree to which it can influence, or is influenced by, the other entities in the network. Typically, the concept of ties is understood in its widest sense, referring to any kind of linkage ranging from equity and ownership to social relationships between individuals. In the airline industry case, there are relatively few actors that make up a large part of the industry (50 airlines make up around 85 percent of global RPK), so it appears feasible for the purpose of examining alliancing behaviour to view the entire industry as the wider network, as the 'task environment'[8] or 'focal net'.[9] Within this wider network which, in the case of the airline industry, constitutes almost the entire industry, the airline alliance groups represent formal multilateral clusters of firms.

A network can be conceptualised as consisting of *nodes* and *links*.[10] In other words, what makes up a network is its members (who they are, and how they are positioned in relation to each other), and also the types of links between different members. It is suggested here that one of the main factors influencing both a firm's positioning in a network and the nature and extent of its interactions is that firm's resource endowment. Due to differences in resource endowment (see Chapter 3), firms differ to often a fairly large degree in their expectations from, and contributions to, a network. Thus, it is possible to characterise the structure of a network by the division of work amongst firms in it.[11] Clearly, some positions in a network provide more leverage over fellow members than others.[12] The industrial network perspective points us thus again towards the importance of power constellations within an airline alliance group: we can translate the term 'resource endowment' as route structure, and market dominance, of a specific airline. Airlines that dominate a market that is considered attractive by other airlines, will obtain a better network position, in the sense that they will be coveted and sought-after alliance partners. This in itself does not necessarily mean that these airlines will join an alliance group – often, it is airlines that dominate an attractive market which can choose to stay outside any alliance group, and base their own cooperative strategy on a portfolio – of-bilateral approach (see Chapter 1). But on the other hand, airlines that dominate a centrally located hub, will often benefit from alliance group integration, and will be sought-after alliance partners by those carriers that operate in more remote home markets. These issues were covered in Chapter 3, which discussed airline positioning in an alliance group from the resource dependence perspective.

In addition to differences in node characteristics (such as airlines' resources), the industrial network perspective also accounts for differences in tightness of links between partners. Tight links, or strong relationships, preclude facile partner switching, and create a certain stabilising inertia within the system (see Chapter 3). Relationships between partners can be strong due to social ties, they can be based on partners' investment in the relationship, and they can be based on mutual trust. It is here that formal networks – such as multilateral alliances – can create much stronger and longer-lasting ties than purely social networks, because formal networks are based on contracts, and involve costs sunk into the alliance. These previous investments deter partners from quick defection. One example of airlines cementing the relationship between them is the exchange of shares. Often, these swaps are minor, but they serve as a pledge of mutual commitment to the relationship.

The following table lists some salient characteristics of networks and alliances as they have been described in academic literature, and depicts the corresponding characteristics of airline alliances.

Table 9.2 Networks, alliances and airline alliance groups

	'Networks'	'Alliances'	Airline Alliance groups
Degree of formality	informal	formal	formal
Time to formation	long	short to medium	short to medium
Temporal orientation	long-term	short to medium-term	long-term
System of relationship	multilateral	mostly dyad	dyad and multilateral
Position primarily defined by...	social brokerage	resources	first resources, later (some) social brokerage
Social ties and brokerage are relevant...	at the outset	at high levels of integration	at high levels of integration
Development	member fluctuation	stages, lifecycle	member fluctuation
Part of organisation typically involved in relationship	individual actors / whole firm	part of firm	whole firm
Firm's behaviour in cooperation shaped by	'contagion',[13] mutual adaptation, trust	contract; trust	contract, mutual adaptation, later increasingly trust

In brief, airline alliance groups can be characterised as networks that are formal (i.e. based on contracts), and where a firm's position is primarily defined by its resource endowment. They are more hierarchically structured than social networks, but they display more flexibility and greater complexity than a bilateral (or dyadic) alliance would. While dyadic alliances between two firms typically concern a specific task, product, or geographical market, and often go through stages and a lifecycle from formation to dissolution, formal networks contain bilateral agreements that might undergo such lifecycle stages, but the network itself changes shape through member fluctuation and/or environmental contingencies. One can say that a network is under continuous development, that it 'emerges'. Thus, the contractual basis for a formal network must allow for a larger range of contingencies, and be more flexible, since not every contingency in the overall network is predictable and not every type of behaviour or reaction can be contractually stipulated. In other words, it must be kept together by more than clauses in a contract.

One further important characteristic of this type of formal network is that the links within it comprise both the ties between actors (in this case, airlines), and the ties between the actor and the network itself. Concretely, an alliance member airline has ties to other carriers (though not necessarily equally tight ties with every member of the group), but also a direct tie to the alliance group superstructure. In a somewhat clinical view, extant literature discusses the so-called 'participatory federation'[14] where members retain an active role in federation management both concerning issues between members, and issues between members and the federation management itself. How this is to be put into practice, and whether it is feasible at all (given the pressure on efficiency in the airline industry) remains doubtful. There can be situations where in fact an airline manager is faced with having to honour three types of obligations: to his own firm, to an alliance partner, and to the alliance group itself. Establishing priorities can be difficult. If alliance integration is to go ahead to the extent that there will be a governing superstructure, there will be a requirement for member airlines to renounce a significant amount of decision making autonomy. In other words, there seems to be a need for a hierarchical structure – but there also might be reluctance on the side of airline managers to concede this power to the superstructure.

Related to this is the issue of a formal network implying the existence of a defined, negotiated, hierarchy: alliance-related decision making occurs, at least in a limited way, on a level *above* the individual airline. An important distinction is whether this level might consist of inter-partner negotiation for consensus (such as alliance types I and III), or whether it is embodied by a unitarian supra-organisation, which exercises authority over all members (such as alliance types II and IV). This distinction is important because it touches the question of the degree of authority that the network has over the individual firm, in other words, at what point the alliance will function as a hierarchically superior *superstructure* to all individual actors. As long as decision-making and authority remain at inter-partner level (Types I and III), the network analogy does in fact apply very well to airline alliance groups. To understand the case of an alliance group with a strong governance body (Types II and especially IV), a comparison with large and diversified organisations – such as the Multinational Corporation (MNC) – might be useful to account for the role of hierarchy. The following two sections will discuss governance issues of formal networks by comparing them with the concepts of multinational corporations (MNCs) and federations.

Perspective 3: Airline alliance groups as 'multinational corporations'

One can identify analytical similarities between a multinational corporation (as understood by recent management literature) and a multilateral alliance:

increasingly, the complexity of MNCs and their attractiveness for organisational research no longer stems from the circumstance that they are multi*national*. Their organisational complexity is based increasingly on the fact that the MNC is a grouping of more or less autonomous, more or less heterogeneous organisational units (where national and cultural diversity is just one of several dimensions of complexity), which displays both centripetal (e.g. internalisation and establishment of hierarchy) as well as centrifugal (e.g. subsidiary autonomy[15]) forces simultaneously. Thus, research now ceases to see the MNC as a 'monolithic' organisation. For example, it has been suggested to replace the 'classic' definition of an MNC as an entity that controls assets in two or more countries by a definition that better reflects current realities, as for example in the following definition:

> An enterprise (a) comprising entities in two or more countries, regardless of legal form and fields of activity of those entities, (b) which operates under a system of decision-making permitting coherent policies and a common strategy through one or more decision making centres, (c) in which the entities are so linked, by ownership or otherwise, that one or more of them may be able to exercise a significant influence over the activities of others, and, in particular, to share knowledge, resources, and responsibilities with others.
> (Ghoshal and Westney, 1993)

It is interesting to note that this definition of MNCs does not require an organisation to be bound together by ownership ties in order to qualify. If the requirements listed above are applied to airline alliance groups, the following picture emerges.

Requirement (a) is met: an airline alliance group consists of several entities (i.e., airline members) in different countries. The international aspect is relevant both in terms of 'soft' factors such as different management cultures, but also in terms of differing national legislation. In the airline case, this often has an impact on airline ownership, labour relations and cost structures.

Requirement (b) can be partially met, depending on the hierarchical structure of the airline alliance group: there are several possible decision making centres within an airline alliance group: Fiat by a dominant partner (Type II, for example, Swissair on Qualiflyer), fiat by a steering committee (Type IV, for example, Star alliance at least to a limited extent), consensus sought in negotiations (Type III, for example, oneworld), and decisions taken entirely by the airline, but which are influenced by its position within the alliance (Type I; this occurs in all existing airline alliance groups). In current reality, the requirement for coherent policies is not always granted because in airline alliance groups there is still very limited authority given to any governance superstructure. The same applies to common strategies. However, it is possible to say that the tighter integrated the alliance (i.e., the closer it comes to a Type II or Type IV hierarchy), the more requirement (b) is met. The main and most important difference to an MNC is that in an airline alliance group the partner is still a separate company that at least theoretically has the option to leave the alliance.

Requirement (c) is partially met. Access to, and sharing of, some resources is still limited, mainly due to regulatory limitations (route rights on a large number of international routes outside intra-EU traffic still pertain to a designated carrier). Sharing of resources can and does occur in terms of joint marketing, joint airport facilities and joint IT infrastructure. As to the requirement for one or several entities exercising 'significant' influence over others, this occurs in some, but not all cases of airline cooperation, mainly in relations between a trunk airline and its feeders, or in the case of one airline's equity investment in another. These cases are still limited.

Thus, airline alliance groups, especially those that have matured into a hierarchically governed structure, offer more than just a remote resemblance to modern large, multinational, and diversified firms. The problems inherent in governing these complex organisation types are quite similar, too: how are these dispersed and diversified structures managed and kept marching into what is hoped to be a common direction? How tight has control over dispersed subunits to be in order for the firm as a whole to evolve in a coherent way? Monitoring and tightly managing far-flung and highly diverse units is costly and resource-consuming. This is the main challenge of MNC management, and modern MNC management literature no longer takes for granted the 'classical' idea of corporate headquarters (representing the owners of the firm) directing in every minute detail the operations of subsidiaries and regional operations. Instead, the focus is increasingly on autonomy and even entrepreneurship at lower organisational levels. For the MNC, the rationale behind this is mainly that local operations are better suited to operate in a country- or region- specific context – hence the slogan 'Think global, act local'. As with airline alliance groups, the core issue is that of coordinating the actions of a heterogeneous group of autonomous but interdependent organisations.

It has been proposed[16] that a governance structure's control over individual units of a large and complex organisation can actually be quite loose, as long as it is made sure that managers across all units share a common basic mindset, in other words, as long as they agree on certain organisational values and norms, on the company mission, and on the 'way things are done'. This shared, joint mindset would then enable them to steer and direct their own subunits in a way coherent with overall organisational policy without the need for tight supervision and direction from headquarters. Symptomatic of this thinking are the exercises that especially large companies stage for their staff in order to create a 'team spirit', and which sometimes verge on the esoteric (retreats at supposedly attractive locations, outward-bound-style adventure exercises and so on), and the related indoctrination sessions which many young recruits have to undergo during their corporate traineeships before they are fully inserted into their professional roles. The idea is to give them a 'mental programming' that will increase the likelihood that their actions (and beliefs) reflect the overall organisation culture, without the need for permanent control or direction. In the airline reality, however, a common mindset is very difficult to establish across a large organisation, and even more so if it has to be established across fairly heterogeneous units, as in the case of an airline alliance group, where all 'subunits' are de facto autonomous firms with their own agenda, and responsibilities to different sets of shareholders. Another non-negligible constraint is the time and resource pressures on airline managers, and this became abundantly clear in the authors' interviews with senior airline managers: few (if any) would see a point in themselves or their subordinates spending time and money in yet more 'teambuilding' exercises, when their main job is to manage their airline in increasingly difficult conditions.

Another strong argument against the concept of cognitive homogeneity (or organisation-wide shared mindsets) in a multilateral federation can be derived from recent research on national economies and regional trade areas. The so-called 'club convergence theory'[17] holds that there can be more homogeneity (in structural as well as cognitive terms) *between* different 'clubs' (here: regional trade areas) than *within* them. For example, AFTA member Thailand is economically more similar to (Mercosur member) Brazil than to fellow AFTA members Laos or Myanmar.[18] These differences, in turn, imply 'heterogeneous policy goals' within one club, or, simply put, that each club member might pursue a different agenda, and are a member of that club for different reasons. The same principle can in fact be observed with multilateral alliance groups in general, and it is interesting to note the analytical parallels between formal networks of independent firms and economic associations of sovereign nations (where the European Union would have a higher level of 'member integration' than, say, Mercosur or NAFTA). Translated to the case of airline alliances, it can indeed be seen that airlines such as (oneworld member) LAN Chile and (Star member) Air New Zealand, both of which are serving geographically remote markets and do not dominate a centrally located global hub, have policy goals (and alliancing rationales) that are more similar to each other than between, say, LAN Chile and British Airways within oneworld. In other words, airline alliance groups do not represent cognitive or strategic clusters. Members do not see things the same way just because they belong to the same alliance group. They are structurally different, they have different policy goals, and their reasons for joining an alliance vary. It is difficult to see a possibility for a profoundly common mindset in a heterogeneous club. And this heterogeneity leads to one of the most problematic issues in alliance building, namely that of 'local rationales'.

The problem of local rationales

The difficulties in consensus-finding in actual alliance coordination meetings were one of the main topics that were brought up in the authors' discussions with airline senior management (see Chapter 4). On one hand, alliance members clearly seek to create a more stable operating environment for the individual airlines. They also seek to establish an alliance governance structure that would facilitate more streamlined, and more rapid, decision-making. But even if there is consensus among members to build such a structure, the building process itself is likely to be fraught with difficulties, due to each airline's individual agenda.

At this stage it is important to underline one fundamental analytical difference between the organisational form of a *firm*, and the organisational form of a *federation* of firms. A firm is an organisational unit that is autonomous, with clear boundaries, purpose, and an internal hierarchy, at the top (or apex) of which stands a governing entity. Any actor (individual employees, managers, or departments) within the firm's boundary will be more tightly integrated with fellow actors, than with elements from outside that boundary; there are also relatively higher costs to transferring actors and goods across boundaries than within them. Thus, a firm displays a relatively higher structural density than its environment. The actors within the firm are organised through a hierarchy, and in practice there are strong, and fairly long-term contractual ties between actors and the apex of this hierarchy (for example, contracts ensuring behavioural compliance from the employee's side, and the payment of salaries from the apex's side). This can be called a 'hierarchical loop', where behavioural compliance is rewarded.

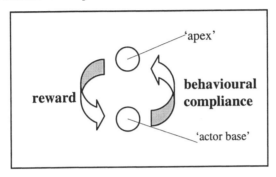

Figure 9.2   The hierarchical loop

The result of a hierarchical loop is what can be called 'local rationales', or thinking in terms of 'I owe obedience to the one who pays me'. This is what induces managers to set one's own firm first.

If one now assumes the – from a hierarchical standpoint – simplest form of governed federation, namely that of a Type IV alliance where there is a superstructure – such as an alliance management company – that has been given authority over alliance members, the result is a double loop hierarchy, where contracts exist also to ensure the existence of the cooperation itself. The individual actor would still owe compliance to, and be rewarded by, the apex of his own firm. But beyond that, he and his firm also owe at least *some* behavioural compliance to the alliance superstructure.

In the organisational form of an alliance group with a governance superstructure there are, then, not just the final goals of each member firm as ends towards which individual managers or departments are rewarded to work, but in addition to this, and to some extent superimposed to the individual goals, there is the superstructure's goal of ensuring group survival and prosperity.

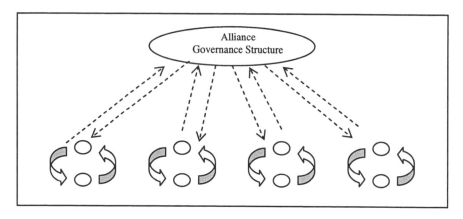

Figure 9.3   A simple form of double-loop hierarchy

If an airline is a member of a hierarchically governed federation (Type IV), this implies that decisions on ensuring compliance and rewarding of its managers are no longer taken on behalf of the individual airline only. In other words, the boundaries between the immediate task environment (the alliance group) and the airline itself have become permissible, and even decisions within the airline-internal hierarchy will be influenced by contingencies that are external to the airline to a much larger extent than would be the case with a non-allied airline. In the extreme, the boundaries would reach a degree of permissiveness where the apex of the individual airline (its senior management and directors) would cease to exist, or remain only with a symbolic, or coordinating   function – behavioural compliance would be commanded directly from the apex of the superstructure (the alliance management superstructure), which would in the extreme then also issue rewards – in other words, in this extreme scenario, managers of individual airlines would be *de facto* employees of, and responsible to, the alliance management superstructure. The individual airline would be no more than a sort of profit centre within a large organisation.

One factor preventing this from happening too easily lies in the fact that, in the case of emerging alliance groups such as those in the airline industry, the superstructure is not prior to its base. In other words, it is the base which conceives, and builds, the superstructure. There is no readily-conceived structure that is superimposed on member airlines, no freshly created and instituted higher hierarchical level. Instead, the alliance governance superstructure is very slowly being *built up* by its constituents – its future base. These constituents (the airlines) also decide to what extent to invest the superstructure with authority over them. In concrete terms, this means that as managers from airlines, who are paid by, and owe allegiance to, their respective firms, set to build up an alliance superstructure, they are likely to continue their behavioural allegiance to their own company during this alliance-building phase, even if they have received the official order to build an alliance superstructure which would eventually take authority over their firms. This can be illustrated with the typical following statement, made by a senior manager in an interview:

> I don't think that the people involved tend to be very committed to [alliance group] ... at the meetings I go to – and I think I've been to three governing body meetings and I've been at a couple of management team meetings which is the next level down, I think those people are, at the meetings, very dedicated to [alliance group], but, as I said earlier, the problem is that when they get back to base, other things dominate.

In view of these difficulties, it can be expected that emerging alliance groups will for a considerable time remain at the stage of Type I and Type III alliances, even though an officially stated goal might be to reach a Type IV structure.

The complication inherent in Type I and Type III alliances is that there is no clear 'apex', no alliance group leadership structure. Individual airlines are still required to comply with alliance-level directives which favour the persistence and prosperity of the cooperation or the alliance itself. But there is no clear direction as to what that compliance should entail, and no clear 'reward' structure. Thus, one can consider these types of alliances *incomplete hierarchies*, multi-apex, or 'polycephalous' (multi-head) organisations in that they consist of several apices (or 'heads'), each governing – and being supported by – its own 'body'. Their cooperation will need constant and ever-recurring coordination between these heads – the recurrent meetings and alliance sessions which many airline managers have come to dread, since they distract them from their main job of running an airline.

Conclusions and practical implications: The virtue of clusters

The perspectives discussed above have pointed to three key issues that pose challenges to the building and governance of airline alliance groups. First, the heterogeneity in airline strategies and alliancing rationales. Second, the lack of an overarching authority over the alliance group. And third, the lack of an organisational blueprint. This means that airline alliance groups are emerging, as their members daily 'invent' and 'enact' the cooperation. The alliance, and especially its governance structure, is thus a product of negotiation – and not so much of deliberation.

The unstable and very competitive operations environment of airlines induced them to cooperate and imposed the need for 'organized coordination of interdependence';[19] however, the retained autonomy of the organisational members poses certain limits on the potential for central coordination, let alone governance. In the interviews conducted by the author, this problem was mentioned very frequently (see also Chapter 4). A senior manager at one airline, which is a member of a relatively tightly integrated alliance group, described it this way:

> If the staff cannot see in a fairly tangible sense some quick payback from the

investment in their participation, because of course the way they tend to describe it is 'I've got a real job back in Head Office, I'm not sure why I'm doing this', and, worse, 'I'm not quite sure why I'm doing this except I'm doing what I'm supposed to do, I have to do it because I'm now a member of [alliance group X] where they should be participating in the development of [alliance group X] as an entity with a clear vision as to their value to [alliance group X] and more importantly, the value to their individual airline, and that's one of the challenges that we've had, that we've really only just started to work on.

What does this mean in concrete alliance management terms? First of all, local rationales still prevail in alliance building. Airline managers think first and foremost in terms of their own firm, and the higher a manager's hierarchical level, the stronger this tendency can be expected to be. It is unlikely that an alliance group governance body will, in the short or even medium term, take (or rather: be given) significant authority over members. In other words, alliance groups are likely to remain loose.

This means also that it can be expected still to take a considerable amount of time before alliance groups settle down to such an extent that they would provide a stable operating environment to the individual airline; which was one of the main reasons why airlines seek alliances in the first place. Airline alliance groups are still in flux, and airlines need to guard their standalone capability that was discussed in Chapter 3. One development that can be expected to continue in the future will be that of cluster building: cemented with equity ties or not, some airlines will speed up alliance building by establishing joint-venture types of very tight collaboration between just a small number of firms – typically two or three. In fact, these clusters of higher density within an alliance group provide an airline with a number of advantages that it would seek in a larger alliance group, without having to incur the risk of sinking too much cost into membership of an as-yet unstable larger structure:

Table 9.3 Clusters versus Type III / IV alliances

	Type III	**Cluster**	**Type IV**
Number of members	>4	2-4 (typically)	> 4
Nature of ties	loose, horizontal (consensus-seeking, 'democratic')	tight, horizontal (joint ventures, possibly involving equity)	tight, vertical (member bound to alliance governance body)
Time to build-up	medium	medium–fast	very slow
Stability	low	high	medium for long build-up phase, later high
Scope benefits	high	low–medium	high
Scale benefits	low	medium–high	possibly medium–high
Individual airline's influence in group management	medium	medium–high	low–medium

Examples for clusters include the Lufthansa joint ventures and equity ties with carriers in Europe; another cluster is the tie between Air France and KLM. As can be seen from the above table, clusters do offer most of the benefits of a large, hierarchical airline alliance group, with the notable advantage that they are built up much faster, and the fact that they involve fewer members that cooperate on a joint venture basis leaves the individual airline more room to negotiate its own position – there would therefore be less of a requirement for the individual airline to relinquish authority to a governance structure, as would be the case in a Type IV alliance. On the other hand, and again this is due to the smaller number of members, decision-making processes are faster than those of alliance-wide consensus seeking that would occur in a Type III alliance. In addition, it is organisationally easier for a cluster to expand into non-marketing areas such as joint IT systems, or joint procurement. Clusters can be expected to be seen by managers as a more efficient thing than their alliance groups and as the next best thing to a merger – given that full mergers in this industry are likely to be difficult in a significant number of cases.

Notes

1 Solberg, 2000.
2 ibid.
3 Easton, 1992.
4 e.g. the authority to ratify decisions reached at group level.
5 Borys and Jemison, 1989.
6 ibid.
7 See Dacin et al., 1999, for a discussion on the concept of embeddedness.
8 Astley and Fombrun, 1983.
9 Alajoutsijärvi et al., 1999.
10 Thorelli, 1986.
11 Easton, 1992.
12 Madhavan et al., 1998.
13 "contagion" (Gulati, 1998) refers to a behavioural domino effect, where firms imitate partners' practices and procedures, thereby establishing homogeneous industry, group, or sector practices.
14 Provan, 1983.
15 Birkinshaw, 1997, discusses corporate entrepreneurship and initiatives at subsidiary level.
16 Hedlund 1986; 1995.
17 Quah, 1996.
18 Proff, 2002.
19 Pfeffer and Salancik, 1978.

References

Alajoutsijärvi, K., Möller, K. and Rojenbröijer, C. (1999), Relevance of Focal Nets in Understanding the Dynamics of Business Relationships. *Journal of Business-to-Business Marketing*, Vol. 6, No. 3, pp. 3-35.
Astley, W. and Fombrun, C. (1983), Collective Strategy: Social Ecology of Organizational Environments. *Academy of Management Review*, Vol. 8, No. 4, pp. 576-687.
Birkinshaw, J. (1997), Entrepreneurship in Multinational Corporations: The Characteristics of Subsidiary Initiatives. *Strategic Management Journal*, Vol 18, No 3, pp. 207-229.
Borys, B. and Jemison, D. (1989), Hybrid Arrangements as Strategic Alliances: Theoretical Issues in Organizational Combinations. *Academy of Management Review*, Vol. 14, No. 2, pp. 234-249.
Dacin, M.T., Ventresca, M. and Beal, B. (1999), The Embeddedness of Organizations: Dialogue & Directions. *Journal of Management*, Vol. 25, No. 3, pp. 317-356.
Easton, G. (1992), Industrial networks: A review. In: Axelsson, B. and Easton, G. (eds), Industrial Networks: A New View of Reality, London: Routledge.
Ghoshal, S. and Westney, E. (1993), Introduction and Overview. In: Ghoshal, S. and Westney, E., Organization Theory and the Multinational Corporation. New York: St Martin's Press.
Gulati, R. (1998), Alliances and Networks. *Strategic Management Journal*, Vol. 19, pp. 293-317.

Hedlund, G. (1986), The Hypermodern MNC – A Heterarchy?. *Human Resource Management*, Vol. 25, No. 1, pp. 9-35.

Hedlund, G. (1995), Assumptions of Hierarchy and Heterarchy, with Applications to the Management of the Multinational Corporation. In: Ghoshal, S. and Westney, D. (eds.), Organization Theory and the Multinational Corporation. New York: St Martin's Press.

Madhavan, R., Koka, B. and Prescott, J. (1998), Networks in transition: How industry events (re) shape interfirm relationships. *Strategic Management Journal*, Vol. 19, pp. 439-458.

Pfeffer, J. and Salancik, G. (1978), The External Control of Organizations. New York: Harper & Row.

Proff, H. (2002), Business unit strategies between regionalisation and globalisation. *International Business Review*, Vol. 11, No. 2, pp. 231-250.

Provan, K. (1983), The Federation as an Interorganizational Linkage Network. *Academy of Management Review*, Vol. 8, No. 1, pp. 79-89.

Quah, D. (1996), Regional Convergence Clusters Across Europe. *European Economic Review*, Vol. 40, pp. 951-958.

Solberg, C.A. (2000), Standardization or Adaptation of the International Marketing Mix: The Role of the Local Subsidiary / Representative. *Journal of International Marketing*, Vol. 8, No. 1, pp. 78-98.

Thorelli, H. (1986), Networks: Between Markets and Hierarchies. *Strategic Management Journal*, Vol. 7, No.1, pp. 37-51.

Chapter 10

Success and Failure Factors of Airline Alliances

Introduction

Generally speaking, airline alliances in the past have had a poor record of success. They have been found unstable and have often lasted relatively short times.[1] In the mid-1990s it was estimated that less than one-third of the international alliances in the airline industry had been successful.[2] Research by the Lared Group indicated in 1997 that 55 per cent of airline alliances disintegrate within three years.[3] These findings are, however, not much different from other industries; research by Andersen Consulting indicated that some 60 per cent of alliances in various industries have already failed or are plagued by under-performance.[4] However, the major airline alliance groups which have been around for some five years now have experienced a relatively steady growth.

Assessing whether an alliance is a success or a failure is not necessarily a straightforward task. First of all, the assessment can be made from the alliance's perspective as a whole, or from an individual airline's perspective. As we have discussed in the chapter concerning alliance performance, one difficulty in assessment relates to the time continuum: in other words, when in the life span of an alliance is the assessment made. Moreover, combining these dimensions, it is possible that, in the beginning, an alliance can be seen as a success for one airline but not for another, and later the fortune may be reversed.

The focus of this chapter is to present factors that may contribute to the success of an alliance. The discussion is drawn partly from the generalisation of findings in other industries, where alliances have been managed longer than in the airline industry – past academic research has focused particularly on joint ventures in manufacturing industries. Research on airline alliances has suggested it to be crucial for the alliance success that the partners are compatible, there is a minimum of power imbalances, and the alliance success is monitored periodically through clear and understandable mechanisms. These conclusions applied, at least, to alliances where the partners were fairly similar in size.[5] In settings where the partners are very different in terms of size and extent of operations – like in today's large alliance groups – the key success factors may be somewhat different.

As usual, it is perhaps easier to pinpoint hazards or causes for failure rather than to suggest what the best practices would be to ensure successful alliance management; consequently, research on alliances in general has produced an endless list of causes for failures. Booz-Allen & Hamilton research[6] has shown that, according to 500 CEOs surveyed, the major reasons for alliance failures were:

- wrong partner selection
- overly optimistic expectations
- lukewarm commitment
- poor communication
- undefined roles
- unclear value creation
- loose agreement
- little relationship building
- weak business plan
- lack of alliance experience
- differing partner styles.

Very relevant to the airline industry, Koza and Lewin (2000) summarised two key reasons for alliance failures; first, the failure to grasp and articulate the strategic intent for the alliance, and second, the lack of recognition of the close interplay between the overall strategy of the company and the role of an alliance in that strategy. In addition, as a critical success factor, they emphasised the conscious balancing of loyalty to the network and to the member company (ibid., p. 149). As to causes for failures, Ariño and Doz[7] talk of a perception gap between expectations and intermediate results; in particular, the misinterpretation of the causes of the expectation shortfall results in problems in alliances. More specifically, research by the Lared Group indicated in 1997 that 75 per cent of airlines attributed the disintegration of an alliance to the incompatibility of corporate culture or personality.[8]

Research by Andersen Consulting[9] has concluded that alliances in general misfire because firms fail to recognise the following five 'truths':

- alliances are more like diplomatic and pragmatic pairings than exclusive bilateral marriages;
- integration for alliances is very different from that of mergers;
- no one governance model fits all alliances as goals, duration, resource contribution and values may differ dramatically;
- alliance expertise needs to be spread throughout the organisation, not just based on a small cadre of experts;
- alliance performance can be measured, including intangibles of trust and culture.

Success drivers in airline business

Compatibility between alliance partners is a prerequisite for alliance success. Ohmae (1989) proposed that there are four criteria for compatibility: trust and understanding, flexibility during the alliance, cultural compatibility, and mutual benefits. It also has been suggested that partner reputation, degree of shared decision making, and strategic similarities between partners all have significant positive relationships to benefits to partner firms from alliance participation.[10] Based on findings from alliance success in various industries, we propose the key determinants of success for strategic airline alliances as follows:

- understanding one's own and other firms' premises and objectives for alliance;
- understanding the value of airline's own capabilities and know-how;
- understanding the roles of partners in the alliance;
- finding a balance between commitment and flexibility;
- selection of partners;
- drafting of the legal agreement;
- determining responsibilities of partners;
- building efficient structure for alliance governance;
- providing resources for alliance management;
- getting the whole organisation's commitment;
- ensuring the flow of information;
- building a system to evaluate the performance of the alliance;
- recognising the challenges due to differences in national and corporate cultures;
- recognising the role of management styles and personalities of executives in making the coalition work.

The most important determinants will be discussed in more detail below.

Premises and objectives

The foundation for a successful alliance relationship lies in understanding the airline's own strategic standing in the competitive field, and having a clear understanding of reasons behind joining an alliance and its objectives concerning the alliance arrangement. In other words, a strategy for alliances needs to be built. In the volatile environment of today's airline industry, many of the alliance strategies of airlines appear to be emerged strategies rather than carefully planned strategies. It is vital to understand the objectives of other airlines when forming or joining an alliance – reasons to join and objectives set for alliances can naturally be very different for different airlines. Building alternative scenarios for the future – including such issues as the evolution of regulation and development of demand in air transport – helps an airline clarify those objectives and understand how those objectives might evolve in case the environment changes from the most likely scenario.

It seems that in the airline industry a key motivation to join alliances is simply the fear of being left out of the restructuring of the industry. In other words, all the other firms are doing it, so we cannot risk not doing it. While it appears that the pros and cons of joining the alliance movement are not always thoroughly assessed, this 'not-being-left-out' may be a perfectly sound argument for joining an alliance in today's turbulent airline industry. An example of such an assessment is the questioning by a small or medium-sized European flag-carrier as to whether the economies of the future will allow it to operate the whole spectrum of services, from the short-haul feeding services to the intercontinental wide-body services. The scenario may be that, in the future, it will be nearly impossible to operate a wide-body fleet of less than ten aircraft profitably and the airline would ultimately be forced to focus on services within their European market only.

Another factor could be the changes in the industry regulation. For instance, it may soon be that the European Commission allows significantly more freedom in rationalising the airline industry in Europe. This would obviously mean that mergers and acquisitions will become more of a realistic option for European airlines. Then we can speculate whether it is likely that Trans-Atlantic or European-Asian M&As will be allowed. Perhaps the restructuring will be allowed within major markets first, among European players in this case, and the small and medium-sized airlines would be well advised to start preparing for large European carriers' efforts to acquire smaller European airlines. If the regulation in the sense of prohibiting airline industry consolidation is eased, for many carriers much of the rationale for alliances will disappear and many of the alliances would thus become useless.

Further, airlines must try to assess the costs and benefits of joining an alliance versus not joining an alliance. The starting point, of course, is that an alliance should add value to the airline. Also, the assessment of the inputs that they can bring into the alliance, and the value of that input to the other partners are needed. Naturally the value of inputs provided by other partners to one's company should be assessed. In addition to efficiency gains and strengthened market position, an alliance should provide an airline a chance to learn better practices.

In preparation for an eventual membership in an alliance, one should not forget such a trivial thing as studying the lessons from earlier alliances. There is a myriad of studies made by consulting firms and academics on the experiences of alliances; zooming out of one's own industry is often an eye-opening experience. Forming a company task force that gets thoroughly familiar with such research may be a relatively small investment that can prove extremely valuable in the alliance process.

Finding suitable partners

The challenge in managing strategic alliances is that the relationships between partners evolve in ways that are very difficult to predict.[11] This is certainly true for the airline industry, perhaps more so than has been the case in any of the manufacturing industries. It is necessary to see what the role of the airline is currently and the way it may evolve in the future; an airline's role has to be understood within the industry in general and also within a particular alliance group. Very relevant to the airline alliances, Ring[12] makes a distinction between 'right' partners and 'good' partners. 'Right' partners bring to the alliance such value that is consistent with its objectives, whereas 'good' partners are likely to employ similar managerial logic.

A crucial thing not to forget is that an airline seldom has complete freedom in choosing its partners. First of all, the ideal partner may already have a close relationship with a key competitor, and we cannot think of living in the same household, so to speak. Also, particularly for small airlines, the issue is not necessarily about us choosing a partner but rather about us being accepted by one of the larger potential partners. The further the evolution of alliance groups, the less room there seems to be for manoeuvring. On the other hand, as there are fewer and fewer non-allied carriers, in their growth ambitions alliance groups may start courting smaller airlines in competing groups and try to get them to change sides.

Past research on alliances in various industries[13] has suggested that the four key criteria for successful partner selection are the following:

- partner assets are complementary;
- business and management cultures of partners are compatible;
- there is trust and integrity in the relationship;
- partners have a shared understanding of the termination of the alliance.

The recent history of the airline industry alliances shows that the use of the dating and engagement analogy is rather appropriate. Airlines have had limited alliances with several partners, typically in the form of code-sharing, and some of those partnerships have developed into more serious relationships where the partners work jointly to integrate numerous functions. In the 1990s, the airline alliance relationships also resembled an odd cross-breed of Argentine tango and some sort of square-dance: dancing was very intimate and passionate but partners were swapped very frequently. It has quite frequently happened that partners break up after having dated for a few years or even longer. The reasons for break-ups appear somehow very familiar to human beings: an airline finds such features in the partner that it cannot tolerate, or the partner does not 'fit into the airline's plans' anymore, or another partner seems more capable of providing the airline with economic safety, or just that the grass may seem to be greener on the other side of the fence.

Using the human relationship analogy, it is possible to speculate on whether Delta, Singapore Airlines and Swissair 'grew apart' in the late 1990s because the partners were just not committed enough and dated too many other partners simultaneously. Perhaps the handsome Lufthansa dumped Finnair as its northern European partner because SAS seemed to have more to offer; obviously Finnair would have liked to continue the relationship with the strong partner. When

Austrian Airlines decided to join the Star Alliance, maybe it saw Lufthansa as a more reliable provider of economic security than Swissair – and quite right so, indeed, we can say with hindsight.

Human life suggests that partners who come from the same kind of background are more likely to have a lasting relationship. Relationships between people with very different cultural background, education level, wealth, areas of interests, etc., may find partnerships very challenging. This would seem to apply to the relationships between firms, too. In the airline industry, the features of airlines that will most likely have a bearing on the success of the relationship include the following:

* size of the firm
* route network
* ownership structure
* corporate culture.

In addition, the reputation of a partner airline evidently has an impact on the outcome of the alliance. Saxton's (1997) studies in various industries suggested that reputation has value to a potential partner as a signal of the worth of both a firm and the asset obtained via an alliance. In addition, a positive reputation signals that a partner is perhaps trustworthy and decreases the perceived likelihood that the partner will defect.

In a relationship where one partner is large and another small, the power imbalance is bound to create friction. It all comes down to how dependent the airlines are on one another. For a large carrier it is possible to live without a particular small partner, but for a small airline the relationship with a large airline or group may be essential for survival. The factor that makes a small airline accept imbalance in a relationship is, of course, the fact that changing partners is costly in many ways. Figure 10.1[14] illustrates three possible outcomes of an alliance, where there are different partners in an alliance that initially looked promising. Obviously the direction that the alliance takes is dependent on the degree of integration. If functions are integrated too tightly, there is a risk of power struggles between partners and the unsolvable differences of opinion may lead to the disintegration of the alliance. On the other hand, if there is too little integration, there is not enough sharing in the relationship and that, too, may lead to a separation.

Concerning route networks the simple rationale appears to be that the less overlap there is the better. In case of extensive overlap, one partner must give up part of the operations and it may often be the less powerful partner, that is, the smaller partner; this is bound to create dissatisfaction with the relationship.

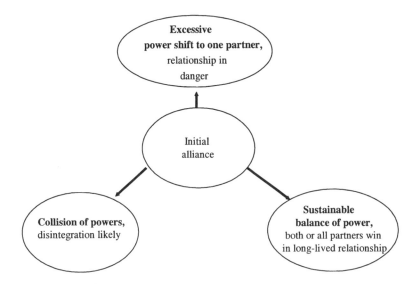

Figure 10.1 Possible outcomes of an alliance among different partners

As to ownership, it appears that companies that have a high share of government ownership may experience difficulties in relationships with airlines that are mostly or completely controlled by non-government owners. The potential difficulties stem from the fact that, at least until today, government-owned or controlled airlines have stronger obligations towards national interests, such as supporting domestic employment, ensuring services to less developed or historically closely connected regions even when it is not economically sustainable, and promoting tourism in the airline's home country. Obviously a privately owned partner, especially of different nationality, has little understanding for such obligations.

Adriana Faoro, manager of Atlantic Excellence alliance marketing for Delta Air Lines, said in 1997 that the representatives of the four member airlines (Austrian, Delta, Sabena, Swissair) represented very different cultures and faced a significant challenge of working together. 'We had to learn to talk the same language basically', she said.[15] So, corporate cultures of airlines differ, even if the differences are narrowing. In the 1980s, the chairman of Sabena, which coincidentally went bankrupt a few years ago, called his own airline 'an expensive flying embassy', while at the same time, say, American Airlines was managed using the strictest methods of control paying relentless attention to efficiency and profitability. So, some airlines have been managed as commercial enterprises for decades but others have been more or less departments within governments' infrastructure. In these airlines there are generations of managers and other employees that may find it difficult adjusting to the realities of the truly competitive airline industry. These differences in corporate culture are mostly visible in the level of hierarchy, appreciation of initiative and innovativeness, level of cost consciousness and control, and empowerment in terms of how much independence managers have in decision-making.

Governance structure

It has been suggested that firms are eager to build alliances but are poor in managing the relationship. In fact a study by Coopers and Lybrand in the mid-1980s suggested that while executives spent 23 per cent of their time developing alliance plans and 19 per cent on drafting legal documents, they spent only eight per cent actually managing the alliance.[16] A key factor for the success of an alliance would seem to be a widely accepted, efficient yet simple structure for the day-to-day management of the relationship. Within a partner airline there could be a task force or special group that has a role of an internal consultant, a co-ordinator between company functions and departments, and a provider of training for company personnel or personnel in non-airline partners such as travel agents.

As alliances are often demanding organisational structures, an airline must assess critically its resources and skills in managing the relationships with an alliance and other partners. This really is a key issue, as evidence from other industries suggests that too often partnership management is left for such persons in the organisation that are 'easily available' or have nothing better to do. Partnership management is typically so demanding – especially when there are different national and corporate cultures involved – that the management of the alliance should never be left to side-tracked managers, but rather the best talent in the company should be found.

The task force or whatever structure that has been built to co-ordinate and run the day-to-day management of an alliance should develop such tools for alliance management that can be used in all the alliances; the fact is that most airlines have numerous alliance agreements and therefore airlines must systematically build competence in managing these alliances. Tools that help managing alliances may include manuals for alliance agreement negotiation, checklists for contract building, or reports of benchmark cases.

It is risky to suggest any particular model for alliance governance because – as proposed many times earlier in this book – the premises and objectives of airlines in alliances may vary remarkably. So, there is no single right governance structure, but the structures need to be adjusted to different markets, to different partners and to different areas of co-operation. Gemini Consulting, for instance, has proposed a framework where there are three stages of integration level in the alliance: co-ordination, shared strategies, and unified equity. Along those stages, the forms of co-operation develop from mere sharing of experiences to common control of operations, which in fact can be seen as a virtual merger of operations.

Degree of integration and trust

As co-operation between partners exceeds simple exchange agreements, the need for tighter co-ordination and integration of efforts increases; in a fully multilateral alliance network a single member's decisions will affect a large part of the network. The degree of integration between members will to a large extent define the organisational boundaries in an alliance. An interesting facet of the alliances is its exclusiveness,[17] or the degree to which an alliance is insulated from other alliances. This constitutes the outside boundaries of the alliance, as a high degree of integration between airlines typically precludes them from seeking co-operation with carriers from outside the group. We have earlier[18] suggested that tight linkages within an alliance may imply significant compromise in the form of sunk costs, either in terms of concrete expenses or in terms of opportunities given up. In addition, members of an alliance are likely to relinquish some amount of authority to a joint governing entity.

There are two mechanisms, in addition to contractual stipulations, which can to some extent mitigate the risks involved at high levels of integration, namely trust and alliance-specific investments. It is possible to observe an interesting interrelation between these two factors: (the tighter the co-operative integration between partners, the higher the need for trust between them.) At the same time, we may observe a higher level of investment, and thus risk that is required) Sunk costs in airline alliances occur, for example, through investments in joint station operations. The resulting form of trust through partner's refraining from opportunistic behaviour has been called 'deterrence-based trust'.[19] At this level of trust, the sunk cost can be considered as a 'safeguard of goodwill'.[20] With partners discouraged from behaving in an opportunistic manner, closer interaction is facilitated and secured. Co-operation over a period of time allows the build-up of knowledge about partners' behaviour and priorities, and another form of trust may emerge. This form is not based only on deterrence, but rather on familiarity,[21] awareness of a common cause and, ultimately, identification with the alliance itself. The development of trust within an alliance over time is important in the alliance context. However, as trust is discussed in detail elsewhere in the book we do not go deeper into it here.

Organisation's commitment

Joining an alliance inevitably means that certain practices in the airline will be questioned and perhaps changed. As organisations are often reluctant to adopt new practices and may oppose changes in the organisation or in the way things are done, it will be difficult to get full commitment to the alliance from the employees. This is exacerbated in the airline industry by the fact that employees have seen partners come and go, and it is a challenge for the management to convince employees that this very alliance is now the right one, and thus worth investing time and effort as it will last a long time. Moreover, economic uncertainty like after

September 11th, with massive lay-offs of staff makes it even harder for the employees to commit themselves to the alliance.

How does one obtain commitment from the organisation? Evidence from many industries suggests that, first of all, involvement and example shown by the top management is essential. Secondly, the benefits of alliances must be clearly demonstrated and substantiated to all employees, emphasising the aspect of something to gain for each and every department and employee. Clear demonstration of benefits means that the pros and cons are exemplified in such a way and in such concrete terms that each level of the organisation can understand them. Third, there should be an incentive scheme built into driving through the required changes in the organisation and its practices; even here the old truth applies that if there is no gain for one personally making an extra effort, why bother in the first place.

Maybe the fundamental reason for KLM's decision to withdraw from the alliance with Alitalia was the lack of commitment from the Italian counterpart. Lack of commitment can be considered risk-increasing for the other partner. 'Continuation of the alliance with Alitalia under the present circumstances constitutes an unacceptable business risk, which could jeopardise (KLM's) financial position, the development and profitability of its own company, and its attractiveness as an alliance partner', were KLM's cited reasons for the disengagement.[22]

Ensuring flow of information

Research by Ariño and Doz (2000), for instance, has emphasised the role of communication between members as a pre-requisite for alliance success. All functions or major departments of an airline should be represented in the task force of alliance management, even if their role would not be crucial in terms of input to the relationship management. The presence would ensure that all functions and departments would be kept up-to-date on the development in the alliance relationship. It has been recommended in past studies that a specific company internal database be built for the alliance management; this database could include the alliance contract and its interpretations, budget and investments for particular alliance activities, and follow-up of the alliance performance (for example growth in the load factors on code-shared routes). It has also been recommended that firms build intranet sites for facilitating discussion and flow of information concerning alliances. These sites could and should include, for instance, a common FAQ (Frequently Asked Questions) section.

Performance evaluation

There is a chapter in the book dedicated particularly to performance measurement, and therefore the theme is only briefly mentioned here. Performance measurement should try to continuously assess the success of the alliance both from the own airline's perspective and for the alliance as a whole. Recapitulating what has been discussed in the chapter on performance assessment, it is worth emphasising that it would be useful to build performance criteria for various functions and even for individual alliance managers in an airline.

Managing cultural differences

Past research has pointed to cultural differences as a key reason for alliance failure. Perhaps the particular danger in the airline industry is that it is, by nature, very much an international business and people in that business travel a lot and consider themselves very experienced and skilful when it comes to managing in a multicultural setting. However, the skills in multicultural management may in reality be much weaker than believed, because airlines in most countries have been run a lot like national corporations, as opposed to firms which are truly international. Therefore, the management typically consists of only nationals of that country and the management's overall exposure to multinational environments is, in fact, quite limited. True, there are airline managers who have run foreign sales offices of the airline for years, but relevant management experience here would refer to, say, managing quite independent and complex major foreign subsidiaries in a number of countries. Especially in Europe, there appears to be a need for airlines to start hiring managers from other industries, and also from other countries. This would enhance the airline's capabilities to respond to the ever-increasing challenges presented by the intensifying international co-operation with firms from different cultures.

As to differences in corporate cultures, there is little an airline can do about it except allocating, or perhaps recruiting, such 'diplomat' managers to alliance liaison functions that have an appreciation for and understand the implications of differences in corporate cultures. Again, as airlines have been national icons in many countries and highly respected firms in their own environment, the danger is that in many airlines there is unwarranted confidence in the way things are done by the firm. Of course, studying the history and activities of partner airlines helps to paint a picture of the way those airlines think and work. Concerning the strong personalities in airline top management, particularly in European countries, there has been typically one major airline, and its CEO and other top executives have been high profile figures in their respective countries. This may easily build egos that are not always the easiest to work with if flexibility and compromise are required.

In conclusion

In addition to the numerous factors contributing to an alliance success as discussed above, it would appear that broadly, from an individual airline's point of view, the success of an alliance boils down to the issue of being able to strike a balance between benefits and risks. Benefits are typically those related to market presence, resource utilisation and learning new practices, whereas risks are related to the sunk costs, lost flexibility and sovereignty, and foregone opportunities.

The balance between benefits and risks would appear to be linked to the degree of integration in an alliance. It seems that in the light of airline alliancing history, it would be wise for airlines to pay particular attention to safeguarding their proprietary skills. To put this in another way, airlines would need to make sure that they do not compromise on their ability to operate alone, without partners; turbulence in the industry suggests that the day may come when an airline has no partners but must stand on its own feet. These core skills may be related to, for example, information technology management or the understanding of consumer behaviour. Of course, the challenge is to benchmark one's own skills and competencies with those of other carriers. This, however, is a good start for understanding the basis of alliancing in the first place. Moreover, as the failure is often attributed to not getting enough value out of the alliance, particular attention should be paid to learning from the alliance – it appears that this would enhance at least the experience of success in many alliances.

Notes

[1] See e.g. Brouthers et al., 1995; Gant, 1999.
[2] Lindqvist, 1996.
[3] Segil, 1998.
[4] *Management Review*, 2000.
[5] Bissessur, 1996.
[6] Pekar and Harbison, 1998, in Mockler, 1999, 198.
[7] 2000, 173.
[8] Segil, 1998.
[9] *Management Review*, 2000.
[10] Saxton, 1997.
[11] Doz and Hamel, 1998, xi.
[12] Ring, 2000, 158.
[13] See e.g. Faulkner, 1995.
[14] Modified from Adarkar et al., 1997
[15] *Aviation Week & Space Technology*, 17 November 1997.
[16] Gulati et al., 1994.
[17] Easton, 1992.
[18] See Kleymann and Seristö, 2000.
[19] Sheppard and Tuchinsky, 1996; Gulati et al., 2000.
[20] Child and Faulkner, 1998.
[21] Gulati, 1995.
[22] *ATI*, 2000.

References

Adarkar, A., Adil, A., Ernst, D. and Vaish, P. (1997), 'Emerging Market Alliances: must they be win-lose?', *McKinsey Quarterly*, no. 4., pp. 121-137.

Ariño, A. and Doz, Y. (2000), 'Rescuing Troubled Alliances...before It's too Late', *European Management Journal*, vol. 18, no. 2, pp. 173-181.

ATI on-line news service, May 9, 2000.

Aviation Week and Space Technology, 17 November, 1997.

Bissessur, A. (1996), *The Identification and Analysis of the Critical Success Factors of Strategic Airline Alliances*. Unpublished Ph.D. thesis, Cranfield University, Bedford, UK.

Brouthers, K., Brouthers, L. and Wilkinson, T. (1995), 'Strategic Alliances: Choose your Alliances', *Long Range Planning*, vol. 28, no. 3, pp. 18-25.

Child, J. and Faulkner, D.(1998), *Strategies of Cooperation. Managing Alliances, Networks, and Joint Ventures*. Oxford University Press, Oxford.

Doz, Y. and Hamel, G. (1998), *Alliance Advantage: the Art of Creating Value through Partnering*. Harvard Business School Press, Boston.

Faulkner, D. (1995), *International Strategic Alliances: Cooperating to Compete*, McGraw-Hill, New York.

Gant, J. (1995), 'The Science of Alliance', *Euro Business*. September, 1995, pp. 70-73.

Gulati, R. (1995), 'Does Familiarity Breed Trust? The Implications of Repeated Ties for Contractual Choice in Alliances', *Academy of Management Journal*, vol. 38, pp. 85-112.

Gulati, R., Khanna, T. and Nohria, N. (1994), 'Unilateral Commitments and the Importance of Process in Alliances', *Sloan Management Review,* vol. 35, no. 3, pp. 61-75.

Gulati, R., Nohria, N. and Zaheer, A. (2000), 'Strategic Networks', *Strategic Management Journal*, vol. 21, pp. 203-215.

Kleymann, B. and Seristö, H. (2000), 'Levels of Airline Alliance Membership: Balancing Risks and Benefits', Proceedings of the Air Transport Research Group Annual Conference in Amsterdam.

Koza, M. and Lewin, A. (2000), 'Managing Partnerships and Strategic Alliances: Raising the Odds of Success', *European Management Journal*, vol. 18, no. 2, pp. 146-151.

Lindqvist, J. (1996), 'Marriages made in Heaven?', *The Avmark Aviation Economist*, vol. 13, no. 1, pp. 12-13.

Management Review, January 2000, p. 7.

Mockler, R. (1999), *Multinational Strategic Alliances*. John Wiley & Sons, Chichester, England.

Ohmae, K. (1989), 'The global logic of strategic alliances', *Harvard Business Review*, March/April, pp. 143-154.

Pekar, P. and Harbison, J. (1998), 'Implementing alliances and acquisitions', The 1998 Strategic Alliances Conference, New York.

Ring, P.S. (2000), 'The three T's of Alliance Creation: Task, Team and Time', *European Management Journal*, vol. 18, no. 2, pp. 152-163.

Saxton, T. (1997), 'The Effects of Partner and Relationship Characteristics on Alliance Outcomes'. *Academy of Management Journal*, vol. 40, no. 2, pp. 443-461.

Sheppard, B. and Tuchinsky, M. (1996), 'Micro-OB and the Network Organization.' In Kramer, R. and Tyler, T. (eds.): *Trust in Organizations*. Sage, Thousand Oaks.

Chapter 11

A Look into the Future

The purpose of this chapter is to depict some key variables which impact the shape of the alliancing scene of the future. Our views are in line with past research, which has shown that when there is a high degree of uncertainty in the future of an industry, firms wish to keep their options open as much as possible. It seems that airline managers typically consider further consolidation to be inevitable, but want to preserve their capability to stand alone in case the move towards consolidation is blocked by authorities or by the conflicting interests of members. The future of alliancing is likely to be shaped primarily by two forces, external and internal. Externally, for instance the stand which regulatory authorities take on competition issues and government subsidies will influence the need for, and extent of, co-operative agreements. Internally, the character of these multilateral networks will be very much shaped by key actors' perceptions of alliancing and their subsequent enactment of cooperation. This chapter emphasises the internal variables because, first, much of the external factors are beyond the control of airline management, and second, because the external ones have been well researched and documented by past research. Also, the examination of the variables internal to a process is closer to the very theme of this book, managing strategic airline alliances.

And yes, we are fully aware of the irony of placing a discussion on the future of the airline industry under the heading of 'Chapter Eleven'. However, no pun is intended.

How did we get here

Alliances have only slowly moved onto the centre stage of airline management. After more than two decades of cooperative agreements mostly on the technical (e.g. KSSU, Atlas) and marketing sides of the business, and some early experiments, e.g. by SAS, with establishing a network of equity ties, it is only since the early 1990s, and clearly linked to a privatisation wave of airlines and growing passenger expectations for global seamless connections, that alliancing, and, even more importantly, living within an alliance group, have become crucial issues to airline managers. The role and nature of airline alliances for the last few decades is illustrated in Table 11.1.

Table 11.1 Building alliances in the airline industry

	Before 1980s	**1980s**	**1990s**
Prevalence of airline alliances	Very rare	Rare	Very common
Stated role of alliances in airline strategies	Quite insignificant.	Increasingly important for some medium-sized airlines.	Essential for practically all kinds of airlines; 'a must' for varying reasons.
Nature of building alliances	Very limited scope. Technical in nature. Often stemmed from national interests.	Bilateral. Often equity involved. Marketing driven.	Bilateral and multi-partner. Strong groupings around largest airlines. Broadening scope: sourcing, production, marketing, branding.

In the volatile environment of today's airline industry, many of the alliance strategies of airlines appear to be emergent rather than carefully planned strategies. Building alternate scenarios for the future – including such issues as the evolution of regulation and development of demand in air transport – helps an airline clarify its objectives and understand how those objectives might evolve in case the environment changes from the most likely scenario.

It seems that the three main features of alliancing as perceived by the industry actors themselves are:

- Alliancing in some form is necessary and inevitable.
- Actors, however, are striving to maintain their firms' autonomy as much as possible.
- The final shape, structure and extent of alliances is yet to emerge.

Scenarios for the future

It seems that most airlines consider it a must to participate in the alliancing game – the opportunity cost of not participating might prove too high. What is much less clear, however, is in which direction alliancing itself will develop. We suggest that the two main factors shaping the future of alliancing are the stand taken by regulatory and competition authorities on one hand, and the daily enactment of alliancing by key actors on the other. Assuming first that the stand on competition issues and regulation taken by authorities is of crucial importance to the industry, it is possible to depict three broad scenarios.

The first, extreme, scenario assumes worldwide open skies (i.e. full freedom for an airline to operate the international routes it deems appropriate), less industry regulation, the abolishment of government subsidies to airlines, and permission to restructure the industry through mergers and acquisitions. We would call this a *Restructuring* scenario, where the airline industry would be turned essentially into what most competitive industries are today. However, it appears that airlines are somewhat pessimistic or cautious concerning the changes to come. The second scenario projects slow, *gradual advancement* in deregulation, but does not assume that governments would be favourable to mergers of major carriers. Since alliancing and the deepening integration of alliances seem to provoke the opposition of competition authorities, airlines are assumed to continue their activities of forming joint ventures with other airlines. It appears that the next episode in the consolidation evolution of this industry, after more than a decade of alliance-building is the forming of joint ventures between airlines – parallel to alliances – for various purposes such as sourcing, sales and distribution and maintenance. The third scenario is what we call *Turning back the clock*, which would imply breaking up or loosening of existing alliances due to co-ordination problems and insurmountable power conflicts between partners, continued government ownership in airlines particularly in Europe, continued subsidies to poorly performing firms, emphasis of national interests and tightening control by authorities on alliances. Admittedly these three scenarios are depictions of somewhat extreme situations; Figure 11.1 illustrates the boundaries within which the future of alliancing is likely to develop.

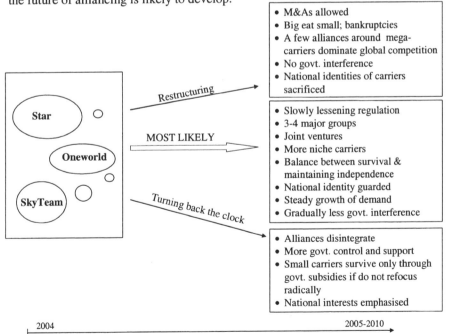

Figure 11.1   Scenarios for airline alliancing

Table 11.2 summarises those variables that may have an impact on airlines' strategies concerning alliancing. These variables can also be seen as components of the future scenarios within these extremes. The demand for air transport, the availability of air transport infrastructure, the evolution of deregulation and governments' actions in protecting weak airlines, the nature of competition, and very importantly the way alliancing is perceived by key actors determine how airlines approach alliancing in the future. As to the experiences by airlines from alliances so far, airline management faces considerable challenges in making the alliances work: there is the pressure from authorities, demands by unions, perhaps mixed ownership by government and private parties, and the normal challenges of different cultures in different countries and firms, differing organisational arrangements in airlines, and strong personalities as airline executives. In the table we have emphasised those 'sub-scenarios' that would appear most likely. It is because of the ambiguity inherent in trying to accommodate often countervailing pressures, strategic rationales, independence concerns, serving 'two masters' (e.g. the alliance and the firm) at a time, that made us refrain from assigning any 'most likely' tag to the last column, which deals with actors' perceptions of alliancing.

Thus, there are several external variables having a great impact on alliancing in the airline strategy framework, such as demand development, infrastructure, regulative environment and government participation, changes in the competitive environment and finally the broader changes in the organisation of distribution in the travel industry. Yet, internally the way airline management perceives the alliances as a feasible component in their strategic arsenal has apparently as great an impact on the future of alliancing, and we address that in the following.

The internal dynamics of alliancing

In brief, the task environment of the alliance can still be considered to be relatively unstable, mainly due to the following dimensions of uncertainty in multilateral alliance coordination:

- 'Multilateralism': Cooperation between two partners may influence relations with a third, or the group as a whole.
- Indeterminacy: The 'polycephalous', or multi-headed organisation invents itself, on the basis of the local rationalities of actors who owe allegiance to their firm, but not to any superstructure.
- Strong perceived ambiguity: This is related to the previous point. There is no blueprint of what the alliance group should look like. In addition, alliancing itself has not reached the status of a strong and unambiguous institution.
- Resource interdependencies are more difficult to manage due to strong partner heterogeneity – there are significant power asymmetries and a large diversity as to resources and policy goals.

Table 11.2 Variables having an impact on airlines' strategies concerning international alliances

DEMAND		INFRASTRUCTURE • Airports • Air space	DEREGULATION	GOVERNMENT PROTECTION OF WEAK AIRLINES	COMPETITION		DISTRIBUTION CHANGES	MANAGERS' VIEW ON ALLIANCING
Volatility	Growth rate				Players	Challengers		
Low	> 4%	Significantly improved	Significant progress • Worldwide open skies • Cross-border M&A allowed	Protection abolished • No subsidies • Bankruptcies • Purely competitive principles • Full privatisation of govt. owned airlines	Between alliances mainly	Start-ups & low-costs do not succeed: do not intrude to scheduled traffic.	Alliances strengthen • Co-operation • More bargaining power • New technologies	Shared vision and unity of purpose in alliances. "Alliance first."
Medium	2-4%	Remain as is	Status quo	Some protection • Government injections of cash • Gradual, slow privatisation	Mixed field	Balanced division into scheduled traffic & low-cost traffic.	Distribution sector remains fragmented. Limited progress in co-operation between airlines.	Harmonious cooperation of members, which are still watchful of their own interests.
High	< 2%	Congestion worsens	More regulation • Limits on alliances • National interest important	Increasing protection • Subsidies distorting competition • Privatisation halted • Unions' rules	Between individual airlines	Low-costs and focused airlines challenge incumbents; new 'rules' of the game.	Distribution channel, i.e. travel agencies consolidate • Increased bargaining power	Irresolvable conflicting interests between members. "Our airline first."

The dimensions of uncertainty listed above can be assumed to influence the degree of integration into an alliance (a superstructure) of individual airlines and thus in the aggregate, the stability of the alliancing task environment.

The following model tries to summarise the dynamics of multilateral alliancing:

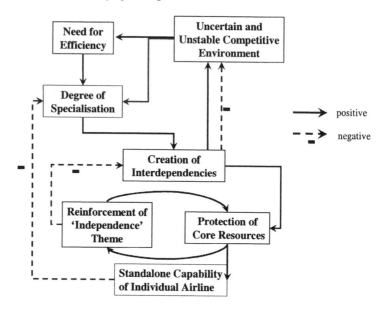

Figure 11.2 The dynamics of multilateral alliancing

The primary assumption is that the stability of the firm's task environment (i.e. the alliance group, or at least allian*cing* in case of an airline opting for a portfolio of bilaterals approach) is influenced by both exogenous and endogenous factors. Exogenous factors stem from the wider environment and include industry regulation, economic cycles, prices for fuel and aircraft, etc. The endogenous factors refer to those which are residing within the task environment itself, both at firm (for example, the degree of a firm's specialisation) and alliance group (for example, interdependencies between firms) levels.

In an uncertain and unstable task environment, firms are pushed toward a generalist position, in order to be fit across a wider range of environmental variations; in other words, the environmental stability is positively related to the degree of specialisation. On the other hand, the instability of the environment paired with industry characteristics (very capital intensive and at the same time very low margin) establishes an imperative on firms to be highly efficient; environmental stability is negatively linked to the need for efficiency. This, in turn, favours specialisation.

Thus, the *first ambiguity of airline alliances* is that the instability of the environment both favours and obstructs specialisation. Specialisation is, however, to some extent unavoidable – it can be said that in an industry where scope benefits are a significant determinant of competitiveness, every firm is to some extent a specialist. As explained in Chapter 3, specialists in an unstable environment tend to federate with each other. This specialisation in a network of actors can be said to increase interdependencies between them. Provided – and this is one of our base assumptions – that a firm's primary aim is survival and the preservation of its identity, one major reaction at management level to the perception of interdependencies is a reinforcement of myths (or stories told) relating to 'independence', and to 'avoidance' of these dependencies. This is because allegiance to one's own firm is a strong institution. The reaction at firm level is to protect the firm's core resources. This protection of core resources is tightly related to the establishment of a standalone capability, which in turn somewhat reduces the possible degree of specialisation. At the same time, the protection of core resources also reinforces (and is reinforced by) the managerial allegiance to the airline's self-identity. In other words, managers tend to think more in favour of their own firm, rather than the alliance. And this, in return, sanctions core-resource protecting behaviour even more. This loop can be considered a case of *fortress building*, where institutional forces and resource protection efforts jointly act to shield the firm from dependencies. Fortress building in itself is caused by interdependencies; but it is countervailing to them because it aims at reducing the degree of integration between organisations. The degree of integration between partners, in turn, can be expected to significantly influence the stability of the task environment.

The above model depicts the interaction and recurrence of processes that shape the phenomenon of multilateral alliancing. It illustrates the challenges to alliance consolidation in times of continued environmental instability, and it combines the behavioural and structural aspects of the alliancing process. What this rather schematic model does not depict, however, is the distinction between specific and unspecific dependencies, in other words, what facilitates or precludes the retention of standalone capability of a firm, and possibly constitutes a source of power over other firms. Interdependencies can create risk or reduce risk in a focal airline's immediate task environment. As explained in Chapter 3, they create risk in case of specific dependencies from one airline's side on a partner or on an alliance. They can reduce risk if every other partner also has a specific dependency on that alliance. This, however, requires the existence of a superstructure at federation level, to which all partners agreed to submit and to which they are all equally bound. The dilemma here is that in the present case of alliancing in the airline industry, the *building* of the superstructure has still not attained the level of a strong (and enforced, or at least legitimately sponsored) institutionalised norm.

This then constitutes the *second ambiguity of alliancing*: partners will all benefit from a stable and predictable task environment, but each of them is reluctant to contribute to the building of such an environment. This reminds us of a game-theory like scenario. The root of the problem seems to be that local rationales still override any meta-rationale, and there is no hierarchically superior 'authority' in place to impose these meta-rationales, nor is there any 'issue sponsor' who could legitimately create such an 'authority'.

A look into the future of airline alliance groups

This 'game' can be expected to be played for many more rounds, each round being a result and a slight variation of the previous ones. Observing the way the 'game' evolves can help to further illustrate the concept of 'alliance competence' that was introduced in Chapter 3: the alliance competence of an airline can be said to lie in its ability to avoid specific dependencies and retain a certain standalone capability.

These two are in fact closely related issues, because the nature of (inter-) dependencies defines the character of the task environment – the structural set-up of the alliance group – and thus the way (and if at all) a firm can maintain its standalone capability. Predicting any sort of 'outcome' is difficult, and would depend on the respective force of each of the factors involved. It can nevertheless be observed that within alliance groups that consist of different airline types (Local Champions, Global Connectors), the moves of 'fortress building' and 'retention of standalone capabilities' have different characteristics with each type of airline. For example, one step towards a more hierarchical alliance structure can be seen in the moves by larger airlines of the Global Connector type to hierarchically control smaller airlines whose route systems qualify them as feeders to the Global Connector's hub airports. A significant contributor to the alliancing competence of this type of airline is their ability to control and dominate a relatively large market in order to ensure high-volume feeding to their global hubs. Lufthansa's current strategy is a very good example for such 'empire building' (note the difference between building a 'fortress' – mainly defensive – and an 'empire', which includes offensive moves).

Then, one possible future set-up of an airline alliance group would be that of a democratically governed society of peers, where a small number of equal partners (with non-overlapping route systems) would convene to form a 'polis', but each of them would hierarchically control a set of smaller airlines (this, too, is very much in line with the original concept of the 'polis', which knew several classes of citizens) within their geographical core area. Some smaller airlines of the Local Champion type, those who managed to retain their standalone capability, might also form part of the 'citizenry' of such a 'polis'.

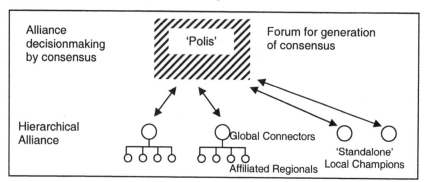

Figure 11.3 A possible future structure of an airline alliance group

As discussed in Chapter 3, the Local Champions which dominate an attractive, remote market will find it relatively easier to be specifically dependent on alliancing as such, but not on any one alliance group or particular partner airline. The Local Champions that manage to retain their standalone capability would benefit from a superstructure that has enough authority to prevent too heavy within-competition in the alliance group, but is loose enough to allow that firm the pursuit of any policy that would allow them to retain their standalone capability. Possibly, this could mean cooperation with other firms from outside that alliance group. Their alliancing competence would hence be very much dependent on their capability to protect their (attractive) core resources and the retention of those link resources that save them from specific dependencies. Finnair's move to retain, even strengthen, their Far Eastern route system (a linkage resource) is a good example of this.

The 'polis' model can indeed be considered one probable outcome of the alliancing process in the medium term because it does not require the immediate creation of a hierarchically superior locus of full authority that is external to all actors. The foregoing discussion has tried to show how difficult this creation is likely to be. The described dilemmas of federating on a multilateral alliance still apply in a 'polis', but they do so in a more moderate form, mainly because of reduced actor number and -heterogeneity. A cluster, as discussed in Chapter 9, can be a precursor to such a 'polis', or be at its very core.

It is then possible to predict these alliances to move in the medium term towards a form where some hierarchies will occur, especially *within* the alliance (e.g. one member airline hierarchically controlling other carriers) but that at alliance group level these hierarchies will be incomplete, in that managers of alliance member airlines try to construct an external locus of full authority where their own hierarchical allegiance is still to their firm; in other words, they are still rewarded for acting in favour of their own firm, rather than any superstructure. The superstructure of a 'polis' (the forum for consensus) can be expected to move towards being a strong, but still fairly unspecific institution (i.e. an institution that is an accepted and integral part of actors' mindsets but the specific rules constituting it are not clearly established and are still subject to ongoing negotiation). Any attempt to institutionalise alliancing beyond the current fairly vague level is likely to meet resistance by the 'countervailing' institutional force of allegiance to actors' own airline, a very strong institution in itself.

It is the relative instability inherent in continuously (re-)negotiated environments that requires member firms of especially the Local Champion type ultimately to strive to retain their standalone capability, even if they seek full integration into an alliance group.

In conclusion

It is likely that the airline industry will experience turbulent times also in the future. The industry is strongly affected by the general economic turns in the world, the health concerns related to virus outbreaks in some parts of the world, and political uncertainties including the risk of terrorism may be an integral part of the future air travel scenario. The overall tendency in the world economy is for more freedom and less regulation, which will lead to a more competitive airline industry on one side and to thin margins on the other. The low-cost carriers have brought low fares to consumers, resulting in pressure for the established carriers to lower their fares. As to costs, airlines are facing a de-facto cartel of fuel suppliers, a limited choice of aircraft from two major manufacturers, and local monopolies in terms of airspace and airport services; consequently, a large share of the operating costs are really beyond the control of airline management. Moreover, in many airlines the management is facing strong unions and political pressures from the local governments, so the tools to respond to the tightening competition may be very much restricted. For those airlines that are members in alliance groups, the pressure to offer a more compatible or homogeneous product may make it increasingly difficult to differentiate one's product. Therefore, while it seems that the industry will become increasingly competitive, there will remain considerable pockets of market which are too small to attract much competition.

However, if the survival of major carriers either in Europe, North America or Asia is at risk, the governments are still likely to interfere and provide shelter for the flag carriers. This may be seen as distorting competition, but is in the best interest of the national and world economies, at least in the short term – the world economy simply cannot do without a reliable and well functioning global air transport system.

Then, what can airlines do in such an unstable business environment? The answer is by no means simple, and naturally it is easier said than done. First of all there are two opposite demands: on one hand, airlines should try to maintain their standalone capability; on the other hand, they should maintain and develop competence in alliancing. Standalone capability is necessary as the industry is unstable and alliance arrangements may change quickly, possibly resulting in a situation where a carrier has no partners. Alliancing competence is important, as it seems that staying outside of alliancing in the long term is a very challenging option, especially for airlines that have the 'burden of history', primarily in the form of high operating costs. Moreover, on a more general note, the history of the industry has shown that when difficult times follow prosperous times – as they always do – airlines are often not prepared enough to tighten the belt. Therefore it would be important to steer a very conservative course in terms of costs even when the demand is high and margins thick.

Overall the air transport environment is likely to remain turbulent. The alliancing route is going to be bumpy, too. For those responsible for the steering of strategic airline alliances, there are no dull days in sight, as the tightrope walk between retaining autonomy and alliance group integration is going to be a primary task for airline managers in the foreseeable future.

Index